World Wisdom
The Library of Perennial Philosophy

The Library of Perennial Philosophy is dedicated to the exposition of the timeless Truth underlying the diverse religions. This Truth, often referred to as the *Sophia Perennis*—or Perennial Wisdom—finds its expression in the revealed Scriptures as well as the writings of the great sages and the artistic creations of the traditional worlds.

The Perennial Philosophy provides the intellectual principles capable of explaining both the formal contradictions and the transcendent unity of the great religions.

Ranging from the writings of the great sages of the past, to the perennialist authors of our time, each series of our Library has a different focus. As a whole, they express the inner unanimity, transforming radiance, and irreplaceable values of the great spiritual traditions.

Tripura Rahasya: The Secret of the Supreme Goddess appears as one of our selections in The Spiritual Classics series.

Spiritual Classics Series

This series includes seminal, but often neglected, works of unique spiritual insight from leading religious authors of both the East and West. Ranging from books composed in ancient India to forgotten jewels of our time, these important classics feature new introductions which place them in the perennialist context.

T0159628

Cover image: Statue of Trimurti, Elephanta cave, South India.
Back cover statue: The Goddess Umâ, Nepal, 9th-10th century.

Tripura Rahasya:
The Secret of the Supreme Goddess

Translated by
Swami Sri Ramanananda Saraswathi
(Sri Munagala S. Venkataramaiah)

World Wisdom

Tripura Rahasya: The Secret of the Supreme Goddess

The text, Foreword to the 1959 Edition, Introduction,
Introductory Note, and Index published by arrangement
with V.S. Ramanan, President, Board of Trustees,
Sri Ramanasramam, Tiruvannamalai 606 603.

Preface and Foreword to the 2002 Edition
© 2002 World Wisdom, Inc.

ISBN 13 for fourth printing
978-0-941532-49-5

Library of Congress Cataloging-in-Publication Data

Tripurârahasya. English.
Tripura rahasya : the secret of the supreme goddess / translated by
Ramanananda Saraswathi.
p. cm. — (Spiritual classics series) (The library of perennial philosophy)
ISBN 0-941532-49-6 (pbk. : alk. paper)
1. Tripurasundarî (Hindu deity) I. Ramananda, Saraswati, Swami,
1867-1936. II. Title. III. Series: Spiritual classics (Bloomington, Ind.)
IV. Series: Library of perennial philosophy.
                                    BL1225.T73T7513 2002
                                       294.5'514—dc21
                                           2002012898

Printed on acid-free paper in the United States of America

For information address World Wisdom, Inc.
P.O. Box 2682, Bloomington, Indiana 47402-2682
www.worldwisdom.com

Contents

Preface to the 2002 Edition

The ancient Sanskrit text, the *Tripura Rahasya: The Secret of the Supreme Goddess,* is a dialogue of instruction given to the seeker Parasurâma by his newly found guru, Dattatreya. The warlike Parasurâma, after having challenged and having been spared by the Man-God Rama, now seeks Truth and salvation. He explains to the sage Dattatreya that despite intensive efforts to understand spiritual instruction, "Even now I understand nothing of the workings of the universe. Where does it rise from, in all its grandeur? Where does it end? How does it exist? I find it to be altogether transient."

Surely such questions will resonate in the souls of modern seekers as well. Thus, this edition of Swami Sri Ramanananda Saraswathi's English translation of the ancient text is intended to make available to modern seekers and scholars alike a valuable resource in their respective pursuits. The chronicler of the dialogue, the Sage Harithayana, concludes the *Tripura Rahasya* by observing that "obstruction to wisdom is destroyed by reading it," but this certainly presupposes both a readiness for spiritual instruction and a grounding in Hindu thought and practice, as would have been the case for the ancient seeker Parasurâma.

Modern seekers in the West will find in the *Tripura Rahasya* ancient wisdom in the form of numerous parables, aphorisms, and direct instruction in the principles of Advaita Vedanta, which is perhaps the most accessible presentation of Hindu thought for the Western mind. To assist those readers who seek in the *Tripura Rahasya* immediate nourishment for the soul, a index has been added at the end of this edition, as well as some comments below that are intended to provide additional keys to a deeper understanding and appreciation of this profound text.

Students of Hinduism, and particularly of Advaita Vedanta, will be pleased to have a new English edition of the ancient text available to them at last. The *Tripura Rahasya* has long been treasured by great expounders of Advaita Vedanta, for example by the ancient sage Shankara, and it was a favorite of the more recent sage Sri Ramana Maharshi, who often quoted from it. Readers especially interested in the philosophies of India will find in this book a beautifully realized synthesis of Advaita Vedanta and Tantra, two of the most important schools of thought which arose in ancient India, and whose two great exponents were Shankara and Abhinavagupta, respectively.

Because of its great antiquity and continued application through the ages, it can be argued that the *Tripura Rahasya* is thus one of the greatest classics of Hindu spirituality. Alert readers may detect themes common to certain classics of ancient Western literature but often with deeper metaphysical dimensions. For example, in his book *Am I My Brother's Keeper?*, Ananda K. Coomaraswamy compared it to Plato's *Republic*, inasmuch as it outlines an ideal city-state, though of a characteristically Indian utopia. This is the "City of Resplendent Wisdom" ruled by a philosopher king, understood in Hindu terminology as the man who is spiritually liberated in this life (*jivan-mukta*). More deeply understood, this philosopher king is the uncreated Self (*atman*), or pure Intelligence (*chit*). The citizens of this city, seen allegorically, have all been illuminated by the Supreme Goddess.

The Sanskrit word *Tripura* refers to the Supreme Goddess envisaged as a manifestation of the most profound wisdom of the Self. *Rahasya* means "secret," referring in this case to the spiritual Reality which cannot be understood by reason alone or through the life of the senses. The subject matter of the book comprises a series of wise and charming stories told by the ancient sage Dattatreya, which ultimately concern the nature of man's relationship with the Real, under the guise of the Supreme Goddess *Tripura*. This perspective finds fascinating parallels in Western traditions concerning Sophia, or the divine Mother. It also echoes the mystical traditions of Kabala and Sufism which make references to the *Shekinah*, or *Sakinah* as the Divine Presence, or the essentially merciful nature of God. For the student of comparative religion, and most especially comparative mystical traditions, further study of these relationships between East and West could bear much fruit. Striking parallels may also be discerned between the intellectual content of this text and other Eastern and Western traditions of non-dualistic spirituality, such as Taoism and the Rhineland mysticism of Meister Eckhart.

The reading of an ancient and foreign text like the *Tripura Rahasya*, with its many levels of symbolism and meaning, would perhaps be greatly illuminating for the Western reader if that reader could see it through the eyes of our own ancient sages such as Plato or Plotinus. An open and questing mind that is receptive to symbolism in its many forms, and that welcomes the wisdom it conveys, should find itself transported through the text into the ancient soul of India where men viewed the question of spiritual liberation in this life as a necessary and vital part of existence. This was a world of wandering contemplatives and men who sought out direct spiritual guidance because they had a profound need to know the Real. In the pages that follow, the reader will encounter the wondrous tale of the soul itself, where the personification of Pure Intelligence interacts with personifications of Ignorance, Delusion, Mind, Desire, Passion, Greed and all the various aspects of human nature. The story unfolds through the medium of tales which delight and amuse, but they also open the door to the cave of wisdom and invite entry to all, regardless of specific religious affiliation.

For whatever reason they come to the *Tripura Rahasya*, readers who appreciate the wisdom literature of the ancient worlds will discover in it that irresistible combination of depth and simplicity which characterizes the best examples of that literature.

World Wisdom
Bloomington, Indiana
March 2002

Foreword to the 2002 Edition

Tripura Rahasya is an ancient, prime text on *Advaita* in Sanskrit. Essentially it represents a dialogue between Dattatreya and Parasurama. Later on, this was communicated to Haritayana. Hence the alternative name to the text is *Haritayana Samhita*.

Tripura Rahasya was highly commended by Bhagavan Sri Ramana Maharshi for study by seekers. There was no English translation until the present one was made by Munagala Venkataramiah (Swami Ramanananda Saraswati) in 1938.

The main lesson of this work is that *vichara* (Self-enquiry) is essential for the release of man from the cycle of birth and death. Although *sadhana* is essential for Self-realization it should not be taken that the Self is got anew. For, *there is no moment when the Self is not the Self.* The basis of *sadhana* is the rejection of all such ideas as "me" and "mine". After the process of analysis and rejection (of all that is non-Self) what remains is the Pure Self. This is to be sought. Earnest devotion to the Lord on the part of the seeker aided by the grace of the Lord enables one to reach the goal.

The position of *Tripura Rahasya* regarding "the world" is that it is not different from the Lord. Time and space and the whole of creation are projections of consciousness. The universe arises out of Abstract Intelligence like an image on a mirror. Sri Ramana Maharshi has pointed out that *the world is unreal if viewed apart from the Self and real if viewed as the Self.*

Tripura Rahasya states that the ignorant take the gross universe to be Shakti whereas the wise know Her as their own Pure Being, eternally shining as "I". . . "I". . . "I".

Tripura literally means "three cities". Actually it signifies the three states of human consciousness—wakefulness, dream, and deep sleep. The underlying, unchanging consciousness in all these states is metaphorically called Devi Sri Tripura (Shakti).

This is a powerful guide for serious seekers on the path.

The translator, Munagala Venkataramiah (later on Swami Ramanananda Saraswati), a staunch devotee of Sri Maharshi, has done outstanding service to the world of seekers by recording and compiling the dialogues with the master between 1935 and 1939 under the title *Talks with Sri Ramana Maharshi.*

Sri V. S. Ramanan
President
Sri Ramanasramam
Tiruvannamalai, India

Foreword to the 1959 Edition

Tripura Rahasya was considered by Bhagavan Sri Ramana Maharshi as one of the greatest works that expounded advaita philosophy. He often quoted from it and regretted that it was not available in English. As a consequence Sri Munagala Venkataramaiah (now Swami Ramanananda Saraswathi) took up the work of translation in 1936 as another labour of love, adding just one more English translation to his already extensive store. This was first published in parts in the Bangalore Mythic Society s Journal (Quarterly) from January 1938 to April 1940 and afterwards collected into book form, of which five hundred copies were printed and privately circulated. The ´shramam has since taken over the copyright and made it one of their official publications.

The work originally in Sanskrit is widely known in India and has been translated into a number of local languages, but I do not know of any previous translation in English. It is regarded as one of the chief text-books on Advaita, the reading of which alone is sufficient for Salvation. Sri Ananda Coomaraswamy quotes from it with appreciation in his book, "Am I My Brother's Keeper?"

I for one much appreciate the present translation which will now be easily available for all who know English. Sri Ramanananda Saraswathi has put us under a great obligation by his painstaking work. It will surely be a gratification to him to know that his labour of love has at last found a permanent abiding-place and will not be lost to future generations, for many of whom it must become a Spiritual text book.

October 16, 1959, Sadhu Arunachala
Sri *Ramanasramam* (Major A. W. Chadwick, O.B.E.)

Introduction

Sri Tripura Rahasya is an ancient work in Sanskrit which has been printed all over India. The latest and best edition was brought out in the Kâshi Sanskrit Series in 1925. The book is said to have been printed once before and issued in loose leaves. There was also an edition in book form printed in Belgium towards the end of last century.[1]

The esteem in which the work is held for its sanctity may be gauged from an account of it given in the Preface to the Mâhâtmya Khanda. Mahâdêva originally taught the Highest Truth to Vishnu who in turn taught Brahmâ in the Celestial regions. Later Vishnu incarnated on Earth as Sri Dattâtreya, the Lord of the *Avadhûtas* (the naked sages), and taught it to Parasurâma with the injunction that it should be communicated to Haritâyana who would later seek the Truth from him. Parasurâma thus realized the Self by the guidance of Sri Datta and dwelt on the Malaya Hill in South India.

In the meantime, a Brahmin, by name Sumanta, living on the banks of the Sarasvati had a son, Alarka by name, who used to hear his mother called "Ai" by his father. Being a child, he too addressed his mother "Ai". He died in his childhood, and his last words on his death-bed were only "Ai". This sound is however sacred to the Goddess. Having been uttered in all innocence and purity of mind, it conferred unexpected merit on the dying child. He was later born as Sumedha, a son to Harita. Haritâyana is his patronymic. His spirituality developed as he grew up and he sought Parasurâma to learn the highest good from him, who in turn imparted to him the knowledge which he had gained from Dattâttreya. Parasurâma told him also that his master had predicted the compilation of the knowledge of the Highest Truth by Haritâyana for the benefit of mankind.

Haritâyana was worshipping Sri Minâkshi in the temple at Madurai in South India. Narada appeared to him and said that

---

1. The original Sanskrit text unfortunately appears to have been out of print for some years.

he had come from *Brahmaloka* in order to see what Haritâyana was going to present to the world in the form of an *Itihasa* (history) containing the Supreme Spiritual Truth. Haritâyana was bewildered and asked how the Saint expected it of him. Narada said: "There was an assembly of saints in Brahmaloka. Markandeya asked Brahmâ about the Sacred Truth. Brahmâ said that it would be brought out by you in the form of a holy book. So I came to ask you about it." Haritâyana was at a loss and pleaded inability to reproduce the Sacred Truth learned from Parasurâma. Narada then meditated on Brahmâ who appeared before them and asked what the matter was. When Narada put the whole matter before him, he turned to Haritâyana and blessed him, endowing him with the ability to produce the book at the rate of four chapters a day. He also referred to Haritâyana's past and attributed his present inability to remember what he learnt to the casual and undisciplined utterance of the sacred syllable in his past incarnation. Brahmâ further enjoined Narada to be the first to read Haritâyana's work when it should be completed.

The work was thus written by Haritâyana and is also called after his name *Haritâyana Samhita*. It is said to consist of 12,000 *slokas* in three sections—The *Mâhâtmya Khanda* (Section on the Greatness of Sri Devi), *Jnâna Khanda* (Section on Supreme Wisdom), and *Charya Khanda* (Section on Conduct). Of these the first consists of 6,687 *slokas;* the second of 2,163 *slokas;* and the third is not traceable. The section on Greatness contains the prelude to the work and later treats mostly of the manifestations of the Supreme Being as Durga, Kâli, Lakshmi, Sarasvati Lalita, Kumâri, etc. and their exploits are found in *Brahmanda Purâna, Mârkandeya Purâna* and *Lakshmi Tantra.* Its contents mostly cover the ground of *Durgâ Saptasati* and of *Lalitâ Upâkhayana.*

Sri Vidyâ (worship of the Supreme Being as Goddess) has a very holy tradition traced to the Vedas. There are two principal divisions, known as *kâdi vidyâ* and *hâdi vidyâ*. The former was practised by Indra, Chandra, Manu, Kubêra, etc.; it is the simpler of the two and also more common. The other was practised by Lopamudra and approved of the wise.

Sri Tripura Rahasya, also known as *Haritâyana Samhita,* begins with *Aum namah* "Salutations to *Aum*" and ends with *Sri tripuraiva namah* "Tripura is only *Hrim*". *Aum* is well known as the sacred syllable signifying the Highest Being in the abstract; so also *Hrim* is the sacred symbol of the same as the Goddess. The contents of the book are thus enclosed by these two symbols— the most sacred in the Vedas and the work is equally sanctified.

In *Sutra Bhasya* (the commentary on Brahmâ Sûtras), Sri Shankara has used the story of Samvarta as found in *Tripura Rahasya,* in his commentary on "Apica Smaryate Sutra", with approval.

There is a lucid commentary in Sanskrit on *Haritâyana Samhita.* It is named *Tâtparya Dipika* and written in 4932 of Kali Era (i.e., 1831 A.D.) by one Dravida Srinivasa, son of Vydianatha Dikshita of the village of Mahapushkara in South India.

As for its philosophy, there is no real reason to distinguish it from Vedânta. Scholars however call this system the *Tantri* or the *Sakta,* and point out some apparent differences between this and Advaita Vedânta. This system teaches that the Supreme Reality is no other than Abstract Intelligence. "Intelligence" signifies Self—luminosity and "Abstraction" denotes its unlimited nature. No other agent can be admitted to exist apart from It in order to reveal It. The apparent variety is only due to *Vimarsa,* the gross aspect of Its absolute freedom known as *Svatantra* which at times unfolds the Pure Self as the Cosmos and at others withdraws Itself and remains unmanifest. Abstraction and manifestation are inherent in the Pure Self; these two aspects are given the names Siva and Sakti respectively. There cannot be manifestation beyond the Supreme Intelligence; therefore Cosmos and the Self are only the same, but different modes of Reality. Realization of the Truth is thus quite simple, requiring only constant remembrance on these lines (*anusandhânam*) that Reality is not incompatible with the world and its phenomena, and that the apparent ignorance of this Truth is itself the outcome of Reality so that there is nothing but Reality.

Creation and Dissolution are cycles of Self-expression and Abstraction due to Swatantra. There are no Sankalpa-Vikalpas (modifications) in the state of dissipation and the Self remains as Chit in absolute purity and unchanging. The Self is uniform and undivided. The dispositions of the individuals of the previous *Kalpa* (creation) remain uncognised but potential, awaiting to become manifest in the alternating mode. The tendency in the direction of manifestation is *Mâyâ* which later displays as *Avidyâ* (ignorance) when the predispositions are in their full swing. *Chit, Mâyâ* and *Avidyâ* are thus the same Reality. Cosmos is an expression in the medium of consciousness and thus not unreal as some would have it.

Here the Reality of the Cosmos is on account of the medium of expression, i.e., consciousness, which does not contradict the statement that forms, etc., are unreal. There is thus no fundamental difference between Tantra and Vedanta. Yet the Pandits say that *Mâyâ* is made subservient to *Brahmâ* in *Vedânta*, that its application is limited to gross manifestation and that it is therefore gross which in ultimate analysis resolves itself into void; whereas according to *Tantra, Mâyâ* is an aspect of Reality and should resolve itself into *Chit* on ultimate analysis. This cannot be a valid objection. For, where does the above void rest? It must resolve itself into *Chit.*

The favourite example of the world being an image reflected in consciousness, as images in a mirror is common to both systems, as mentioned in *"vishvam darpan drasyaman tulyam nijantaragatam"* in *Dakshinâmoorti Stotra* of Sri Sankara.

Without trying to find differences where they do not exist, let the earnest student apply the infallible test of the peace of mind brought about by the different modes of expression of the Reality and be satisfied and happy.

Munagala S. Venkataramaiah
(now Swami Ramanananda Saraswathi)

Introductory Note

Jamadagni was a Brahmin saint who lived in the forest with his wife Renuka and his sons, of whom Parasurâma was the youngest, the most valiant and the best renowned. The country was then ruled by Haihayas, a certain clan of Kshattriyas. Some of them came into clash with Parasurâma but fared the worse. They dared not challenge him afterwards. Their rancour, however, remained, and they could not resist their longing for revenge. They seized their opportunity when Parasurâma was far away from the hermitage, attacked his saintly father and killed him. On the son's return, the mother narrated the unprovoked murder of the saint; she also desired that her husband's body should be cremated on the banks of the Ganges and that she might as a *Sati* mount the funeral pyre.

Parasurâma vowed that he would clear the earth of the Kshattriya vermin. He placed his father's corpse on the shoulder and took his living mother on the other and set out along to the Ganges. While passing through a forest, an *Avadhutha*, by name Dattatreya, saw Renuka and stopped the young man who carried her. The *Avadhutha* addressed Renuka as Sakti incarnate, of unparalleled might and worshipped her. She blessed him and told him of her life on earth and her resolve to end it. She also advised her son to look to Dattatreya for help when needed. Parasurâma went on his way and fulfilled his mother's desire.

He then challenged every Kshattriya in the land and killed them all. Their blood was collected in a pool in Kurukshetra, and Parasurâma offered oblations to his forefathers with it. His dead ancestors appeared and told him to desist from his bloody revenge. Accordingly, he retired into mountain fastnesses and lived as a hermit.

Hearing on one occasion of the prowess of Rama, his wrath rekindled and he came back to challenge him. Rama was born of Dasaratha who, though a Kshattriya, escaped his doom by a ruse. Rama accepted Parasurâma's challenge and got the better of him.

Parasurâma returned crest-fallen and on his way met an *Avadhuta* named Samvarta, the brother of Brihaspati. Later he encountered Sri Dattatreya who instructed him in the *Truth* and so led him to salvation.

Dattatreya

There was once a dutiful wife whose husband was, however, a licentious wretch. This couple unwittingly disturbed Rishi Mandavya, who had been placed on a spear by a misguided king. The Rishi, who was in agony but not dying, cursed them, saying that the husband would die at sunrise and the wife be left a widow. Widowhood is most abhorrent to a Hindu lady and considered worse than death. By the force of her dutiful wifehood she resisted the curse of the Rishi; the Sun could not rise; and the Gods were rendered impotent.

The Gods in council resolved to approach Anasuya—the ideal of wifehood—to ask her to prevail on the other lady to relent. Anasuya promised her that she would restore her dead husband to life; and so the matter ended satisfactorily for all.

The three chief Gods then agreed to be born as sons to Anasuya. Brahman was born as the Moon, Siva as Dhurvasa and Sri Narayana as Datta. The last is also called "Datta Atreya," of which the latter world is the patronymic derived from Atri, the husband of Anasuya. Sri Dattatreya is the foremost in the line of divine teachers incarnate on earth.

Chapter I

1. Salutation to *Aum* (undifferentiated Brahman, and yet the Primal and Blissful cause), the transcendental consciousness shining as the unique mirror of the wonderful universe:

Note: The one undifferentiated Brahman signified by *Aum* polarises as *Sat-chit-ananda* taking shape as Parameswari who, in Her crystal purity, displays the variegated phenomena which gyrate in equipoise within Her. Neutral Brahman and the polarised Brahman are thus interchangeable. The idea of the mirror implies the non-separateness of the object from the subject (conscious being).

2. (Harithayana said: . . .)

"Undisturbed you have heard, O Narada! the *Mahatmya* (The Gospel) of Sri Tripura, which teaches the way to Transcendence."

Note: Thus begins the latter part of the book; the first part deals with a narrative of Devi (Sakti-Sri Tripura), Her worship and Her grace. Tripura literally means the three cities. They are the states—*Jagrat, Svapna* and *Shushupti.* The undercurrent of consciousness in all of them, remaining unaffected, is metaphorically called the Resident Mistress by name Sri Tripura. The procreative faculty generating new beings and the link of altruistic love connecting the offspring to the parent are personified in the *Mother.* Hence the feminine termination of Tripura.

"The way to transcendence" signifies that interest in Tripura purifies the mind and creates the zeal for enquiry into the Truth. The listener is now fit for the ensuing discourse on wisdom.

3. I shall now discourse on wisdom, which is unique because one will be permanently freed from misery, by hearing it.

4. This is the concentrated extract of the essence of the Vedic, Vaishnava, Saiva, Satkta and Pasupata lore taken after a deep study of them all.

5-7. No other course will impress the mind so much as this one on Wisdom which was once taught by that illustrious master

Dattatreya to Parasurâma. The teaching was born of his own experience, logical in sense and quite unique in its nature. One who cannot apprehend Truth even after hearing this must be dismissed as a silly fool to be ranked among the insentient and accursed of God; Siva himself cannot make such a one gain wisdom.

8. I now proceed to relate that incomparable teaching. Listen! Oh, the lives of Sages are most sacred!

9-11. Narada, too, served me to learn the same from me; for, service to sages enables one to comprehend their innate kindness, just as the sense of smell helps one to detect the intrinsic odor of musk.

As Parasurâma, the son of Jamadagni, already pure-minded and pleasing to all, was listening to the Gospel of Tripura from the lips of Dattatreya, he became abstracted in devotion and so growing still for a time, his mind became still purer.

12-13. Then as the mind relaxed, his eyes glowed in rapture and his hair stood on end, as if his ecstasy could not be contained within but must escape through the very pores of his body. He then fell to the ground before his master Datta.

14. Again he arose, and being filled with ecstasy his voice choked with emotion as he said: 'Lucky am I; blessed am I; through Thy Grace O Lord!'

15. That expanse of Grace called Siva, here incarnate as my Guru, is indeed gracious to me; gaining whose pleasure even the Lord of creation looks a pigmy.

16. Does not the God of Death verily merge into the Self, if only one's master is pleased with one?

That Supreme Being is gracious indeed, just in so much as is my Master, for reasons unknown to me.

Note: The meaning is that the Guru, being God, is mercy incarnate and requires no incentive to show grace.

17. The Guru's grace gained, I have gained all! Thou hast now kindly opened out to me the glory of Tripura.

18. I now desire fervently to worship Her Transcendental Majesty. Kindly tell me, my Master, how it is to be done.

19-22. Being thus requested, Datta Guru satisfied himself as to the fitness of Parasurâma, whose zeal for and devotion to

Tripura worship were intense; and he duly initiated him into the method of Her worship. After initiation into the right method, which is more sacred than all others and leads directly to Realization, Parasurâma learned from the sweet lips of Sri Guru all the details regarding recitation figures for worship and different meditations, one after another—like a honey bee collecting honey from flowers. Bhargava (*i.e.*, Parasurâma) was overjoyed.

23. Being then permitted by his holy master, he thirsted to practise the sacred lore; he went round his master, made obeisance to him and retired to the Mahendra Hill.

Note: To walk round gently and peacefully, always keeping the centre to one's right, is a sign of respect to the object in the centre.

24. There, having built a clean and comfortable hermitage, he was engaged for twelve years in the worship of Tripura.

25. He incessantly contemplated the figure of that Holy Mother Tripura, performing at the same time his daily tasks and the special ceremonies connected with Her worship and recitations; twelve years thus passed in a flash. Then on a certain day while the son of Jamadagni was sitting at ease, he fell into a reverie.

27. "I did not understand even a little of what Samvarta told me whom I met formerly on the way.

28. I have also forgotten what I asked my Guru. I heard from him the Gospel of Tripura, . . .

29. . . . but it is not clear to me what Samvarta said in reply to my query on creation.

30. "He mentioned the story of Kalakrit, but went no further, knowing that I was not fit for it.

31. "Even now I understand nothing of the workings of the universe. Where does it rise from, in all its grandeur?

32. "Where does it end? How does it exist? I find it to be altogether transient.

33. "But worldly happenings seem permanent; why should that be? Such happenings seem strangely enough to be unconsidered.

34. "How strange! They are at *par* with the blind man led by the blind!

35. "My own case furnishes an example in point. I do not even remember what happened in my childhood.

36. "I was different in my youth, again different in my manhood, still more so now; and in this way, my life is constantly changing.

37-38. "What fruits have been reaped as the result of these changes is not clear to me. The end justifies the means as adopted by individuals according to their temperaments in different climes and in different times. What have they gained thereby? Are they themselves happy?

39. "The gain is only that which is considered to be so by the unthinking public. I however cannot deem it so, seeing that even after gaining the so-called end, the attempts are repeated.

Note: Since there is no abiding satisfaction in the gain, it is not worth having.

40-41. "Well, having gained one purpose, why does man look for another? Therefore, what the man is always after should be esteemed the only real purpose—be it accession of pleasure or removal of pain. There can be neither, so long as the incentive to effort lasts.

42. "The feeling of a need to work in order to gain happiness (being the index of misery) is the misery of miseries. How can there be pleasure or removal or pain so long as it continues?

43-45. "Such pleasure is like that of soothing unguents placed on a scalded limb, or of the embrace of one's beloved when one is lying pierced by an arrow in the breast; or of the sweet melodies of music heard by an advanced consumptive!

46. "Only those who need not engage in action, are happy; they are perfectly content, and self-contained, and they experience happiness which extends to all the pores of the body.

47. "Should there still be a few pleasurable moments for others, they are similar to those enjoyed by one who, while writhing with an abdominal pain, inhales the sweet odor of flowers.

48. "How silly of people with innumerable obligations ever to be busy seeking such moments of pleasure in this world!

49. "What shall I say of the prowess of undiscriminating men? They propose to reach happiness after crossing interminable hurdles of efforts!

50. "A beggar in the street labors as much for happiness as a mighty emperor.

51-52. "Each of them having gained his end feels happy and considers himself blessed as if he had reached the goal of life. I too have been unwittingly imitating them like a blind man following the blind. Enough of this folly! I will at once return to that ocean of mercy—my Master.

53. "Learning from him what is to be known, I will cross the ocean of doubts after boarding the boat of his teachings."

54. Having resolved thus, Parasurâma of pure mind immediately descended the hill in search of his Master.

55. Quickly reaching the Gandhmadan Mountain, he found the Guru sitting in the *padmasana* posture as if illuminating the whole world.

56. He fell prone before the Master's seat and, holding the Guru's feet with his hands, pressed them to his head.

57. On Parasurâma saluting him thus, Dattatreya gave him his blessings, his face lit with love, and he bade him rise saying:

58. "Child! rise up. I see you have returned after a long time. Tell me how are you? Are you in good health?"

59. He rose as commanded by his Guru, and took his seat in front of and close to him as directed. Clasping his hands, Parasurâma spoke with pleasure.

Note: Clasping the two hands with fingers directed towards the object, is a sign of respect.

60. "Sri Guru! Ocean of Mercy! Can any one drenched with Thy kindness ever be afflicted by ailments even if destiny so decree?

61. "How can the burning pains of illness touch one who is abiding in the refreshing moon of Thy nectarlike kindness.

Note: The moon is believed to be the store of nectar with which the *pitris* feed themselves.

62–64. "I feel happy in body and mind, being refreshed by Thy kindness. Nothing afflicts me except the desire to remain in unbroken contact with Thy holy feet. The very sight of Thy holy feet has made me perfectly happy, but there are a few long-standing doubts in my mind.

65. "With Thy kind permission I desire to propound them."

66. Hearing the words of Parasurâma, Dattatreya the Ocean of kindness, was pleased and said to him.

67. "Ask at once, O Bhargava, what you so much want to know and what you have so long been thinking about. I am pleased with your devotion and shall answer your questions with pleasure."

Thus ends the First Chapter known as the Interrogatory of Bhargava in *Sri Tripura Rahasya*.

Chapter II

Obligatory Sense towards Action Condemned
and Investigation Recommended

1. Ordered thus, Parasurâma, again saluting the son of Saint Atri with humility, began to ask:

2. "Bhagavan, dear and esteemed Master! Oh, Omniscient one! Ocean of Mercy! Once before for good reason I was furious with the kingly class.

3. "Twenty-one times I strode the land exterminating them all, including suckling babes and those in the womb collecting their blood in a pool.

4. "My forefathers were pleased with my devotion to them; however, they ordered me to desist from such carnage. My wrath was at last appeased.

5. "On hearing of the renowned Rama the very incarnation of Hari in Ayodhya, my wrath was rekindled. Blinded by fury and proud of my prowess, I challenged him.

6. "I was defeated by that great Lord and my pride was humbled. However, out of his innate kindness he let me go with my life because I was a Brahmin.

7. "As I was returning mortified by defeat, I realized the vanity of the ways of the world.

8. "Unexpectedly I met Samvarta, the Lord of the *Avadhutas*, and instinctively recognised him to be like fire in embers.

Note: Samvarta, the brother of Brihaspati, looked like a maniac wandering in the forests. Narada once directed the emperor Nivritta to him and instructed him how Samvarta could be recognised. The King accordingly met the Sage and prayed for his help in the performance of a sacrifice, in which Brihaspati prompted by Indra had refused to officiate. Samvarta agreed, though hesitatingly, and later completed it in spite of the wrath of Indra. Indra attempted to break up the function but was rendered impotent by the Sage (*see Asvarnedha Parva* in the *Mahabharata*).

9. "His greatness was like red hot coal hidden in embers. Every inch of his body filled one with exhilaration so that I had a refreshing feeling in his mere proximity.

Note: Sensation of Peace or of *ananda* is the symptom of *Satsanga*.

10. "I asked him to tell me about his state. His answer was clear cut and expressive of the essence of the sweet nectar of Eternal life.

11. "I could not pursue the conversation then and felt like a beggar maid before a queen. However I prayed to him and he directed me to Thee.

12. "Accordingly I have sought shelter at Thy holy feet, just as a blind man who is entirely dependent on his friends.

13. "What Samvarta said is not at all clear to me. I have learnt the Gospel of Tripura well. It is undoubtedly an incentive to devotion to Her.

14. "She is incarnate as Thou, and always abides in my heart. But what have I gained after all?

Note: Prayers to God are only selfish in the beginning, yet they not only fulfill one's desires but also purify the mind so that devotion to God grows in intensity and the devotee desires nothing more than God. Then God shows His Grace by manifesting as his Guru.

15. "Lord, kindly explain what Samvarta told me before. It is certain that I cannot realize the goal until it is made known to me.

16. "Whatever I do in ignorance thereof looks like mere child's play.

17. "Formerly I pleased the Gods, including Indra, with various ceremonies, observances, gifts and presents of food.

18. "Later I heard Samvarta say that the fruits of all these acts are only trivial. I consider those acts of no account which yield only trifling results.

19. "Misery is not absence of happiness, but limited happiness. For as happiness recedes misery pours in.

20. "This is not the only miserable result of action, but there remains a still worse one, the fear of death, which cannot be mitigated by any amount of activity.

21. "My devotional practices before Tripura are similar. All these mental conceptions are nothing but child's play.

22. "The practices may be according to Thy instructions, or different. Again they may be with discipline or without discipline, since the Sastras differ about this.

23. "Meditations may also differ according to individual tastes and temperaments. How can that be? Devotion is just as imperfect as *Karma*.

24. "How can transient mental concepts of devotion produce intransient results of high Truth? Moreover, the practices are continuous and there seems to be no end to these obligatory duties.

25. "I have noticed that Samvarta, the Lord, is quite happy, being completely free from any sense of obligation to act and its disastrous results.

26. "He seems to laugh at the ways of the world, to stride unconcerned up the road of fearlessness, like a majestic elephant refreshing itself in a lake of melted snow when the surrounding forest is on fire.

27. "I found him absolutely free from any sense of obligation and at the same time perfectly happy in his realization of Eternal Being. How did he gain that state? And what did he tell me?

28. "Kindly explain these points, and so rescue me from the jaws of the monster of *Karma.*"

29. Praying so, he fell prostrate and took the Master's feet in his hands.

Seeing Parasurâma doing so and feeling that he was now ready for Realization.

30. Sri Datta, whose very being was love, said gently: "Oh child Bhargava! Lucky are you—your mind being thus disposed.

31-33. "Just as a man sinking in the ocean suddenly finds a boat to rescue him, so also your virtuous actions of the past have now placed you on the most sacred heights of Self-Realization. That Devi Tripura, who is the conscious core of the heart and therefore knows each one intimately, swiftly rescues Her unswerving devotees from the jaws of death, after manifesting Herself in their hearts.

34. "As long as a man is afraid of the nightmare, obligation, so long must he placate it, or else he will not find peace.

35. "How can a man stung by that Viper, obligation, ever be happy? Some men have gone mad as if some poison had already entered their blood and were torturing their whole being.

36. "While others are stupefied by the poison of obligation and unable to discriminate good from bad.

37. "Wrongly do they ever engage in work, being deluded; such is the plight of humanity stupefied by the poison of the sense of obligation.

38. "Men are from time immemorial beings swallowed up by the terrific ocean of poison, like some travellers once on the Vindhya range.

39. "Oppressed by hunger in the forest, they mistook the deceptive *Nux Vomica* fruits for some delicious oranges.

40. "And in their voracious hunger they ate them up without even detecting the bitter taste. They then suffered torment from the effects of the poison.

41. "Having originally mistaken the poisonous fruit for an edible fruit, their reason being now blinded by poison, they eagerly sought relief from pain.

42. "And in their agony they took hold of and ate thorn-apples, thinking them to be rose-apples.

Note: Thorn-apples are used for extracting a poisonous alkaloid. The fruit is fatal or produces insanity.

43. "They became mad and lost their way. Some becoming blind fell into pits or gorges.

44. "Some of them had their limbs and bodies cut by thorns; some were disabled in their hands, feet or other parts of the body; others began to quarrel, fight and shout among themselves.

45. "They assaulted one another with their fists, stones, missiles, sticks, etc., till at length thoroughly exhausted, they reached a certain town.

46. "They happened to come to the outskirts of the town at nightfall, and were prevented by the guards from entering.

47-49. "Unaware of the time and place and unable to gauge the circumstances, they assaulted the guards and were soundly thrashed and chased away; some fell into ditches; some were caught by crocodiles in deep waters; some fell headlong into wells and were drowned; a few more dead than alive, were caught and thrown into prison.

50. "Similar is the fate of the people who, deluded with the quest of happiness, have fallen into the snares of the task-master of action. They are bewildered in their frenzy and destruction awaits them.

51-52. "You are fortunate, Bhargava, in having transcended that distracted state. Investigation is the root-cause of all, and it is the first step to the supreme reward of indescribable bliss. How can any one gain security without proper investigation?

53. "Want of judgment is certain death, yet many are in its clutches. Success attends proper deliberation till eventually the end is without doubt accomplished.

54. "In deliberation is the ever-present weakness of the Daityas and Yatudhanas (Asuras and Rakshasas); deliberation is the characteristic of the Devas (Gods), and therefore they are always happy.

55. "Owing to their discrimination they depend on Vishnu and inevitably conquer their enemies. Investigation is the seed capable of sprouting and flourishing into the gigantic tree of happiness.

56. "A deliberating man always shines over others. Brahmâ is great because of deliberation; Vishnu is worshipped because of it.

57-58. "The Great Lord Siva is omniscient for the same reason. Rama, though the most intelligent of men, came to disaster for want of judgment before attempting to capture the golden deer; later with due deliberation, he spanned the ocean, crossed over to Lanka, the island of the Rakshasa brood, and conquered it.

Note: The reference is to the *Ramayana*. Ravana, the arch enemy of Rama, induced one of his lieutenants to assume the shape of a golden deer and entice Rama away from his hermitage so that Ravana could forcibly carry away Sita, who would thus be left unprotected. The ruse succeeded; and later ensued the great battle in which Ravana and others were killed and Sita was recovered. Thus did Rama vindicate himself.

59. "You must have heard how Brahmâ also becoming on an occasion infatuated, acted rashly like a fool and consequently paid the penalty with one of his five heads.

Note: Brahmâ had originally five heads. He and Vishnu were once contesting each other's superiority. Just then a huge column of light appeared in front of them and they wondered what it was. They agreed that he who found either end of the column earlier, should get the palm. Vishnu became a boar and sought the bottom; Brahmâ became a swan and flew up towards the top. Vishnu returned disappointed. Brahmâ at the point of despair came across a swrewpine flower. He stopped its descent and asked wherefrom it was coming. All that it knew was that it was falling from space and nothing more. Brahmâ persuaded it to bear false witness and claimed superiority over his rival. Siva was enraged, snipped off that head which spoke the lie, and declared himself as the column of light.

60. "Unthinkingly, Mahadeva conferred a boon on the Asura and was immediately obliged to flee in terror for fear of being reduced to ashes.

Note: There was once an Asura by name Bhasma. He did penance and pleased Siva who appeared before him and asked him what he wanted. Bhasma desired that his mere touch should reduce any object to ashes. Siva conferred the boon; Bhasma wanted to test it on him; Siva took to flight. In order to save him from that predicament, Vishnu appeared as a voluptuous damsel before the purusing Asura and enticed him. He became amorous and made advances to her. She asked him to go to a spring in front of them and rub himself with water, before embracing her. He was taken in. On his hand touching his body, he fell down, a heap of ashes.

61. "On one occasion, Hari having killed the wife of Bhrigu became the victim of a terrible curse and suffered untold miseries.

62. "Similarly have other Devas, Asuras, Rakshasas, men and animals become miserable by want of judgment.

63. "On the other hand, great and valiant are the heroes, O Bhargava, whom judgment ever befriends. Eternal homage to them.

64. "Common people, becoming foolishly involved in regard to their sense of action, are perplexed at every turn; if on the other hand, they think and act, they will be free from all misery.

65. "The world has been in the coils of ignorance from time immemorial; how can there be discernment so long as ignorance lasts?

66-68. "Can the sweet waters of dew collect in tropical sandy deserts which are already scorched by heat? Similarly, can the refreshing touch of discernment be sought in the red-hot flue over the furnace of long burning ignorance? Discernment is, however, gained by proper methods, the most effective of which is also the best of all, and that is the supreme grace of the Goddess who inheres as the Heart Lotus in every one. Who has ever accomplished any good purpose, without that Grace?

69. "Investigation is the Sun for chasing away the dense darkness of indolence. It is generated by the worship of God with devotion.

70. "When the Supreme Devi is well pleased with the worship of the devotee, She turns into *vichara* in him and shines as the blazing Sun in the expanse of his Heart.

Note: Devi: Goddess. *Vichara:* (Thought), discrimination, investigation, deliberation, judgment.

Devi is there in ignorance, in worship, in *vichara* and later, like fat in the milk, the curds and the churned butter successively.

71-72. "Therefore that Tripura, the Supreme Force, the Being of all beings, the blessed, the highest, the one consciousness of Siva, who abides as the Self of self, should be worshipped sincerely, exactly as taught by the Guru. The fore-runner of such worship is devotion and praiseworthy earnestness.

73-76. "The antecedent cause of these is again said to be the learning of the *mahatmya* (Gospel). Therefore, O Rama, the *mahatmaya* was first revealed to you; having heard it, you have now progressed well. *Vichara* is the only way to attain the highest Good. I was indeed anxious about you; and there is very good reason for such anxiety until the mind turns towards *vichara* from the overpowering disease of ignorance, just as one is anxious for a patient who is delirious, until one sees that the system shows signs of a favorable turn.

77. "If once *vichara* takes root, the highest good has for all practical purposes, been reached in this life. As long as *vichara* is absent from a human being, the most desirable form of birth, so long is the tree of life barren and therefore useless. The only useful fruit of life is *vichara*.

79-81. "The man without discrimination is like a frog in the well; just as the frog in the well does not know anything either of good or of bad and so dies in his ignorance in the well itself, in the same way men, vainly born in *Brahmanda*,[1] do not know either good or bad regarding themselves and are born only to die in ignorance.

82. "Confounding dispassion *(vairagya)* with misery, and pleasures of the world with happiness *(sukha)*, a man suffers in the cycle of births and deaths, powerful ignorance prevailing.

83-84. "Even though afflicted by misery, he does not cease further indulgence in those causes antecedent to it (namely, wealth, etc.); just as a jack-ass pursues a she-ass even if kicked a hundred times by her, so also it is with the man and the world. But you, O Rama, becoming discriminating have transcended misery."

Thus ends the Second Chapter in *Tripura Rahasya*.

---

1. *Brahmanda:* Egg of Brahmâ (*i.e.*, the Universe).

Chapter III

The Antecedent Cause for Learning the Gospel. Association with the Wise Must Precede "*Vichara*"

1. Having listened to Dattatreya's words, Parasurâma was delighted and continued his questions in all humility:

2. "O Bhagavan! It is precisely as my Lord Guru has just said. Truly, a man will ever head for destruction in his ignorance.

3. "His salvation lies in investigation *(vichara)* alone. The remote and proximate causes have also been mentioned by Thee, and they have been traced to *mahatmya*. I am in great doubt on this point.

4. "How does that happen and what is again its proximate cause? Can it be that it is natural (like courage to a hero)? Then why is it not shared by all?

5-6. "Why have I not got it as yet? Again, there are others who are more troubled and who suffer more than I. Why have they not got this means? Kindly tell me."

Thus asked, Datta, the Ocean of Mercy, answered:

7. "Listen, Rama! I shall now tell you the fundamental cause of salvation. *Association with the wise* is the root cause for obliterating all misery.

8-9. "Association with the sages is alone said to lead to the highest good. Your contact with Samvarta has led you to this stage of enlightenment, which is the fore-runner of emancipation. On being approached, the sages teach the greatest good.

10. "Has any one ever got anything great, without contact with the wise? In any case, it is the company which determines the future of the individual.

11. "A man undoubtedly reaps the fruits of his company. I shall relate to you a story to illustrate this:

12. "There was once a king of Dasarna by name Muktachuda. He had two sons: Hemachuda and Manichuda.

15

13. "They were comely, well-behaved and well-learned. At one time they led a hunting party, consisting of a great retinue of men and warriors, into a deep forest on the Sahya Mountains which was infested with tigers, lions and other wild animals. They were themselves armed with bows and arrows.

14. "There they shot several deer, lions, boars, bisons, wolves, etc., having killed them by the skilful use of their bows.

16. "As more wild animals were being hunted down by the royal hunters, a tornado began to rage, pouring down sand and pebbles.

17. "A thick cloud of dust screened the sky; and it became dark like night, so that neither rocks, trees nor men could be seen.

18. "The mountain was shrouded in darkness, so that neither hills nor valleys could be seen. The retinue hurried away afflicted by the sands and pebbles hurled down by the tornado.

19. "A few of them took shelter under rocks, others in caves, and still others under trees. The royal pair mounted on horses and rode away into the distance.

20. "Hemachuda ultimately reached the hermitage of a sage, which had been built in a fine garden of plantain, date and other trees.

21. "There he saw a charming maiden whose body, bright as gold, shone like a flame of fire.

22-23. "The prince was bewitched at the sight of the girl, who looked like the Goddess of Fortune, and spoke to her thus: 'Who are you, fair lady, who live fearlessly in such a dreadful and solitary forest? Whose are you? Why are you here? Are you alone?'

24. "On being spoken to, that spotless maiden replied: 'Welcome, prince! Please sit down.

25. "Hospitality is the sacred duty of the pious. I notice you have been overtaken by the tornado and afflicted.

26. "Tie your horse to the date-palm. Sit here and take rest, and then you will be able to listen to me in comfort."

27-29. "She gave him fruits to eat and juices to drink. After he had refreshed himself, he was further treated with her charming words which dropped like sweet nectar from her lips.

'Prince! there is that well-known sage, Vyaghrapada, and ardent devotee of Siva, by whose penance all the worlds have been transcended, and who is eagerly worshipped even by the greatest saints for his unparalleled wisdom both with regard to this and other worlds.

30. "I am his foster child—Hemalekha is my name. There was a *Vidyadhari* (celestial damsel), Vidyaprabha by name, and very beautiful.

31. "One day she came here to bathe in this river, the Vena, to which Sushena, the King of Vanga, also came at the same time.

32. "He saw the celestial beauty bathing. She was the fairest in the world, lithe in body and with the most beautiful breasts.

33. "He fell in love with her which love she returned.

34. "Their love consummated, he returned home leaving her pregnant.

35. "Afraid of slander, she caused an abortion. I was however born alive from that womb.

36. "As Vyaghrapada came to the river bank for his evening ablutions, he picked me up because of his great love for all, in order to bring me up with a mother's care.

37. "He who offers righteous protection is said to be the father. I am therefore his daughter by virtue of this and devoted to him.

38-39. "There is certainly no fear for me anywhere on earth on account of his greatness. Be they Gods or Asuras, they cannot enter this hermitage with bad motives; if they did they would only be counting their own ruin. I have now told you my story. Wait here, Prince, a little.

40. "That same lord, my foster-father, will soon be here. Salute him and hear him with humility; your desire will be fulfilled, and you may leave here in the morning.'

41. "Having heard her and becoming enamored by her, he was silent for fear of giving offence; yet he became distressed in mind.

42-46. "Noting the prince love-stricken, that highly accomplished girl continued: 'Bravo Prince! Be steady! My father is about to come. Tell him all.' As she was saying this Vyaghrapada the great saint arrived, carrying a basket of flowers culled from the forest for worship. Seeing the sage coming, the prince rose up from his seat, prostrated before him mentioning his own name, and then took his seat as directed. The sage noticed that the man was love-stricken; taking in the whole situation by his occult powers, he pondered on what would be the best course in the circumstances; and ended by bestowing Hemalekha on the young man as his life-partner.

47-49. "The prince was filled with joy and returned with her to his own capital. Muktachuda, his father, was also very pleased and ordered festivities in the kingdom. He then had the marriage performed ceremoniously, and the loving couple passed a very happy honeymoon in the palace, in forest retreats, and in holiday resorts. But the infatuated prince noticed that Hemalekha was not as amorous as himself.

50. "Feeling that she was always unresponsive, he asked her in private: 'My dear! How is it you are not as attentive to me as I am to you?

51. "Thou fairest of girls radiant with smiles! How is it that you are never keen on seeking pleasure or enjoying it? Are not these pleasures to your taste?

52. "You look indifferent even during the greatest pleasures. How can I be happy if your interest is not awakened?

53. "Even when I am close to you, your mind seems to be elsewhere; when spoken to, you do not seem to listen.

54. "As I hold you in close embrace for a long while, you seem unconscious of me, and then ask me, 'Lord, when did you come?'

55. "None of the carefully planned arrangements seem to interest you and you do not take part in them.

56. "When I turn away from you, you remain with your eyes closed; and so you continue whenever I approach you.

57. "Tell me how I can derive pleasure with nothing but an artist's model which is what you are, seeing your indifference to all enjoyments.

58. "What does not please you cannot please me either. I am always looking to you, trying to please you like a lily looking up at the moon.

Note: Kumuda, a certain lily, blossoms only in the night and is therefore said to be the beloved of the Moon, as the lotus blossoming in the day is said to be the beloved of the Sun.

59. "Speak, dear! Why are you like this? You are dearer to me than even life. I adjure you! Speak and so relieve my mind."

Thus ends the Third Chapter in the section on the potency of the association with the wise, in *Tripura Rahasya.*

Chapter IV

Disgust for Worldly Enjoyments is Inculcated
So That Dispassion Might Be Developed

1-3. "On hearing the sweet words of her infatuated lover, who was all the time pressing her to his bosom, that stainless girl, wishing to teach him, smiled gently and spoke with good sense as follows: 'Listen to me, O Prince. It is not that I do not love you, only that I am trying to find what the greatest joy in life is which will never become distasteful. I am always searching for it, but have not attained it as yet.

4. 'Though always looking for it, I have not reached any definite decision, as is a woman's way. Will you not kindly tell me what exactly it is and so help me?'

5. "Being thus coaxed, Hemachuda laughed derisively and told his beloved: 'Women are indeed silly.'

6-8. "For do not even the birds and beasts, nay the crawling insects know what is good and what is bad? Otherwise, how are they guided in the pursuit of good, and how do they escape from bad? That which is pleasing is clearly good and that which is not so, is bad. What is there in it, my dear, that you are always given to thinking about it? Is it not silly?' Hearing her lover speak thus, Hemalekha continued:

9. "True that women are silly and cannot judge rightly. Therefore should I be taught by you, the true discerner.

10. "On being rightly taught by you, I shall stop thinking like that. Also, I shall then be able to share in your pleasures to your entire satisfaction.

11. "O King, subtle judge that you are, you have found happiness and misery to be the result of what is pleasing or otherwise.

12. "The same object yields pleasure or pain according to circumstances. Where is then the finality in your statement?

13. "Take fire for example. Its results vary according to seasons, the places and its own size or intensity.

14. "It is agreeable in cold seasons and disagreeable in hot seasons. Pleasure and pain are, therefore, functions of seasons; similarly of latitudes and altitudes.

15. "Again, fire is good for people of certain constitutions only and not for others. Still again, pleasure and pain depend on circumstances.

16-17. "The same reasoning applies to cold, to riches, to sons, to wife, to kingdom and so on. See how your father, the Maharaja, is daily worried even though he is surrounded by wife, children and wealth. Why do not others grieve like this? What has happened to enjoyments in his case? He is certainly on the look-out for happiness; are not his resources all directed to that end?

18. "No one seems to possess everything that is sufficient for happiness. The question arises: Cannot a man be happy, even with such limited means? I shall give you the answer.

19. "That cannot be happiness, my Lord, which is tinged with misery. Misery is of two kinds, external and internal.

20. "The former pertain to the body and is caused by the nerves, etc., the latter pertains to the mind and is caused by desire.

21. "Mental distraction is worse than physical pain and the whole world has fallen a victim to it. Desire is the seed of the tree of misery and never fails in its fruits.

22. "Overpowered by it, Indra and the Devas, though living in celestial regions of enjoyment and fed by nectar, are still slaves to it and work day and night according to its dictates.

23. "Respite gained by the fulfilment of one desire before another takes its place, is not happiness because the seeds of pain are still latent. Such respite is enjoyed by the insects also (which certainly do not typify perfect happiness).

24. "Yet is their enjoyment distinctly better than that of men because their desires are less complex.

25. "If it is happiness to have one desire among many fulfilled who will not be thus happy in this world?

26. "If a man, scalded all over, can find happiness by smearing unguents on himself, then everyone must be happy.

27. "A man is happy when embraced by his beloved; he is unhappy in the same act under other circumstances.

*

* *

30. ". . . Or do you mean to say that the enjoyment of man is enhanced by his sense of beauty?

31. "Beauty is only a mental concept, as is evident from the similar feeling in similar enjoyments of lovers in dreams. (I shall tell you a story to illustrate the point.) There was once a most handsome scion of a king—fairer than Cupid himself.

32. "He was wedded to an equally beautiful damsel and was very devoted to her.

33. "But she fell in love with a servant of the royal household who deceived the young prince very skilfully.

34. "This servant used to serve liquor in excess so that the prince got drunk and lost his senses, on retiring, a wily harlot was sent to keep him company.

35-38. "The unchaste princess and the servant were then able to carry on; and the foolish prince was embracing the other woman in his intoxication. Yet he thought within himself that he was the happiest of men to have such an angel for his wife who was so devoted to him. After a long time, it happened that the servant in the pressure of work left the liquor on the prince's table and occupied himself otherwise. The prince did not drink as much as usual.

39-42. "Becoming voluptuous, he hastily retired to his bed-room, which was sumptuously furnished, and enjoyed himself with the strumpet, without recognising her in the heat of passion. After some time, he noticed that she was not his wife and on this confusion asked her 'where is my beloved wife?'

43-48. "She trembled in fear and remained silent. The prince, who suspected foul play, flew into a rage and holding her by her hair drew his sword and thus threatened her, 'Speak the truth or your life will not be worth a moment's purchase.'

Afraid of being killed, she confessed the whole truth, taking him to the trysting-place of the princess. There he found her with her lovely and delicate body in close and loving embrace of the dark, ugly, loathsome savage who was his servant. . . .

51. "The prince was shocked at the sight.

52. "Shortly afterwards he pulled himself together and began to reflect as follows: ' Shame on me who am so addicted to drink!

53. "Shame on the fools infatuated with love for women. Women are like nothing but birds flitting above the tree tops.

54. "Ass that I was, all the time loving her even more than life.

55. "Women are only good for the enjoyment of lecherous fools. He who loves them is a wild ass.

56. "Women's good faith is more fleeting than streaks of autumnal clouds.

57-59. "I had not till now understood the woman who, unfaithful to me, was in illicit love with a savage, all the time feigning love to me, like a prostitute to a lecherous fool.

60. "I did not in my drunkenness suspect her in the least; on the other hand, I believed that she was as much with me as my own shadow.

61-64. "Fie! is there a fool worse than myself, who was deceived by this ugly harlot at my side and enthralled by her professions of love? Again, what has the other woman found in preference to me in a loathsome brute?

65. "The prince then left society in disgust and retired into a forest."

Hemalekha continued "So you see, O Prince, how beauty is only a concept of the mind.

66. "What pleasure you have in your apprehension of beauty in me, is sometimes even exceeded by others in their love of their dear ones—be they fair or ugly. I will tell you what I think of it.

67. "The fair woman that appears as the object is only the reflection of the subtle concept already in the subjective mind.

68-69. "The mind draws an image of her beauty in conformity with its own repeated conceptions. The repeatedly drawn image becomes clearer and clearer until it appears solidly as the object. An attraction springs up (and enslaves the mind) by constant mental associations.

70. "The mind, becoming restless, stirs up the senses and seeks the fulfillment of its desires in the object; a composed mind is not excited even at the sight of the fairest.

71. "The reason for the infatuation is the oft-repeated mental picture. Neither children nor self-controlled yogis are excited in the same way (because their minds do not dwell on such things).

72. "So whoever finds pleasure in anything, the beauty therein is only mental imagery.

73. "Ugly and loathsome women too are looked upon as delightful angels by their husbands.

74. "If the mind conceives anything as loathsome and not delightful, there will be no pleasure in such.

75. "Fie on human beings who appraise the foulest part of the body as the most delightful.

*

* *

77. "Listen Prince! the idea of beauty lies in one's own desire innate in the mind.

78. "If, on the other hand, beauty is natural to the object of love, why is it not recognised by children too, as sweetness in edibles is recognised by them?

79-81. "The form, the stature and complexion of people differ in various countries and at different times; their ears may be long; their faces distorted; their teeth large; their nose prominent; bodies hirsute or smooth, their hair red, black, or golden, light or thick, smooth or curly; their complexion fair, dark, coppery, yellow or grey.

82. "All of them derive the same kind of pleasure as you, Prince!

83. "Even the most accomplished among men have fallen into the habit of seeking pleasure from woman, for all consider her the best hunting ground for delight.

84. "Similarly also a man's body is thought by woman to be the highest source of enjoyment. But consider the matter well, Prince!

85-86. "Shaped of fat and flesh, filled with blood, topped by the head, covered by skin, ribbed by bones, covered with hair, containing bile and phlegm, a pitcher of feces and urine, generated from semen and ova, and born from the womb, such is the body. Just think of it!

87. "Finding delight in such a thing, how are men any better than worms growing in offal?

88. "My King! Is not this body (pointing to herself) dear to you? Think well over each part thereof.

89. "Analyze well and carefully what it is that forms your food materials with their different flavors, kinds and consistencies?

90. "Every one knows how the consumed foods are finally ejected from the body.

91. "Such being the state of affairs in the world, tell me what is agreeable or otherwise."

"On hearing all this, Hemachuda developed disgust for earthly pleasures.

92. "He was amazed at the strange discourse he heard. He later pondered over all that Hemalekha had said.

93. "His disgust for earthly pleasures grew in volume and in force. He again and again discussed matters with his beloved so that he understood the ultimate truth.

94. "Then realizing the pure consciousness inhering in the Self to be that self-same Tripura, he became aware of the One Self holding all, and was liberated.

95. "He was liberated while yet alive. His brother Manichuda and his father Muktachuda were both guided by him and were also liberated.

96. "The queen was guided by her daughter-in-law and was liberated; so also did the ministers, chieftains and citizens gain wisdom.

97. "There was no one born in that city who remained ignorant. The city was like that of Brahmâ, the abode of happy, peaceful and contented people.

98. "It was known as Visala and became the most renowned on Earth, where even the parrots in the cages used to repeat: 'Meditate, O Man, on the Self, the Absolute Consciousness devoid of objects! There is naught else to know besides pure consciousness; it is like a self-luminous mirror reflecting objects within.

100. "'That same consciousness is also the objects, that is the subject, and that is all—the mobile and the immobile; all else shines in its reflected light; it shines of itself.

101. "'Therefore, O Man, throw off delusion! Think of that consciousness which is alone, illuminating all and pervading all. Be of clear vision.

102-103. "Those holy saints Vamadeva and others having on one occasion heard these sacred words of the parrots, wondered at the wisdom of even the birds of that city and named it the *City of Wisdom*.

104. "The city is today still called by that name," Dattatreya continued. "Association with the sages, O Rama, is thus the root cause of all that is auspicious and good.

105. "By association with Hemalekha, all people gained *jnana* (wisdom). Know then, the *satsanga* (association with the wise) is alone the root cause of salvation.'"

Thus ends the Fourth Chapter on the fruits of *satsanga* in the Section of Hemachuda in *Tripura Rahasya*.

Chapter V

On Bondage and Release

1. Parasurâma, on hearing the master's discourse on the greatness of *satsanga,* was highly pleased and continued to ask.

2. "You have truly said, O Lord, that *satsanga* is the harbinger of all that is worthy, and illustrated the fact with a story.

3. "One's enjoyments are determined by the quality of one's company. The highest good was accomplished by all owing to their association direct or indirect, with Hemalekha, though she was only a woman.

4. "I am anxious to hear how Hemachuda was further guided by her. Please tell me, Thou Lord of Mercy!"

5. Thus requested, Dattatreya said to Parasurâma: "Listen, O Bhargava, I shall now continue the holy narrative.

6. "Having heard what she had to say, the enjoyments ceased to interest him, he developed a disgust for them, and became pensive.

7. "But the force of habit still remained with him. He was therefore unable either to enjoy himself or to desist all of a sudden.

8. "He was however too proud to confess his weakness to his beloved. Some time passed in this way.

9. "When his habits forced him into the old ways he was still mindful of his wife's words, so that he engaged himself in them with reluctance and shame.

10-11. "He repeatedly fell into his old ways by force of habit; and very often he became repentant, realizing the evil of those ways and remembering his wife's wise words. His mind was thus moving to and fro, like a swing.

12. "Neither delicious foods, nor fine clothes, nor rich jewels, nor charming damsels nor caparisoned horses, nor even his dear friends continued to interest him.

13-14. "He became sad as if he had lost his all. He was unable to resist his habits at once nor was he willing to follow them knowingly. He grew pale and melancholy.

15. "Hemalekha, always aware of the change in him, went to him in his private chamber and said, "How is it, my Lord, that you are not as cheerful as before?

16. "You look sad. Why so? I do not see symptoms of any particular ailment in you.

17. "Doctors may hold out the fear of disease amidst the pleasure of life; diseases are due to loss of harmony in the three tempers of the body.

18. "Diseases remain latent in all bodies because disharmony of tempers cannot always be prevented.

19. "Tempers get displaced by food consumed, clothes worn, words uttered or heard, sights seen, objects contacted, changes of seasons and travel in different countries.

20. "Being inescapable, the dislocation of tempers need not claim one's constant attention. There are remedies prescribed for diseases arising from it.

21. "Now tell me, dear, why you are so sad."

22. "When Hemalekha had finished, the prince replied, 'I will tell you the cause of my misery. Listen to me, dear.'

23. "'What you said on the last occasion has barred all means of pleasure for me, so that I can now find nothing to make me happy.

24. "'Just as a man under orders to be executed cannot relish the luxuries provided for him by the State, so also I do not relish anything.

25. "'Just as a man is forced by royal command to do something in spite of himself, so also must I engage in old ways by force of habit. Now I ask you, dear, tell me how I can gain happiness.'

26. "Being thus approached, Hemalekha thought: This dispassion is certainly due to my words.

27. "'There is the seed of the highest good in that field where such symptoms appear. Had my well-calculated words not produced even the slightest turn in this direction, there would be no hope of emancipating him. This state of dispassion only

28

arises in one with whose continued devotion Tripura inherent in the Heart as the Self, is well pleased."

Thinking thus, that wise lady was eager to reveal wisdom to her husband.

30. "Keeping her own wisdom secret at the same time, she spoke with measured words: 'Listen, Prince, to the story of my own past.

31. "My mother formerly gave me a lady-in-waiting who was good by nature, but later associated with an undesirable friend.

32. "This friend was clever in creating new and wonderful things. I also without my mother's knowledge associated with her.

33. "That lady-in-waiting became very friendly with that undesirable companion, and I was obliged to do the same because I loved my friend more than life.

34. "For, I could not remain without her even for a second; so much did she enthrall me by her undoubted purity.

35. "Always loving my friend, I quickly became part of herself. She for her part was all the time close to her friend, a wicked strumpet, who was ever generating new and fascinating things.

36-38. "In secret that woman introduced her son to my friend. That son was an ignorant fool with eyes blood-shot with drink. And my friend went on enjoying him in my very presence. But she, though completely overpowered by him and being enjoyed by him day after day, never left me, and I, too, did not abandon her. And out of that union was born a fool of the same type as his father.

39-41. "He grew up to be a very restless young fellow, fully inheriting his father's dullness and his grandmother's wickedness and creativeness. This boy, *Master Inconstant* by name, was brought up and trained by his father, *Mr. Fool* and his grandmother *Madame Ignorance,* and he became skilled in their ways. He could negotiate the most difficult places with perfect ease and surmount obstacles in a trice.

42. "In this manner, my friend, though very good by nature, became afflicted and silly because of her association with wicked people.

43-44. "What with love for her friend, devotion for her lover, and affection for her son, she began gradually to forsake me. But I could not break with her so easily.

45-46. "Not being self-reliant, I was dependent on her so remained with her. Her husband, *Mr. Fool*, though always in enjoyment of her, mistook me for one of the same sort and tried to ravish me. But I was not what he took me to be. I am pure by nature and only led by her, for the time being.

47. "Even so, there was wide-spread scandal about me in the world, that I was always in *Mr. Fool's* hold.

48. "My friend, entrusting her son *Master Inconstant* to me, was always in the company of her lover.

49. "*Mr. Inconstant* grew up in my care and in due course married a wife with his mother's approval.

50. "*Unsteady* by name, she was ever restless and changeful and could put on different forms to please her husband's whim.

51. "By her wonderful capacity to change and by her exceeding skill and cleverness, she brought her husband completely under her control.

52. "*Mr. Inconstant,* too, used to fly hundreds of miles in a twinkling and return, go here, there and everywhere, but yet could find no rest.

53-54. "Whenever *Mr. Inconstant* wished to go anywhere and whatever he wanted to have in any measure, *Madame Unsteady* was ready to meet his desires changing herself accordingly and creating new environments to please her husband. She thus won his affection entirely.

55. "She bore him five sons who were devoted to their parents. Each one was skilled in his own way. They were also entrusted to my care by my friend.

56-61. "Out of love for my friend, I brought them up with care, and made them strong. Then those five sons of *Madame Unsteady* individually erected splendid palaces, invited their father to their homes and entertained him continually in turns. The eldest of them entertained him in his mansion with different kinds of classic music, with incantations of the Vedas, the reading of scriptures, the humming sounds of bees, the twittering of birds and other sounds sweet to hear.

62-64. "The father was pleased with the son, who arranged for still further sounds for him which were harsh, fearful and tumultuous like the roar of the lion, the peal of thunder, the raging of the sea, the rumblings of earthquakes, the cries from lying-in-chambers, and the quarrels, moans and lamentations of many people.

65-67. "Invited by his second son, the father went to stay in his mansion. There he found soft seats, downy beds, fine clothes and some hard things, others hot or warm or cold, or refreshing things with various designs, and so on. He was pleased with the agreeable things and felt aversion to the disagreeable ones.

68. "Then going to the third son, he saw charming and variegated scenes, things red, white, brown, blue, yellow, pink, smoky grey, tawny, red-brown, black and spotted, others fat or lean, short or long, broad or round, bent or wavy, pleasing or horrible, nauseous, brilliant or savage, unsightly or captivating, some pleasing and others otherwise.

72. "The father was taken to the fourth son's mansion and there he had fruits and flowers to order. He had drinks, things to be licked, to be sucked, and to be masticated, juicy things, some refreshing like nectar, others sweet, sour, pungent or astringent, some decoctions of similar flavors, and so on. He tasted them all.

76-79. "The last son took the father to his home and treated him with fruits and flowers, with various scented grasses, herbs and things of different odors, sweet or putrescent, mild or acrid, others stimulating or soporific and so on.

"In this manner, he enjoyed himself uninterruptedly, one way or another, in one mansion or another, being pleased with some and repulsed by others.

80. "The sons too were so devoted to their father that they would not touch anything themselves in his absence.

81. "But *Mr. Inconstant* not only enjoyed himself thoroughly in his sons' mansions, but also stole away things from them and shared them in secret with his dear wife, *Madam Unsteady,* in his own home, unknown to his sons.

83. "Later, one *Vorax* fell in love with *Mr. Inconstant* and he wedded her; they became very devoted to each other. *Mr. Inconstant* loved *Madam Vorax,* heart and soul.

84-87. "He used to fetch enormous provisions for her, she consumed them all in a moment and was still hungry for more; therefore she kept her husband always on his legs, to collect her food; and, too, he was incessantly in quest of provision for her. She was not satisfied with the service of the father and his five sons put together, but wanted still more. Such was her insatiable hunger. She used to order all of them about, for her needs. In a short time she gave birth to two sons.

88. "They were *Master Flaming-mouth* the elder and *Master Mean* the younger—both of course very dear to their mother.

89-91. "Whenever *Mr. Inconstant* sought *Madam Vorax* in privacy, his body was burnt by the wrathsome flames of *Master Flaming-mouth*; being thus afflicted, he fell down unconscious.

"Again, whenever he fondled the younger son out of his love, he was hated by all the world and he himself became as if dead. *Mr. Inconstant* thus experienced untold misery.

92. "Then my companion, good by nature, was herself afflicted because of her son *Mr. Inconstant's* grief.

93-95. "Being also associated with her two grandsons, *Master Flaming-mouth* and *Master Mean,* she became quite miserable and gave way under the public odium. I too, dear, collapsed in sympathy with her. Thus passed several years until *Mr. Inconstant* dominated by *Madam Vorax* lost all initiative and was entirely in her hands.

96-107. "He was foredoomed and betook himself to the city of ten gates. There he lived with *Madam Vorax,* his sons and his mother, always seeking pleasure but only sharing misery, day and night. Burnt by the wrath of *Flaming-mouth* and treated with contempt by *Master Mean,* he swung hither and thither greatly agitated. He went into the homes of his other five sons but was only perplexed, without being happy. My companion too was so affected by her son's plight that she again collapsed, and yet she continued to live in the same city. *Madam Vorax* with her two boys *Masters Flaming-mouth* and *Mean* was being fed by *Madam Ignorance*—her husband's grandmother, and by *Mr. Fool,* her father-in-law. She got on well with her co-wife *Madam Unsteady* and was even intimate with her. (Ingratiating herself with all of them), she completely dominated her husband *Mr. Inconstant.*

*
* *

"I too continued to live there because of my love for my friend. Otherwise, none of them could remain in the town without me who was their protectress, though I was moribund owing to my friend's moribundity.

"I was sometimes suppressed by *Madam Ignorance,* was made a fool of by *Mr. Fool,* became inconstant on account of *Mr. Inconstant,* grew unsteady with *Madam Unsteady,* contacted wrath with *Flaming-mouth* and looked contemptible with *Master Mean.* I reflected within myself all the moods of my friend, for she would have died if I had left her even a minute. Because of my company, the common people always misjudged me for a strumpet, whereas discriminating men could see that I have always remained pure.

108-111. "For that Supreme Good One, my mother, is ever pure and clear, more extensive than space and subtler than the subtlest; she is omniscient, yet of limited knowledge; she works all, yet remains inactive; she holds all, herself being unsupported; all depend on her, and she is independent; all forms are hers, but she is formless; all belong to her, but she is unattached; though illumining all, she is not known to any one under any circumstances; she is Bliss, yet not blissful; she has no father nor mother; innumerable are her daughters, like me.

112-113. "My sisters are as many as the waves on the sea. All of them, O Prince, are just like me involved in their companions' affairs. Though sharing the lives of my friends, I am in possession of the most potent spell, by virtue of which I am also exactly like my mother in nature.

114. (The tale is resumed.)

115. "When my friend's son retired to rest, he always slept soundly on the lap of his mother; as *Mr. Inconstant* was asleep, all others, including his sons, were also asleep, for no one could remain awake.

116. "On such occasions, the city was guarded by *Mr. Motion,* the intimate friend of *Mr. Inconstant,* who was always moving to and fro by two upper gateways.

117. "My friend, the mother of *Mr. Inconstant,* along with him and her wicked friend—the same was her mother-in-law—watched the whole sleeping family.

118. "I used to seek my mother in that interval and remain blissful in her fond embrace. But I was obliged to return to the city simultaneously with the waking of the sleepers.

119. "This *Mr. Motion,* the friend of *Mr. Inconstant,* is most powerful and keeps them all alive.

120-121. "Though single, he multiplies himself, manifests as the city and citizens, pervades them all, protects and holds them.

122. "Without him, they would all be scattered and lost like pearls without the string of the necklace.

123. "He is the bond between the inmates and myself; empowered by me, he serves in the city as the string in a necklace.

124. "If that city decays, he collects the inmates together, leads them to another and remains their master.

125-131. "In this way *Mr. Inconstant* rules over cities always, he himself remaining under the sway of his friend. Though supported by such a powerful friend, though born of such a virtuous mother and brought up by me, he is never otherwise than miserable, because he is tossed about by his two wives and several sons. He is torn asunder by his sons and finds not the least pleasure but only intense misery. Tempted by *Madame Unsteady,* he grieves; ordered about by *Madam Vorax,* he runs about in search of food for her; stricken by *Flaming-mouth,* he burns with rage, loses his sense and is baffled; approaching *Master Mean,* he is openly despised and reviled by others and becomes as one dead under shame of odium.

132-134. "Already of disreputable heredity, and now infatuated by love for, and tossed about by his wicked wives and sons, he has been living with them in all kinds of places, good or bad, in forests with woods or thorny bushes and infested with wild beasts, in deserts burning hot, in icy tracts pierced by cold, in putrid ditches or in dark holes and so on.

135. "Again and again my friend was stricken with grief on account of her son's calamities and nearly died with sorrow.

34

136. "I too, though sane and clear by nature, dear, got involved in the affairs of her family and became sad also.

137. "Who can hope for even the least happiness in bad company? One may as well seek to quench one's thirst by drinking water from a mirage.

138. "Engulfed in sorrow, my friend once sought me in private.

139. "Advised by me, she soon gained a good husband, killed her own son and imprisoned his sons.

140. "Then accompanied by me, she quickly gained my mother's presence, and being pure, she often embraced my mother.

141. "She at once dived in the sea of Bliss and became Bliss itself. In the same manner, you too can conquer your wrong ways which are only accretions.

142. "Then, my Lord, attain the mother and gain eternal happiness. I have now related to you, my Lord, my own experience of the pedestal of Bliss.'"

Thus ends the Chapter on Bondage in the Section of Hemachuda in *Tripura Rahasya*.

Note:

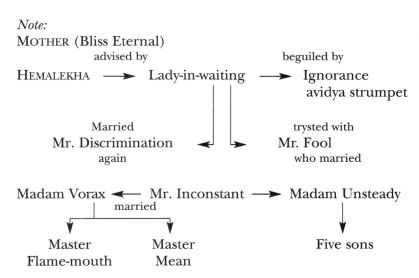

MOTHER (Bliss Eternal)

HEMALEKHA → Lady-in-waiting → Ignorance
avidya strumpet

advised by   beguiled by

Married   trysted with
Mr. Discrimination ← → Mr. Fool
again   who married

Madam Vorax ← Mr. Inconstant → Madam Unsteady
married

Master   Master   Five sons
Flame-mouth   Mean

Chapter VI

On the Merits of Faith for Gaining the Goal and on the Harmfulness of Dry Polemics

1. Hemachuda was astonished at the fantastic tale of his beloved. Being ignorant, he smiled derisively at the tale and asked that wise princess:

2. "My dear, what you have been saying seems to be nothing but invention. Your words have no relation to facts and are altogether meaningless.

3. "You are certainly the daughter of an *Apsaras* (celestial damsel), and brought up by Rishi Vyagrapada in the forest; you are still young and not yet fully grown.

4. "But you talk as if you were several generations old. Your long-winded speech is like that of a girl possessed and not in her senses.

5. "I cannot believe that rigmarole. Tell me where your companion is and who is the son she killed.

6. "Where are those cities? What is the significance of your story? Where is your friend?

7. "I know nothing of your lady-in-waiting. You may ask my mother if you like. There is no other lady besides your mother-in-law in my father's place.

8. "Tell me quickly where such a lady is to be found and where her son's sons are. I think your tale is a myth like the tale of a barren woman's son.

9-11. "A clown once related a story that a barren woman's son mounted a chariot reflected in a mirror and decorated with silver taken from the sheen of mother-of-pearl, armed himself with weapons made of human horn, fought in the battle-field of the sky, killed the future king, subdued the city of aerial hosts and enjoyed himself with dream maidens on the banks of the waters of a mirage.

12. "I take your words to mean something similar. They can never be the truth." After listening to the words of her lover, the wise girl continued.

13. "Lord, how can you say that my parable is meaningless? Words from the lips of those like me can never be nonsense.

14. "Falsehood undermines the effects of one's penance; so how can it be suspected in virtuous people? How can such a one be stainless and numbered among the sages?

15. "Moreover, one who entertains an earnest seeker with hollow or false words will not prosper in this world nor advance in the next.

16. "Listen, Prince. A purblind man cannot have his eyesight restored by merely hearing the prescription read.

17. "He is a fool who misjudges good precepts for falsehood. Do you think, my dear, that I, your wife, would deceive you with a myth when you are so much in earnest?

18-19. "Reason well and carefully examine these apparent untruths of mine. Is not an intelligent man accustomed to judge big things in the world by verifying a few details in them? I now present you my credentials.

20. "Some things used to please you before. Why did they cease to do so, after you heard me on the last occasion?

21. "My words brought about dispassion; they are similarly bound to do so even more in the future. How else can it be? Judge your own statements from these facts.

22. "Listen to me, King, with an unsophisticated and clear intellect. Mistrust in a well-wisher's words is the surest way to ruin.

23. "Faith is like a fond mother who can never fail to save her trusting son from dangerous situations. There is no doubt about it.

24. "The fool who has no faith in his well-wisher's words is forsaken by prosperity, happiness and fame. A man who is always suspicious can never gain anything worthwhile.

25. "Confidence holds the world and nourishes all. How can a babe thrive if it has no confidence in its mother?

26. "How can a lover gain pleasure if he does not trust his beloved? Similarly, how is the aged parent to be happy who has no confidence in his sons?

27. "Would the husbandman till the land, if he had no confidence? Mutual distrust will put an end to all transactions.

28. "How can humanity exist without universal confidence? If you should say, on the other hand, that it is the law of cause and effect, I will tell you; listen to me.

29. "People believe in the law that such a cause produces such a result. Is that not faith?

30. "So then, a man will not dare to breathe in the absence of *Sraddha* (faith) for fear of pathogenic infection, and consequently perish. Therefore believe before you aspire for supreme beatitude.

31. "If again, Prince, you hesitate to depend on an incompetent person, as you may think me to be, that is because you believe that a certain end must be accomplished.

32. "How else can the desired end be approached?" Hearing his beloved's arguments, Hemachuda said to the fair speaker:

33. "If faith should be placed on any one, my dear it should certainly be placed on those worthy of it, in order that one's ends may be served.

34-35. "He who is bent on the highest good should never trust an incompetent person. Otherwise, he comes to grief, like a fish attracted by the tempting bait at the end of a fishing line. Therefore, faith can only be put in the worthy and not in the unworthy.

36. "Fishes and all those men who have ruined themselves in one way and prospered in the other, can verify my statement.

37. "I can only believe you therefore after full ascertainment of your worth; not otherwise. Why then do you ask me if the desired end can be approached?"*(vide* sloka 32 *ante.)*

38. After hearing him, Hemalekha replied: "Listen, Prince, to what I am going to say now.

39. "I answer your point. How is one to be judged, whether one is good or bad?

40. "Is it by reference to accepted standards? What is the authority behind such standards? Are the authors themselves

worthy or unworthy? In this way, there will be no end to argument.

41. "Moreover, the observer's competence must be taken into account. (Thus, too, there will be no finality reached.) Therefore life moves by faith only.

42-45. "I shall tell you the rationale of reaching the Supreme Goal by means of faith. Be attentive. People will not gain anything, either during their life-time or after death, by endless discussions or blind acceptance. Of the two, however, there is hope for the latter and there is none for the former."

(The following anecdote illustrates the point.)

"Once there lived a saint, by name Kausika, on the Sahya Hill near the banks of the Godavari.

46. "He was serene, pure, pious, having knowledge of the Supreme Truth. Several disciples attended on him.

47. "Once when the master had gone out, the disciples started to discuss philosophy, according to their own rights.

48. "There appeared on the scene a Brahmin of great intellect and wide learning, Soonga by name, who successfully refuted all their arguments by his skill in logic.

49-50. "He was a man without faith and without conviction, but an able debater. When they said that the truth must be ascertained by reference to some standard, he argued on the basis of an unending series of standards and refuted them.

51-55. "He rounded off his speech with the following: 'Listen, you Brahmins, standards are not applicable for ascertaining merits or demerits and so arriving at the truth. For erroneous standards are no good as tests. To start with, their correctness must be established. Other standards are required to check them. Are they in their turn infallible? Proceeding in this way, no finality can be reached. Therefore no tests are possible. Ascertainment of Truth being impossible without being tested, nothing can therefore be Truth. This enunciation itself cannot be true, nor the enunciator either. What then is the decision arrived at? That all are nothing, void. This too cannot be supported by reliable facts; hence, the statement that all are void ends in void also.'

56. "Hearing his discourse, some of them were impressed by the force of Soonga's logic and became scholiasts of the void.

57-60. "They got lost in the maze of their philosophy. The discriminating ones among the hearers placed Soonga's arguments before their master and were enlightened by him. Thus they gained peace and happiness. Therefore, beware of arid polemics parading as logic. Use it in the manner in which the holy books have done. That way lies the salvation." Thus addressed by that eminent heroine, Hemachuda was greatly astonished and said: "My dear, I did not realize your sublimity earlier.

61. "Blessed are you that you are so wise! Blessed am I that I have fallen into your company. You say that *faith* bestows the highest good. How does it do so?

62-63. "Where is *faith* expedient, and where not? The scriptures differ in their teachings; the teachers differ among themselves; the commentaries similarly differ from one another; to add to this, one's reasoning is no guide. Which of them is to be followed and which rejected?

64. "Each one stamps his own views with the seal of authority and condemns the rest, not only as worthless but also as harmful, my dear!

65. "That being the case, I cannot decide for myself. What you condemned as the school of the void turns round on others and attacks them.

66. "Why should not that school be respected? It has its own adherents and its own system of philosophy. Explain to me, dear, all these things clearly. They must indeed be already clear to you."

Thus ends the Chapter VI on *Sraddha* (Faith) in Hemachuda Section in *Tripura Rahasya*.

Chapter VII

That the Goal is Gained only after Ascertaining God by Faith, Effort and Approved Logic, and Devotion to Him

1. When Hemalekha was thus asked by her husband, she with her saintly practical knowledge of the state of the universe, spoke to him with increased kindness:

2-5. "Dearest, listen to me attentively. What is known as the mind is, after all, always like a restless monkey. So the ordinary man is always afflicted with troubles. Everybody knows that a restless mind is the channel of endless troubles; whereas one is happy in sleep in the absence of such restlessness. Therefore keep your mind steady when you listen to what I say. Hearing with a distracted mind is as good as not hearing, for the words serve no useful purpose, resembling the fruit-laden tree seen in a painting.

6. "Man quickly benefits if he turns away from dry, ruinous logic and engages in purposeful discussion.

7. "Appropriate effort must follow right discussion; for a man profits according to the zeal accompanying his efforts.

8. "You find, my dear, that aimless discussions are fruitless and that earnest efforts are fruitful in the world.

9. "Discriminating zeal is what enables the husbandman to plough the field in season and the assayer to assay the worth of gold, silver, precious stones, medicinal herbs and the rest. No practical work will be done if people spend all their lives in vain discussions alone. Therefore, one should discard aimless talk and begin immediately to accomplish the highest aim of life as ascertained by appropriate sincere discussion. Nor should one refrain from individual effort, as is the wont of the followers of Soonga.

12. "A man who is in earnest need never be at a loss, will sustained effort ever fail in its purpose?

13. "Men earn their food, gods their nectar, pious ascetics the highest beatitude and others their desires, by individual exertion alone.

14. "Think well and tell me where, when, how and what profit was ever gained by any man who without engaging in action was taken up with dry polemics.

15. "If some stray cases of failure should make one lose faith in individual exertion, that one is certainly accursed of God, because he is his own ruin.

16. "Guided by proper deliberation, accompanied by zeal and engaged in individual efforts, one must take one's own unfailing way to emancipation.

17. "There are said to be many ways to that end. Choose that one among them which is the surest.

18. "Choice is made by right discussion and according to the experience of the wise. Then begin the practice immediately. I shall now explain them in detail. Listen!

19. "That is best which does not again yoke you to suffering. To a discriminating man, pain is apparent in all aspects of life.

20-22. "Whatever has the impression of misery on it cannot be good. Such are wealth, children, wife, kingdom, treasury, army, fame, learning, intellect, body, beauty and prosperity. For they are all of them transient and already in the jaws of death, otherwise called *time*.

23. "Can that be good which is only the seed ready to sprout as pain and grow into misery?

24. "The right means lies beyond these. However, the desire to possess them is born of delusion. The Master Wizard is Mahesvara. He being the creator of the universe, all are deluded by Him.

25-30. "Even a juggler of limited powers is able to deceive his audience although only to a limited degree. The majesty cannot be seen through without reference to him. Of course, the whole audience will not be deluded by him, but who can escape the illusion of Mahadeva?

"Just as there are a few who know how to see through the illusory tricks of the juggler and are not mystified by them, so also men can learn to overcome the universal *Mâyâ* (illusion) if only the Lord is gracious to them. They can never escape from Mâyâ, without His grace.

"Therefore he should be worshipped by those who are anxious to cross the Ocean of *Mâyâ*.

31. "He with whom God is graciously pleased is endowed with *Mahavidya*, the supreme knowledge by means of which his crossing of the Ocean of *Mâyâ* is certain.

32. "Other methods are also put forward as serving this supreme end, but they are bound to fail in their purpose if the Lord's grace be not forthcoming.

33. "Therefore worship the Primal Cause of the universe as the starting point; be devoted to Him; He will soon enable you to succeed in your attempts to destroy the illusion.

34. "Clearly the universe must have some origin.

35. "Although the origin is shrouded in mystery, let us investigate the cause from the visible effect and be guided by the holy scriptures; and then the conclusion will be reached that there is a Creator in no way comparable to any known agents.

36. "Contentious statements to the contrary have been logically refuted by many authoritative scriptural texts.

37. "That system which admits only sensory evidence is merely an apology for philosophy and leads nowhere. Salvation is not its end but damnation is its fruit.

38-40. "Dry logic also must be condemned. Another system declares that the universe is eternal, without beginning or end. It follows that the universe and its phenomena are self-existent; thus lifeless insentient matter is its own agent and keeper, which is absurd, because action implies intelligence and no example can be cited to the contrary. Scriptures also say that the Primal Cause is an intelligent principle, and we know that action always originates from an intelligent source alone.

41-43. "The world is thus traced to its Creator who differs entirely from any agent known to us. Judging from the magnitude of the creation, His power must be immeasurable in the same proportion as the unimaginable vastness of the creation. Such a one must also be able to protect and elevate His own creatures. Surrender therefore unreservedly unto Him.

44-50. "I shall adduce an example as a proof of this. We find in every-day life that a chief, if pleased, even though his means are limited, always ensures the prospects of the man who is sincerely devoted to him.

"If the Lord of the world be pleased, will anything be withheld from the devotee? Tell me. He is the only Solace of the devotees whereas the chiefs are many in the world and not necessarily kind; maybe they are cruel and ungrateful also. Their patronage is also wavering and short-lived. The Supreme Lord has infinite mercy for His devotees, is most grateful and has unlimited powers. Otherwise, would people continue to worship Him from untold ages? Kingdoms not well ordered are known to disintegrate. (But this universe continues as ever.) Therefore this Lord of mercy is well established and also rightly famed.

"Surrender yourself directly and unhesitatingly to him. He will ordain the best for you and you need not ask for it.

51-59. "Among the methods of approach to God, there are (1) worship to overcome troubles, (2) worship to gain wealth, etc., and (3) loving dedication of oneself. The last one is the best and surest in its results.

"In practical life too, a chief entreated by a man in trouble duly affords him relief. The man however loses help or support if he has not shown proper attention to the patron. So also the service born of ambition, bears indeterminate and limited fruits according to its intensity. Devoted service with no ulterior motive takes a long time to be recognised; yet it makes even the petty chief amiable. A human master may take long to recognise unselfish work; but God, the Lord of the universe, the Dweller in our hearts, knows everything and soon bestows appropriate fruits. In the case of other kinds of devotees, God has to await the course of destiny—that being His own ordainment; whereas for the selfless devotee, God, the Lord and the sole Refuge, is all in all and takes care of him without reference to the devotee's predestiny or His own ordained laws. He compensates the devotee quickly, and that is because He is supreme and self-contained without depending on anything else.

60-61. "Predestiny or divine will is powerless before Him. Every one knows how He set aside predestiny and divine laws in the case of His famous devotee, Markandeya. I will explain to you now the fitness of this. Listen, my dearest!

Note: A *rishi* Mrikandu, by name, who was childless, pleased Siva by his penance. When Siva appeared to him, he prayed that a son might be born to him. Siva asked him if he would have a dull boy long-lived, or a sharp boy short-lived. Mrikandu preferred the latter.

So Siva said: 'You will have a very brilliant son; but he will only live for sixteen years.' Accordingly a son was born who was very good and dutiful, and most intelligent and pious, charming all who saw him. The parents were delighted with him but grew sad as he grew up. He asked them the reason for their sadness and they told him of Siva's boon. He said, 'Never mind. I will see' and took to penance. Siva was pleased with his intense devotion and ordained that he should remain sixteen years of age for all eternity.

62. "The current notion that one cannot escape one's destiny is applicable only to weak-minded and senseless wastrels.

63. "Yogis who practise control of breath conquer fate. Even fate cannot impose its fruits on yogis.

64-66. "Destiny seizes and holds only senseless people. Conforming to and following nature, destiny forms part of nature. Nature again is only the contrivance for enforcing God's will. His purpose is always sure and cannot be prevented. Its edge can, however, be blunted by devotion to Him and if it is not so blunted, the predisposing cause must therefore be considered a most powerful factor in a man's life.

67. "Therefore, eschew high vanity and take refuge in Him. He will spontaneously take you to the Highest State.

68. "This is the first rung in the ladder to the pedestal of Bliss. Nothing else is worth while.

69. (Dattatreya continued) "O Parasurâma, hearing this speech of his wife, Hemachuda was delighted and continued to ask her:

70. "Tell me, dear, who is this God, the Creator, the Self-contained One and the Ordainer of the universe to whom I should consecrate myself.

71-72. "Some say He is Vishnu, others Siva, Ganesa, the Sun, Narasimha or similar other avatars; others say Buddha or Arhat; still others Vasudeva, the life-principle, the Moon, Fire, *Karma*, Nature, primordial nature and what not.

73. "Each sect give a different origin for the universe. Tell me which of them is true.

74. "I verily believe that there is nothing unknown to you because that famous and omniscient sage Vyaghrapada has been gracious to you, and profound wisdom shines in you though you are of the weaker sex. Please tell me out of your love to me, O fair one, speaking words of eternal life!"

75. Thus requested, Hemalekha spoke with pleasure: "Lord, I shall tell you the final Truth about God. Listen!

76-78. "God is the All-Seer who generates, permeates, sustains and destroys the universe. He is Siva, He is Vishnu, He is Brahman, the Sun, the Moon, etc. He is the One whom the different sects call their own; He is not Siva, nor Vishnu, nor Brahmâ nor any other exclusively.

79-93. "I will tell you. Heed me! To say, for instance that the Primal Being is Siva with five faces and three eyes. The Creator would in that case be like an ordinary potter making pots, endowed with a body and brain. True, there is no art found in the world, without a body and some intellect. In fact, the creative faculty in men belongs to something between the body and pure intelligence.

Note: The body being insentient cannot act of its own accord; nor can intellect do so without a tool.

"Therefore the mind operates apart from the gross body, in dreams; being intelligent it creates environments suitable to its latent desires. This clearly indicates that the body is only a tool for a purpose and the agent is intelligence. Instruments are necessary for human agents because their capacities are limited and they are not self-contained. Whereas the Creator of the universe is perfect in Himself and creates the whole universe without any external aid. This leads to the important conclusion that God has no body. Otherwise, He would be reduced to a glorified human being, requiring innumerable accessories for work and influenced by seasons and environments, in no way different from a creature, and not the Lord. Moreover, pre-existence of accessories would quash His unique mastery and imply limits to His powers of creation. This is absurd, as being contrary to the original premises. Therefore, He has no body nor the other aids, yet He still creates the world, O Lord of my life! Fools are taken in by the notion of giving a body to the transcendental Being. Still, if devotees worship and contemplate Him with a body according to their own inclinations, He shows them Grace, assuming such a body. For He is unique and fulfils the desires of His devotees.

"Nevertheless, the conclusion must be reached that He is pure intelligence and His consciousness is absolute and transcendental. Such is the consciousness-intelligence in purity, Absolute Being, the One Queen, Parameswari (Transcendental Goddess) overwhelming the three states and hence called *Tripura*. Though She is an undivided whole the universe manifests in all its variety in Her, being reflected as it were, in a self-luminous mirror. The reflection cannot be apart from the mirror and is therefore one with it. Such being the case, there cannot be difference in degrees (*e.g.,* Siva, or Vishnu being superior to each other). Bodies are mere conceptions in the lower order of beings and they are not to the point in the case of God. Therefore, be wise, and worship the one pure, unblemished Transcendence

94. "If unable to comprehend this pure state, one should worship God in the concrete form which is most agreeable to Him; in this way, too, one is sure to reach the goal, though gradually.

95. "Though one attempted it in millions of births, one would not advance except in one of these two ways."

Thus ends the Chapter on the Nature of God in the Section of Hemachuda in *Tripura Rahasya*.

Chapter VIII

Key to the Parable of Chapter V

1-3. Having learnt from the mouth of his wise wife, the true significance of Tripura, who is Pure Intelligence and God in Truth, and also the technique of Tripura's worship from competent teachers as prompted by divine grace, Hemachuda gained peace of mind and took to the worship with intense devotion.

A few months passed in this manner.

Note: God's grace is the *sine qua non* of any kind of knowledge of God.

4. "The Supreme Mother's grace descended on him, and he became totally indifferent to pleasure because his mind was entirely absorbed in the practical investigation of the Truth.

5. "Such a state is impossible for anyone without the Grace of God, because the mind engaged in practical search for truth is the surest means of emancipation.

6. "Parasurâma! Countless aids will not give emancipation if an earnest search for truth is not made.

7. "Once more Hemachuda sought his wife alone, his mind absorbed in the quest for Truth.

8-9. "She saw her husband coming to her apartment, so she went to meet him, welcomed him and offered him her seat. She washed his feet and prostrated before him, as was due to one of his rank, and spoke melting words of sweet love.

10-14. "Dearest! I see you again after such a long time. Are you in good health? Of course, the body is sometimes liable to illness. Do tell me why you have been neglecting me all these days. Not a day passed before without your seeing me and conversing with me. How have you been passing your time? I could never have dreamt that you would be so indifferent to me! What makes you so? How do you spend your nights? You used to say that a moment without me was like eternity to you, and that you

48

could not bear it." Saying this, she embraced him fondly and appeared distressed.

15-17. Though embraced lovingly by his dear wife, he was not moved in the least and said to her: "Dear, I can no longer be deceived by you. I am convinced of your strength and that nothing can affect your inherent happiness. You are a sage and unperturbed. You know this world and beyond. How could anything affect you like this? I am here to ask your advice. Now please listen. Explain to me that tale you once related to me as the story of your life.

18. "Who is your mother? Who is your friend? Who is her husband? Who are her sons? Tell me, what relationship have all these people to me?

19. "I do not clearly understand it. I no longer think it is a lie. I am sure you told me a parable which is full of significance.

20. "Tell me everything in full so that I may understand it clearly. I bow to you reverently. Kindly clear these doubts."

21-23. Hemalekha with a smiling and delighted face heard her husband and thought within herself: 'He is now pure in mind and blessed of God. He is evidently indifferent to the pleasures of life and is also strong in mind. This must be due to God's Grace alone and his former virtues are now bearing fruit. The time is now ripe for him to be enlightened, so I will enlighten him.' She said, "Lord, God's Grace is upon you, and you are blessed!

24-25. "Dispassion cannot arise otherwise. It is the criterion of God's Grace that the mind should be rapt in the quest for truth, after becoming detached from sensual pleasures. I shall now solve the puzzle of my life-story.

26. "My mother is *Transcendence*—pure Consciousness; my friend is *intellect* (discerning faculty); *ignorance* is *Madam Dark,* the undesirable friend of intellect.

27. "The caprices of ignorance are too well known to need elucidation, she can delude any one, making a rope seem to be a serpent and striking terror in the onlooker.

28-33. "Her son is the greatest of illusions—the *mind*; his wife is *thought* or conception or imagination; her sons are five in number, namely, *audition, taste, sight, touch* and *smell,* whose mansions are the respective senses. What the mind was said to steal from them is enjoyment of sensual objects which leaves an impress on the mind to develop later into the proclivities of the mind. Sharing stolen objects with his wife is manifestation of proclivities in dreams. *Dream* is the daughter-in-law of *Delusion* (*i.e.*, ignorance). *Madam Vorax* is *desire*; her sons are *anger* and *greed*; their city is the *body*. What was said to be my most potent talisman is *Realization* of the Self. Mind's friend guarding the city is the vital principle which keeps moving as the *life-breath*. The different cities peopled by them are hells passed in the eternal passage of the soul. The consummation of the discerning faculty is *Samadhi*. My admission into my mother's chamber is *final emancipation*.

34. "Such is in brief the tale of my life. Yours is likewise. Think well and be absolved."

Thus ends the Chapter on the Course of Life in the Section of Hemachuda in *Tripura Rahasya*.

Chapter IX

How that Hemachuda Realized the Self after Analyzing His Own Mind and Plunging Within

1. When Hemachuda understood the significance of his wife's parable he was agreeably surprised. His voice chocked with pleasure as he said to her:

2. "My dear, you are indeed blessed, and clever too; how shall I describe the profound wisdom of the story of your life, narrated to me in the form of a parable.

3. "Up to now I did not know your progress. It has all been made as clear to me as a gooseberry resting on the palm of my hand.

4-5. "I now understand the end of humanity and realize wonderful nature. Please tell me more now: who is this mother of yours? How is she without beginning? Who are we? What is our real nature?"

Asked thus, Hemalekha told her husband:

6. "Lord, listen carefully to what I am going to say, for it is subtle. Investigate the nature of the Self with intellect made transparently clear.

7. "It is not an object to be perceived, nor described; how shall I then tell you of it? You know the mother only if you know the Self.

8. "The Self does not admit of specification, and therefore no teacher can teach it. However, realize the Self within you, for it abides in unblemished intellect.

9. It pervades all, beginning from the personal God to the amoeba; but it is not cognisable by the mind or senses; being itself unillumined by external agencies, it illumines all, everywhere and always. It surpasses demonstration or discussion.

10. "How, where, when, or by whom has it been specifically described even incompletely? What you ask me, dear, amounts to asking me to show your eyes to you.

11-12. "Even the best teachers cannot bring your eyes to your sight. Just as a teacher is of no use in this instance, so in the other. He can at best guide you towards it and nothing more. I shall also explain to you the means to realization. Listen attentively.

13. "As long as you are contaminated with notions of *me* or *mine (e.g.,* my home, my body, my mind, my intellect), the Self will not be found, for it lies beyond cognition and cannot be realized as '*my* Self.'

14. "Retire into solitude, analyze and see what those things are which are cognised as *mine;* discard them all and transcending them, look for the Real Self.

15. "For instance, you know me as your wife and not as your self. I am only *related* to you and not part of you much less your very being.

16. "Analyze everything in this way and discard it. What remains over, transcending at all, beyond conception, appropriation, or relinquishment—know That to be the Self. That knowledge is final emancipation."

17. After receiving these instructions from his wife, Hemachuda rose hurriedly from his seat, mounted on his horse and galloped from the city.

18. He entered a royal pleasure-garden beyond the outskirts of the town and went into a well-furnished crystal palace.

19-20. He dismissed his attendants and ordered the keepers: "Let no one enter these rooms while I am in contemplation— be they ministers, elders or even the king himself. They must wait until you obtain my permission."

21. Then he went up to a fine chamber in the ninth storey which looked out in all directions.

22. The room was well furnished and he sat down on a soft cushion. He collected his mind and began to contemplate thus:

23-30. "Truly all these people are deluded! No one of them knows even the fringe of the Self! But all are active for the sake of their own selves. Some of them recite the scriptures, a few study them and their commentaries; some are busy accumulating wealth; others are ruling the land; some are fighting the enemy; others are seeking the luxuries of life. When engaged in all this selfish activity they never question what exactly the Self may be; now why is there all this confusion? Oh! When the Self is not known, all is in vain and as if done in a dream. So I will now investigate the matter.

"My home, wealth, kingdom, treasure, women, cattle—none of these is *me,* and they are only *mine.* I certainly take the body for the Self but it is simply a tool of mine. I am indeed the king's son, with goodly limbs and a fair complexion. These people, too, are taken up by this same notion that their bodies are their egos."

31-36. Reflecting thus, he considered the body. He could not identify the body as the Self, and so began to transcend it. This body is *mine,* not *me.* It is built up of blood and bones, and is changing each moment. How can this be the changeless, continuous *me.* It looks like a chattel; it is apart from me as is a waking body from the dream, etc. *'I'* cannot be the body nor can the vital force be the Self; mind and intellect are clearly my tools so they cannot be *'I.' 'I'* am surely something apart from all these, beginning from the body and ending with the intellect. *[Note:* The intermediates are (1) the senses, (2) the mind including the thinking, reasoning and coordinating faculties, (3) vital force.] I am always aware, but do not realize that pure state of awareness. The reason of this inability is not clear to me.

37-38. Objects are cognised through the senses, not otherwise; life is recognised by touch, and mind by intellect. By whom is the intellect made evident? I do not know. . . .

I now see I am always aware—realization of that pure awareness is obstructed by other factors (pertaining to the non-self) butting in—Now I shall not imagine them—They cannot appear without my mental imagery of them and they cannot obstruct the glory of the Self, without appearing.

39. Thinking thus, he forcibly arrested his thoughts.

40-41. Instantaneously a blank superseded. He, at the same time, decided that it was the Self, so became very happy and once again he began to meditate. "I will do it again," he said and plunged within.

42. The restlessness of the mind being thus resolutely checked, he saw in an instant a blazing light with no circumference.

43-45. Regaining human consciousness, he began to wonder how this could happen. 'There is no constancy in the experience. The Self cannot be more than one. I will repeat and see,' he said and dived again. This time he fell into a long sleep and dreamt wonderful dreams. On waking up, he fell furiously to think:

46-48. "How is it that I was overpowered by sleep and started to dream? The darkness and light which I saw before must also be in the nature of dreams. Dreams are mental imagery, and how shall I overcome them?

"I shall again repress my thoughts and see," he said, and plunged within.

His mind was placid for a time. He thought himself sunk in bliss.

49-54. Shortly after, he regained his original state, owing to the mind again beginning to function. He reflected: "What is all this? Is it a dream or a hallucination of the mind? My experience is a fact but it surpasses my imagination.

"Why is that bliss quite unique and unlike any that I have experienced before? The highest of my known experiences cannot compare with even an infinitesimal part of the state of bliss I was in just now. It was like sleep in so far as I was not externally aware. But there was a peculiar bliss at the same time. The reason is not clear to me because there was nothing to impart pleasure to me. Although I attempted to realize the Self, I do not do so. I probably realize the Self and also see others like darkness, light, dreams or pleasure, etc. Or is it possible that these are the stages of development for the realization of the Self? I do not understand it. Let me ask my recondite wife."

55-61. Having thus resolved, the prince ordered the door-keeper to ask Hemalekha to come to him. Within an hour and a half, she was climbing the steps of the mansion like the Queen of Night moving across the sky. She discovered the prince, her consort, in perfect peace of mind, calm, collected and of happy countenance. She quickly went to his side and sat by him. As she nestled close to him he opened his eyes and found her sitting close to him. Directly he did so, she quickly and fondly embraced him and gently spoke sweet words of love: "Lord, what can I do for Your Highness? I hope you are well. Please tell me why you called me up to this place?" Thus addressed, he spoke to his wife in his turn:

62-66. "My dear! I have, as advised by you, retired to a solitary place where I am engaged in investigating the Self. Even so, I have diverse visions and experiences. Thinking that the constant Self-awareness is dimmed by the uncalled-for interference of mental activities, I forcibly repressed my thoughts and remained calm. Darkness superseded, light appeared, sleep supervened and finally a unique bliss overpowered me for a little while. Is this the Self, or something different? Please analyze these experiences of mine and tell me, my dear, so that I may clearly understand them.

67-69. "After listening to him carefully Hemalekha, the knower of this world and beyond, spoke sweetly thus. 'Listen to me, my dear, closely. What you have now done to repress thoughts with the mind turned inward is a good beginning and praised by the worthy as the best way. Without it, no one has ever been successful anywhere. However, it does not produce Self-Realization for the Self remains realized at all times.

70. "If a product, it cannot be the Self. For, how can the Self be got anew? So then, the Self is never gained. Gain is of something which is not already possessed. Is there any moment when the Self is not the Self? Neither is control of mind used to gain it. I shall give you some examples:

72. "Just as things unseen in darkness are found on its removal by means of a lamp, and are therefore said to be recovered from oblivion.

73-74. "Just as a confused man forgets his purse, but remembers and locates it on keeping his mind unruffled and steady, yet still says that he has gained the lost purse, though the steadying of his mind did not produce it.

75. "So also the control of your mind is not the cause of your Self-Realization; though the Self is always there, it is not recog-

nised by you even with a controlled mind because you are not conversant with it.

76. "Just as a yokel unacquainted with the system cannot understand the dazzling lights of the royal audience-chamber at night and so ignores its magnificence at first sight, so it is that you miss the Self.

77. "Attend dear! Blank darkness was visible after you controlled your thoughts. In the short interval before its appearance and after the control of mind there remains a state free from the effort to control and the perception of darkness.

78. "Always remember that state as the one of perfect and transcendental happiness. All are deceived in that state because their minds are accustomed to be turned outward.

79. "Though people may be learned, skilful and keen, still they search and search, only to be thwarted and they do not abide in that holy state.

80. "They grieve day and night, without knowing this state. Mere theoretical knowledge of sculpture can never make a man a sculptor.

81. "Though he be a pandit well grounded in the theory and the discussion of the philosophy of the Self, he cannot realize the Self because it is not *realizable* but already *realized*. Realization is not attained by going far, but only by staying still not by thought (intellection) but by cessation of thought.

83-85. "Effort towards Realization is like the attempt to stamp with one's foot on the shadow cast by one's head. Effort will always make it recede.

"Just as an infant tries to take hold of his own reflection being unaware of the mirror, so also common people are taken in by their mental reflections on the mirror of the pure, luminous Self and are not aware of the mirror, because they have no acquaintance with the Self.

"Although people understand space, they are not aware of it because they are taken up by the objects in space.

86-88. "They understand the universe in space but have no regard for space itself. Similarly, it is with them in regard to the Self.

"My Lord, consider well. The world consists of knowledge and the objects known. Of these the objects are non-self and perceived by the senses; knowledge is self-evident; there is no world in the absence of knowledge. Knowledge is the direct proof of the existence of objects which are therefore dependent on knowledge. Knowledge is dependent on the knower for its existence. The knower does not require any tests for knowing his own existence. The knower therefore is the only reality behind knowledge and objects. That which is self-evident without the necessity to be proved is alone real; not so other things.

89-91. "He who denies knowledge has no ground to stand on and so no discussion is possible.

"The subject of knowledge settled, the question arises regarding the existence of objects in the absence of their knowledge. Objects and their knowledge are only reflections in the eternal, self-luminous, supreme Consciousness which is the same as the knower and which alone is real. The doubt that the reflection should be of all objects simultaneously without reference to time and place (contrary to our experience), need not arise because time and space are themselves knowable concepts and are equally reflections. The specific nature of the reflections is the obverse of the objects found in space.

92. "Therefore, Prince, realize with a still mind your own true nature which is the one pure undivided Consciousness underlying the restless mind which is composed of the whole universe in all its diversity.

93. "If one is fixed in that fundamental basis of the universe (*i.e.*, the Self), one becomes the All-doer. I shall tell you how to inhere thus. I assure you—you will be That.

94. "Realize with a still mind the state between sleep and wakefulness, the interval between the recognition of one object after another or the gap between two perceptions.

Note: The commentator compares the rays of light proceeding from the Sun before they impinge on materials. They are themselves invisible, but capable of illumining objects. This explains the third statement above. He also says that consciousness is like water flowing through a channel and later assuming the shape of the beds watered.

95. "This is the real Self, inhering in which one is no longer deluded. Unaware of this Truth, people have become inheritors of sorrow.

Note: The commentator adds that a sage realizing the world as the reflection of the mind treats it as such and is thus free from misery.

96-97. "Shape, taste, smell, touch, sound, sorrow, pleasure, the act of gaining, or the object gained—none of these finds place in that Transcendence which is the support of all there is, and which is the being in all but not exclusively so. That is the Supreme Lord, the Creator, the Supporter and the Destroyer of the universe and the Eternal Being.

98. "Now let not your mind be outgoing; turn it inward; control it just a little and watch for the Self, always remembering that the investigator is himself the essence of being and the Self of Self.

Note: The commentary on this *sloka* says: This *sloka* contains what is not to be done (namely, the mind should not be permitted to be outgoing), what is to be done (the mind is to be turned inwards) and what is to be engaged in (watchfulness). Just a short control is enough; no long control is necessary for the purpose. The question arises: how to look? The investigator, investigation and the object investigated are all one. The mind should be brought to the condition of a new-born baby. Then he feels as if he were separate from all gross materials and only the feeling 'I am' persists.

When the mind is controlled a little, a state will be evident at the end of the effort in which the Self can be realized as pure being, underlying all phenomena but undivided by them, similar to the baby sense.

99. "Be also free from the thought 'I see'; remain still like a blind man seeing. What transcends sight and no sight that you are. Be quick."

Note: Here the commentary says: The Self transcends also the feeling 'I see.' Adherence to that sensation divorces one from the Self. Therefore, let that feeling also vanish, for that state is absolutely unstained by will, sensation or thought. Otherwise, there will be no perfection in spite of innumerable efforts.

Again the word 'sight' includes the waking and dream states and 'no sight' signifies deep sleep. That which is threading through these three states and even surpasses the sense 'I am' is what you are. This is the fourth state *Turiya*. (WHICH is the string on which all the diverse objects of the universe are strung and the whole is a garland to Sri Ramana! Translator's comment.)

100. Hemachuda did accordingly, and having gained that state referred to by his wife, he remained peaceful a long time, unaware of anything beside the Self.

Note: The commentator says that he was in *Nirvikalpa Samadhi.*

Thus ends the Chapter on Peace in the Section on Hemachuda in *Tripura Rahasya.*

Chapter X

On Further Instructions by His Beloved, He Got Samadhi in Spite of His External Activities and Remained in the State of Emancipation Even While Alive

1-5. "Hemalekha noticed that her husband had attained supreme Peace and so did not disturb him, He awoke in an hour and a half, opened his eyes and saw his wife nearby. Eager to fall into that state once more, he closed his eyes; and immediately Hemalekha took hold of his hands and asked him sweetly: 'My Lord, tell me what you have ascertained to be your gain on closing your eyes, or your loss on opening them, my dearest. I love to hear you. Do say what happens on the eyes being closed or left open.'

6. "On being pressed for an answer, he looked as if he were drunk and replied reluctantly and languidly, as follows:

7-14. "'My dear, I have found pure untainted happiness. I cannot find the least satisfaction in the activities of the world as sorrow increases when they finish. Enough of them! They are tasteless to me like a sucked orange, only indulged in by wasters, or like cattle incessantly chewing the cud. What a pity that such people should be to this day unaware of the bliss of their own Self! Just as a man goes a-begging in ignorance of the treasure hidden under his floor, so did I run after sensual pleasures unaware of the boundless ocean of bliss within me. Worldly pursuits are laden with misery and pleasures are transient. Still I was so infatuated that I mistook them for enduring pleasures, was often grief-stricken, yet did not cease to pursue them over and over again. The pity of it: men are fools, unable to discriminate pleasure from pain. They seek pleasures but gain sorrow. Enough of these activities which increase the relish for such pleasure.

"My dear, I beg you with hands clasped. Let me fall again into the peace of my blissful self. I pity you that though knowing this state, you are not in it but are ever engaged in vain."

15-27. "The wise girl gently smiled at all this, and said to him: 'My lord, you do not yet know the highest state of sanctity (which is not besmirched by duality), reaching which the wise transcend duality and are never perplexed. That state is as far from you as the sky is from the earth. Your small measure of wisdom is as good as no wisdom, because it is not unconditional, but remains conditioned by closing or opening your eyes. Perfection cannot depend on activity or the reverse, on effort or on no effort. How can that state be a perfect one if mental or physical activity can influence it or if the displacement of the eyelid by the width of a barley grain makes all the difference to it? Again, how can it be perfect if located only in the interior? What shall I say of your muddled wisdom! How ridiculous to think that your one inch long eyelid, can shut up the expanse in which millions of worlds revolve in one corner alone!'

"Listen Prince! I will tell you further. As long as these knots are not cut asunder so long will bliss not be found. (The knowledge acquired is thus not effective.) These knots are millions in number and are created by the bond of delusion which is no other than ignorance of Self. These knots give rise to mistaken ideas, the chief of which is the identification of the body with the Self, which in its turn gives rise to the perennial stream of happiness and misery in the shape of the cycle of births and deaths. The second knot is the differentiation of the world from the Self whose being consciousness is the mirror on which the phenomena are simply reflected. Similarly with the other knots including the differentiation of beings among themselves and from the universal Self. They have originated from time immemorial and recur with unbroken ignorance. The man is not finally redeemed until he has extricated himself from these numberless knots of ignorance.

28-38. "The state which is the result of your closing the eyes, cannot be enough, for it is pure intelligence and eternal truth transcending anything else yet serving as the magnificent mirror to reflect the phenomena arising in itself. Prove, if you can, that everything is not contained in it. Whatever you admit as known to you, is in the knowledge conveyed by that consciousness. Even what may be surmised to be in another place and at a different time, is also within your consciousness. Moreover, what is not apparent and unknown to that intelligence is a figment of imagination like the son of a barren woman. There cannot be anything that is not held by consciousness, just as there cannot be reflection without a reflecting surface.

"Therefore I tell you that your conviction: 'I shall lose it by opening my eyes' or 'I know it,' is the knot awaiting to be cut, and there will be no attainment though, remember, it cannot be the perfect state if it can be attained. What you consider the happy state as accomplished by the movements of your eyelids, cannot indeed be perfect because it is certainly intermittent and not unconditional. Is any place found where the effulgence is not, my lord, of the fire blazing at the dissolution of the universe? All will resolve into that fire and no residue will be left. Similarly also the fire of realization will burn away all your sense of duty so that there will be nothing left for you to do. Be strong, root out your thoughts and cut off the deep-rooted knots from your heart, namely, 'I will see,' ' I am not this,' ' This is non-Self,' and such like.

"Find wherever you turn the one undivided, eternal blissful Self; also watch the whole universe reflected as it arises and subsides in the Self. See the Self both within and without you; yet do not confound the seeing Self within as the Seer of the universal Self without, for both are the same. Inhere in the peace of your true internal Self, devoid of all phenomena."

39-42. At the end of her speech, Hemachuda's confusion was cleared up, so that he gradually became well established in the perfect Self bereft of any distinction of within and without. Being always equable, he led a very happy life with Hemalekha and others, reigned over his kingdom and made it prosperous, engaged his enemies in war and conquered them, studied the scriptures and taught them to others, filled his treasury, performed the sacrifices pertaining to royalty and lived twenty-thousand years, emancipated while yet alive *(Jivanmukta)*.

Note: Scholars say that "One thousand" is a peculiar expression for 'four.' Thus twenty-thousand stands for eighty.

43-61. "The king Muktachuda having heard that his son Hemachuda had become a *Jivanmukta,* consulted his other son Manichuda. Both agreed that Hemachuda was not as before, but that he had changed so that he was no longer affected by the greatest of pleasures or the worst of sorrows; that he treated friend and foe alike; that he was indifferent to loss or gain; that he engaged in royal duties like an actor in a play; that he seemed like a man always intoxicated with wine; and that he did his duty well notwithstanding his absent-minded or other worldly look. They pondered the matter over and wondered. Then sought him in private and asked him the reason of his change. When they had heard him speak of his state, they too desired to be instructed by him, and finally became *Jivanmuktas* like Hemachuda. The ministers were in their turn desirous of attaining that state, and eventually reached it after receiving proper instructions from the king. So were the citizens, the artisans and all classes of people in that city. All of them gained the *summum bonum* (highest good) of life and transcended desire, anger, lust, etc. Even the children and the very old people were no longer moved by passions. There were still worldly transactions in this ideal state, because the people consciously acted their parts as the actors in a drama, in accord with the rest of creation. A mother would rock the cradle with lullabies expressive of the highest Truth; a master and his servants dealt with one another in the Light of that Truth; players entertained the audience with plays depicting Truth; singers sang only songs on Truth; the court fools caricatured ignorance as ludicrous; the academy only taught lessons on God-knowledge. The whole State was thus composed only of sages and philosophers, be they men or women; servant-boys or servant-maids; dramatic actors or fashionable folk; artisans or laborers; ministers or harlots. They nevertheless acted in their professions in harmony with creation. They never cared to recapitulate the past or speculate on the future with a view to gain pleasure or avoid pain, but acted for the time being, laughing, rejoicing, crying or shouting like drunkards, thus dissipating all their latent tendencies.

62. "The rishis, Sanaka and others called it the City of Wisdom when they visited it.

63-68. "Even parrots and cockatoos in their cages spoke words of wisdom, *e.g.,* 'Consider the Self as pure intelligence bereft of objective knowledge.'

"What is known is not different from that intelligence, it is like a series of images reflected in a mirror. Absolute consciousness is the universe; it is 'I,' it is all, sentient and insentient, mobile and immobile. Everything else is illuminated by it whereas it is alone and Self-luminous. Therefore let those sensible people who are desirous of *chit* (pure intelligence) turn away from illusory knowledge and contemplate their own Self— the absolute consciousness—which illumines all the rest, and which is their being too. The town where even the lower animals convey such supreme wisdom is famous to this day as the City of Wisdom on Earth, which reputation it owes to that one wise princess Hemalekha by whose advice Hemachuda became a *Jivanmukta,* all the rest following in his wake."

69. Dattatreya continued: "Thus, you see, Parasurâma, the primary cause of emancipation is association with the wise. Therefore, follow that advice first and foremost."

Thus ends Chapter X on the Section of Hemachuda in *Tripura Rahasya.*

Chapter XI

That the Cosmos Is Not Other than Intelligence

1. After he had listened to this sublime story of Hemachuda, Bhargava was confused and asked:

2-5. "Lord, my Master! What you have related as a wonderful teaching appears to me against the experience of all people in every way. How can the magnificent, objective universe be no other than tenuous consciousness, which is not seen, but only inferred? Pure intelligence devoid of known objects cannot be imagined and therefore cannot be postulated. Thus the whole theme based on it is not at all clear to me. I pray you kindly to elucidate the subject so that I may understand it." Thus requested, Dattatreya continued:

6-30. "I will now tell you the truth of the objective world, as it is. What is seen is absolutely nothing but sight. I shall now give you the proof of this statement. Listen with attention. All that is seen has an origin and there must therefore be an antecedent cause for it. What is origin except that the thing newly appears? The world is changing every moment and its appearance is new every moment and so it is born every moment. Some say that the birth of the universe is infinite and eternal each moment. Some may contest the point saying that the statement is true of a specific object or objects but not of the world which is the aggregate of all that is seen. The scholiasts of *Vijnana* answer them thus: The external phenomena are only momentary projections of the anamnesis of the continuous link, namely, the subject and the worldly actions which are based on them. But the intellect which collates time, space and phenomena is infinite and eternal at each moment of their appearance and it is called *Vijnana* by them. Others say that the universe is the aggregate of matter—mobile and immobile. (The atomists maintain that the universe is made up of five elements, earth, air, fire, water and ether which are permanent and of things like a pot, a cloth, etc., which are transient. They are still unable to prove the external existence of the world, because they admit that happenings in life imply their conceptual nature. It follows that the objects not so involved are useless.)

"But all are agreed that the universe has an origin. (What is then the point in saying that the momentary creations are eternal and infinite? The momentary nature cannot be modified by the qualifications mentioned. There is no use in dressing a condemned man before the executioner's axe is laid on him.) To say however that creation is due to nature (accidental?) is to overstretch the imagination and therefore unwarranted. The Charvakas, nihilists, argue that some effects are not traceable to their efficient causes. There are occurrences without any antecedent causes. Just as a cause need not always foretell an event, so also the event need not always have a cause. The conclusion follows that the world is an accident.

"If a thing can appear without a cause there is no relation between cause and effect, and there can be no harmony in the world. A potter's work may lead to a weaver's products, and *vice versa,* which is absurd. The interdependence of cause and effect is ascertained by their logical sequence and proved by its role in practical life. How then can a universe be an accident?

"They infer the cause where it is not obvious, and trace the cause from the effect. This conforms to the universal practice. Each occurrence must have a cause for it; that is the rule. Even if the cause is not obvious, it must be inferred; otherwise the world activities would be in vain—which is absurd. The conclusion is then reached that every event is a product of a certain condition or conditions; and this fact enables people to engage in purposeful work. So it is in the practical world. Therefore the theory of accidental creation is not admissible.

"The atomists premise a material cause for creation and name it *imponderable atoms.* According to them, the imponderable atoms produce the tangible world, which did not exist before creation and will not remain after dissolution. (They say the existence of the world before or after is only imaginary and untrue, like a human horn—they say.) How can the same thing be true at one time and untrue at another? Again if the primary atoms are imponderable, without magnitude and yet are permanent, how can they give rise to material and transient products endowed with magnitude?"

"How can the same thing be yellow and not yellow—bright and dark—at the same time? These qualities are not in harmony; the whole theory is confused, it is as if one were trying to mix up the immiscible. Again, how did the primordial atoms begin to unite to produce diatoms or triatoms? Was it of their own accord? (which is impossible because, they are insentient) or by God's will? (Then the action is God's and not of the atoms. Otherwise it would be like a king in his palace who, by merely willing to kill the enemy, sent his weapons flying about in the act of destruction.) (It has already been pointed out that God cannot be supposed to operate atoms for the purpose of creation, as a potter does with clay.)

Note: Thus the idea of the beginning of creation is altogether refuted.

"It is also absurd to say that the insentient atoms of matter began creation when the equilibrium of the three forces *Satva*, *Rajas* and *Tamas*, was disturbed. (One of the systems of philosophy believes that three qualities, brightness, activity and darkness, are always there in equilibrium. When disturbed, creation begins; when they revert to equilibrium, the universe is dissolved.) How are the changes in the state of equilibrium brought about? Change is not possible without an intelligent cause. So none of the systems can satisfactorily account for creation. Scriptures alone are the guide for comprehending the metaphysical and the transcendental. The rest are not authoritative because of the individual's limitations, the absence of reliable tests for their accuracy, and of the repeated failures of attempts which ignore God. The universe must have a Creator, and He must be an intelligent principle, but He cannot be of any known type because of the vastness of the creation. His power is past understanding and is dealt with in the Scriptures, whose authority is incontrovertible. They speak of the unique Creator, the Lord who was before creation, being self-contained. He created the universe by His own power. It is in its entirety and all its details, a picture on the screen of His Self like the dream world on the individual consciousness. The individual encompasses his own creation with his ego (as 'I'); so does the Lord play with the universe. Just as the dreamer is not to be confounded with the dream so is the Lord not to be confounded with the creation. Just as a man survives his dream, so does the Lord survive the dissolution of His creation. Just as you remain ever as pure consciousness apart from the body, etc., so is the Lord, unbounded consciousness apart from the universe, etc. Is it not after all only a picture drawn by Him on His Self? How can this unique creation be apart from Him?

There can indeed be nothing but consciousness. Tell me of any place where there is no consciousness; there is no place beyond consciousness. Or can any one prove in any manner anything outside consciousness? Conciousness is inescapable.

31-32. "Moreover, this consciousness is the only existence, covering the whole universe, and perfect all through. Just as there cannot be breakers apart from the ocean and light without the Sun, so also the Universe cannot be conceived without consciousness. The Supreme God is thus the embodiment of pure Consciousness.

33-34. "This whole universe consisting of the mobile and the immobile, arises from, abides in, and resolves into Him. This is the final and well-known conclusion of the Scriptures; and the Scriptures never err. The guide by which one can comprehend the metaphysical and transcendental matters is Scripture alone.

35. "Miraculous powers possessed by gems and incantations cannot be denied, nor can they be fathomed by a man of limited knowledge.

36-40. "Because the scriptures proceed from the all-knowing Lord, they partake of His omniscient quality. The Being mentioned in them is eternally existing even before the birth of the universe. His creation has been without any material aids. Therefore God is supreme, perfect, pure and self-contained. The creation is not an object apart; it is a picture drawn on the canvas of supreme consciousness, for there cannot possibly be anything beyond Perfection. Imagination on the contrary, is impractical. The universe has thus originated only as an image on the surface of the mirror of the Absolute. This conclusion is in harmony with all the facts.

41-45. "Creation is like a magician's trick, and is a city born of divine imagination. O! Parasurâma, you are aware of the mental creations of day-dreamers which are full of people, life and work, similar to this. There are also doubts, tests, discussions and conclusions—all imaginary arising in the mind and subsiding there. Just as castles in the air are mental figments of men so also is this creation a mental figment of Siva. Siva is absolute Awareness, without any form. Sri Tripura is Sakti (energy) and Witness of the whole. That Being is perfect all round and remains undivided.

46-47. "Time and space are the factors of division in the world; of these, space refers to the location of objects and time to the sequence of events. Time and space are themselves projected from consciousness, how then would they divide or destroy their own basis and still continue to be what they are?

48-51. "Can you show the time or place not permeated by consciousness? Is it not within your consciousness when you speak of it? The fact of the existence of things is only illumination of them, and nothing more. Such illumination pertains to consciousness alone. That alone counts which is self-shining. Objects are not so, for their existence depends upon perception of them by conscious beings. But consciousness is self-effulgent—not so the objects, which depend on conscious beings for being known.

52-54. "If on the other hand, you contend that objects exist even if not perceived by us, I tell you—listen! There is no consistency in the world regarding the existence or non-existence of things. Their cognition is the only factor determining it. Just as reflections have no substance in them, outside of the mirror, so also the things of the world have no substance in them outside of the cognising factor, *viz.*, Intelligence.

The detail and tangibility of things are no arguments against their being nothing but images.

55-63. "Those qualities of reflected images depend on the excellence of the reflecting surface, we can see in the case of water and polished surfaces. Mirrors are insentient and are not self-contained. Whereas, consciousness is always pure and self-contained; it does not require an external object to create the image. Ordinary mirrors are liable to be soiled by extraneous dirt whereas consciousness has nothing foreign to it, being always alone and undivided; and therefore its reflections are unique. Created things are not self-luminous and are illumined by another's cognitive faculty. Cognition of things implies their images on our intelligence. *They are only images.* The creation therefore is an image. It is not self-shining; and thus it is not self-aware, but becomes a fact on our perception of it. Therefore I say that the universe is nothing but an image on our consciousness. Consciousness shines notwithstanding the formation of images on it; though impalpable, it is steadily fixed and does not falter. Just as the images in a mirror are not apart from the mirror, so also the creations of consciousness are not apart from it.

64. "Objects are necessary for producing images in a mirror; they are not however necessary for consciousness because it is self-contained.

65-66. . . . "O Parasurâma! note how day-dreams and hallucinations are clearly pictured in the mind even in the absence of any reality behind them. How does it happen? The place of objects is taken up by the peculiar imaginative quality of the mind. When such imagination is deep, it takes shape as creation; consciousness is pure and unblemished in the absence of imagination.

67. "Thus you see how consciousness was absolute and pure before creation and how its peculiar quality or *will* brought about this image of the world in it.

68-69. "So the world is nothing but an image drawn on the screen of consciousness; it differs from a mental picture in its long duration; that is again due to the strength of will producing the phenomenon. The universe appears practical, material and perfect because the will determining its creation is perfect and independent; whereas the human conceptions are more or less transitory according to the strength or the weakness of the will behind them.

70. "The hampering of limitations is to some extent overcome by the use of incantations, gems and herbs, and an unbroken current of 'I' is established.

71. "With the aid of that pure *yoga,* O Rama, observe the creation manifested by one's will like the hallucinations brought about by a magician.

Note: There are said to be some live gems which have extraordinary properties. They are lustrous even in the dark and do not take on different lustres according to the background. They also illumine the objects close to them. One kind is said to be cool to touch and it does not become warm even on contact with the body; another is said to sweat in moonlight; still another makes the owner prosperous; yet another ruins him *(e.g.,* the 'Hope' diamond), and so on.

A vivid account is given of a magician's performance in Ranjit Singh's court. He threw a rope into the air which stood taut. A man climbed up the rope and disappeared.

72. "Objects in the world can be handled and put to use, while mental creations *(e.g.,* dreams) present the same phenomenon.

73. "A magician's creations are only transitory; a *yogi's* creations may be permanent; both are external to the creator, whereas the divine creation cannot be apart from the omnipresent Lord.

Note: Visvamitra, a great *Rishi,* is reputed to have created a duplicate Universe, a part of which consists of the constellations composing Scorpio, Sagittarius, and the Southern Cross. Some trees, plants and herbs in imitation of well-known species *(e.g.,* palmyra corresponding to cocoanut, jungle potatoes and onions insipid to taste and useless, etc.) are among his creations.

74. "Because the Lord of consciousness is infinite, the creation can remain only within Him and the contrary is pure fancy.

75. "Since the Universe is only a projection from and in the mirror of consciousness, its unreal nature can become clear only on investigation, and not otherwise.

76. "Truth can never change its nature, whereas untruth is always changing. See how changeful the nature of the world is!

77-78. "Distinguish between the changeless truth and the changeful untruth and scrutinise the world comprised of these two factors, changeful phenomena and changeless subjective consciousness, like the unchanging light of the mirror and the changing images in it.

79. "The world cannot stand investigation because of its changing unreal nature. Just as the owl is dazzled, and blinded by bright sunlight, so the world parades in glory before ignorance and disappears before the right analysis.

Note: The man sees by sunlight and is helpless in its absence. The owl sees in darkness and is blinded in sunlight. Whose sight is the better of the two? This cannot be determined satisfactorily so the investigation becomes lame.

80-84. "What is food for one, is poison for another *(e.g., decomposed food for worms and men)*. What is one thing to *yogis* and celestials, is another to others. A long distance by one vehicle is short by another.

"Long intervals of space reflected in the mirror are themselves in it and yet unreal.

"In this way, investigation becomes indeterminate by itself. Investigation and the object investigated are both indeterminate, and the only constant factor underlying both is consciousness. Nothing else can stand beside it.

85. "That which shines as 'Is' is Her Majesty the Absolute Consciousness.

"Thus the universe is only the *Self—the One* and one only."

Thus ends the Chapter XI on the Ascertainment of Truth in *Tripura Rahasya*.

Chapter XII

The Appearance of the Reality of the Universe Depends on the Strength of Will of Creation

1. Even after listening to Dattatreya patiently, Parasurâma was still perplexed and asked:

2. "O Lord, what you have said so far about the Universe is the truth.

3. "Even so, how is it that it appears to be real to me and to others who are both intelligent and shrewd?

4. "Why does it continue to seem to be real to me even though I have heard you say otherwise? Please prove to me its unreality and remove my present illusion."

5. Thus requested, Dattatreya, the great sage, began to explain the cause of the illusion which makes one believe the world to be real.

6. "Listen, Rama! This illusion is very old, being no other than the deep-rooted ignorance which mistakes one thing for another.

7. "See how the true Self has been ignored and the body has become identified with the Self. Consider this foul body comprised of blood and bones beside that unblemished, pure intelligence!

8. "Even the gross body becomes mistaken for crystal-clear consciousness by mere force of habit.

9. "So also the universe has repeatedly been taken to be real so that it now looks as if it were actually real. The remedy lies in a change of outlook.

10. "The world becomes for one whatever one is accustomed to think it. This is borne out by the realization of *yogis* of the objects of their long contemplation.

11-12. "I shall illustrate this point by an ancient and wonderful incident. There is a very holy town, Sundara, in the country of Vanga. Here once lived a very wise and famous king,

Susena by name. His younger brother, Mahasena, was his loyal and dutiful subject.

13. "The king ruled his kingdom so well that all his subjects loved him. On one occasion he performed the horse-sacrifice.

Note: This sacrifice can be performed only by the most powerful kings. A horse chosen and dedicated for sacrifice is allowed to roam wherever it pleases. The sacrificer or his lieutenant or group of lieutenants, follows the horse at a distance. The horse is a challenge to the kings in whose country it roams, so that battles are fought until the horse is successfully brought back and the sacrifice performed.

14. "All the most valiant princes followed the horse with a great army.

15. "Their course was victorious until they reached the banks of the Irrawaddy.

16. 'They were so elated that they passed by the peacefully sitting royal sage, Gana, without saluting him.

17. "Gana's son noticed the insult to his father and was exasperated. He caught the sacrificial horse and fought the heroes guarding it.

18-23. "They surrounded him on all sides but he together with the horse entered a hill, Ganda, before their eyes. Noticing his disappearance in the hill, the invaders attacked the hill. The sage's son re-appeared with a huge army, fought the enemy, defeated them and destroyed Susena's army. He took many prisoners of war, including all the princes and then re-entered the hill. A few followers who escaped fled to Susena and told him everything. Susena was surprised and said to his brother:

24-30. "'Brother! go to the place of the sage, Gana. Remember that penance doers are wonderfully powerful and cannot be conquered even by gods. Therefore take care to please him so that you may be allowed to bring back the princes and the horse in time for the sacrifice which is fast approaching. Pride before sages will always be humbled. If enraged, they reduce the world to ashes. Approach him with respect so that our object may be fulfilled.'

"Mahasena obeyed and immediately started on his errand. He arrived at Gana's hermitage and found the sage seated peacefully like a rock, with his senses, mind and intellect under perfect control. The sage, who was immersed in the Self, looked like a calm sea whose waves of thought had quieted down. Mahasena spontaneously fell prostrate before the sage and began to sing his praises, and here he remained for three days in reverential attitude.

31-46. "The sage's son who had been watching the new visitor was pleased, and coming to him said, 'I am pleased with the respect you show for my father, tell me what I can do for you and I will do it at once. I am the son of this great Gana, the unique hermit. Prince, listen to me. This is not the time for my father to speak. He is now in *kevala nirvikalpa samâdhi* and will come out of it only after twelve years, of which five have already passed and seven yet remain.'

"'Tell me now what you desire from him and I will do it for you. Do not underestimate me and think that I am only a head-strong youth not worthy of my father. There is nothing impossible for *yogis* engaged in penance.'

"After hearing him, Mahasena, being wise, saluted him with clasped hands and said: 'Oh child of the sage! If you mean to fulfil my desire I want to make a short request to your wise father when he has come out of his *samâdhi*. Kindly help me to that end if you please.' After he had thus requested, the sage's son replied: 'King, your request is hard to grant. Having promised fulfilment of your desire, I cannot now go back on my word. I must now ask you to wait an hour and a half and watch my yogic power. This, my father, is now in transcendental peace. Who can wake him up by external efforts? Wait! I shall do it forthwith by means of subtle *yoga*.'

"Saying so, he sat down, withdrew his senses, united the in-going and out-going breaths, exhaled air and stopped motionless for a short time; in this way he entered the mind of the sage and after agitating it, re-entered his own body. Immediately the sage came to his senses and found Mahasena in front of him, prostrating and praising him. He thought for a moment taking in the whole situation by his extraordinary powers.

47-49. "Perfectly peaceful and cheerful in mind, he beckoned to his son and said to him: 'Boy, do not repeat this fault.

Wrath wrecks penance. Penance is only possible and can progress without obstruction because the king protects *yogis*. To interfere with a sacrifice is always reprehensible and never to be countenanced by the good. Be a good boy and return the horse and the princes immediately. Do it at once so that the sacrifice may be performed at the appointed hour.'

50. "Directed thus, the sage's son was immediately appeased. He went into the hill, returned with the horse and the princes and released them with pleasure.

51-53. "Mahasena sent the princes with the horse to the town. He was surprised at what he saw and saluting the sage asked him respectfully: 'Lord, please tell me how the horse and the princes were concealed in the hill.' Then the sage replied:

54-66. "'Listen, O King, I was formerly an emperor ruling the empire bounded by the seas. After a long while the Grace of God descended on me and I grew disgusted with the world as being but trash in the light of consciousness within. I abdicated the kingdom in favor of my sons and retired into this forest. My wife, being dutiful, accompanied me here. Several years were passed in our penance and austerities. Once my wife embraced me and this son was born to her when I was in *samâdhi*. She brought me to my senses, left the babe with me and died. This boy was brought up by me with love and care. When he grew up, he heard that I had once been a king; he wished to be one also and besought me to grant his prayer. I initiated him in *yoga* which he practised with such success that he was able by the force of his will to create a world of his own in this hill which he is now ruling. The horse and princes were kept there. I have now told you the secret of that hill.' After hearing it Mahasena asked again:

67. "'I have with great interest heard your wonderful account of this hill. I want to see it. Can you grant my prayer?'

68. "Being so requested, the sage commanded his son saying 'Boy! show him round the place and satisfy him.'

69. "Having said thus, the sage again lapsed into *samâdhi;* and his son went away with the king.

70. "The sage's son entered the hill without trouble and disappeared, but Mahasena was not able to enter. So he called out for the sage's son.

71. "He too called out to the king, from the interior of the hill. Then he came out of it and said to the king:

72-74. "'O King, this hill cannot be penetrated with the slender yogic powers that you possess. You will find it too dense. Nevertheless you must be taken into it as my father ordered. Now, leave your gross body in this hole covered with bushes; enter the hill with your mental sheath along with me.' The king could not do it and asked:

75. "'Tell me, saint, how I am to throw off this body. If I do it forcibly, I shall die.'

76. "The saint smiled at this and said: 'You do not seem to know *yoga*. Well, close your eyes.'

77. "The king closed his eyes; the saint forthwith entered into him, took the other's subtle body and left the gross body in the hole.

78. "Then by his yogic power the saint entered the hill with this subtle body snatched from the other which was filled with the desire of seeing the empire within the bowels of the hill.

79. "Once inside he roused up the sleeping individual to dream. The latter now found himself held by the saint in the wide expanse of ether.

Note: The *ativahika sarira* (astral body), exhaustively treated in *Yoga Vasishta.*

80-82. "He was alarmed on looking in all directions and requested the saint, 'Do not forsake me lest I should perish in this illimitable space.' The saint laughed at his terror and said, 'I shall never forsake you. Be assured of it. Now look round at everything and have no fear.'

83-95. "The king took courage and looked all round. He saw the sky above, enveloped in the darkness of night and shining with stars. He ascended there and looked down below; he came to the region of the moon and was benumbed with cold. Protected by the saint, he went up to the Sun and was scorched by its rays. Again tended by the saint, he was refreshed and saw the whole region a counterpart of the Heaven. He went up to

77

the summits of the Himalayas with the saint and was shown the whole region and also the earth. Again endowed with powerful eye-sight, he was able to see far-off lands and discovered other worlds besides this one. In the distant worlds there was darkness prevailing in some places; the earth was gold in some; there were oceans and island continents traversed by rivers and mountains; there were the heavens peopled by Indra and the Gods, the *asuras,* human beings, the *rakshasas* and other races of celestials. He also found that the saint had divided himself as Brahman in Satyaloka, as Vishnu in Vaikunta, and as Siva in Kailasa while all the time he remained as his original-self the king ruling in the present world. The king was struck with wonder on seeing the yogic power of the saint. The sage's son said to him: 'This sight-seeing has lasted only a single day according to the standards prevailing here, whereas twelve thousand years have passed by in the world you are used to. So let us return to my father.'

96. "Saying so, he helped the other to come out of the hill to this outer world."

Thus ends the Chapter XII on sight-seeing in the Ganda Hill in *Tripura Rahasya.*

Chapter XIII

How Wakefulness and Dream Are Similar in Nature and Objects Are Only Mental Images

1-2. The sage's son made the king sleep, united his subtle body with the gross one left in the hole, and then woke him up.

3. On regaining his senses, Mahasena found the whole world changed. The people, the river courses, the trees, the tanks, etc., were all different.

4-30. He was bewildered and asked the saint:

"O great one! How long have we spent seeing your world? This world looks different from the one I was accustomed to!" Thus asked, the sage's son said to Mahasena: 'Listen King, this is the world which we were in and left to see that within the hill. The same has undergone enormous changes owing to the long interval of time. We spent only one day looking round the hill region; the same interval counts for twelve thousand years in this land; and it has accordingly changed enormously. Look at the difference in the manners of the people and their languages. Such changes are natural. I have often noticed similar changes before. Look here! This is the Lord, my father in *samâdhi*. Here you stood before, praising my father and praying to him. There you see the hill in front of you.

"By this time, your brother's progeny has increased to thousands. What was Vanga, your country, with Sundara, your capital, is now a jungle infested with jackals and wild animals. There is now one Virabahu in your brother's line who has his capital Visala on the banks of the Kshipra in the country of Malwa; in your line, there is Susarma whose capital is Vardhana in the country of the Dravidas, on the banks of the Tambrabharani. Such is the course of the world which cannot remain the same even for a short time. For in this period, the hills, rivers, lakes, and the contour of the earth have altered. Mountains subside; plains heave high; deserts become fertile;

79

plateaus change to sandy tracts; rocks decompose and become silt; clay hardens sometimes; cultivated farms become barren and barren lands are brought under tillage; precious stones become valueless and trinkets become invaluable; salt water becomes sweet and potable waters become brackish; some lands contain more people than cattle, others are infested with wild beasts; and yet others are invaded by venomous reptiles, insects and vermin. Such are some of the changes that happen on the earth in course of time. But there is no doubt that this is the same earth as we were in before."

Mahasena heard all that the sage's son said and fainted from the shock. Then being brought round by his companion, he was overcome by grief and mourned the loss of his royal brother and brother's son and of his own wife and children. After a short time, the sage's son assuaged his grief with wise words: "Being a sensible man, why do you mourn and at whose loss? A sensible man never does anything without a purpose, to act without discernment is childish. Think now, and tell me what loss grieves you and what purpose your grief will serve."

Asked thus, Mahasena, who was still inconsolable retorted: "Great sage that you are, can you not understand the cause of my sorrow? How is it that you seek the reason of my grief when I have lost my all? A man is generally sad when only *one* of his family dies. I have lost *all* my friends and relatives and you still ask me why I am sad."

31-48. The sage's son continued derisively. "King! tell me now, is this lapse into sorrow a hereditary virtue? Will it result in sin if you do not indulge in it on this occasion? Or, do you hope to recover your loss by such grief? King! Think well and tell me what you gain by your sorrow. If you consider it irresistible, listen to what I say.

"Such loss is not fresh. Your forefathers have died before. Have you ever mourned their loss? If you say that it is because of blood relationship that it now causes your grief, were there not worms in the bodies of your parents, living on their nourishment? Why are they not your relatives and why does not their loss cause you sorrow? King, think! Who are you? Whose deaths are the cause of your present grief?

"Are you the body, or other than that? The body is simply a conglomerate of different substances. Harm to any one of the constituents is harm to the whole. There is no moment in which each of the components is not changing. But the excretions do not constitute a loss to the body.

"Those whom you called your brother and so on are mere bodies; the bodies are composed of earth; when lost, they return to earth; and earth resolves ultimately into energy. Where then is the loss?

"In fact you are not the body. You own the body and call it your own, just as you do a garment you happen to possess. Where lies the difference between your body and your garment? Have you any doubt regarding this conclusion? Being other than your own body, what relation is there between you and another body? Did you ever claim similar relationship, say with your brother's clothes? Why then mourn over the loss of bodies, which are in no way different from garments?

"You speak of 'my' body, 'my' eyes, 'my' life, 'my' mind and so on, I ask you now to tell me what precisely you are."

Being confronted thus, Mahasena began to think over the matter, and unable to solve the problem he asked to take leave to consider it carefully. Then he returned and said with all humility "Lord, I do not see who I am. I have considered the matter, and still I do not understand. My grief is only natural; I cannot account for it.

"Master, I seek your protection. Kindly tell me what it is. Every one is overpowered by grief when their relative dies. No one seems to know his own self; nor does one mourn all losses.

"I submit to you as your disciple. Please elucidate this matter to me."

Being thus requested, the sage's son spoke to Mahasena:

49. "King, listen! People are deluded by the illusion cast by Her Divine Majesty. They partake of misery that is due to the ignorance of their selves. Their misery is meaningless.

50. "As long as the ignorance of the self lasts, so long will there be misery.

51-52. "Just as a dreamer is foolishly alarmed at his own dreams or as a fool is deluded by the serpents created in a magic performance, so also the man ignorant of the Self is terrified.

53-55. "Just as the dreamer awakened from his fearful dream or the man attending the magic performance informed of the unreal nature of the magic creations, no longer fears them but ridicules another who does, so also one aware of the Self not only does not grieve but also laughs at another's grief. Therefore, O valiant hero, batter down this impregnable fortress of illusion and conquer your misery by realization of the Self. In the meantime be discriminating and not so foolish."

56-58. After hearing the sage's son, Mahasena said, 'Master, your illustration is not to the point. Dream or magic is later realized to be illusory whereas this hard concrete universe is always real and purposeful. This is unassailed and persistent. How can it be compared to the evanescent dream?' Then the sage's son answered:

59. "Listen to what I say. Your opinion that the illustration is not to the point is a double delusion like a dream in a dream.

Note: The commentary says that the first delusion is the idea of separateness of the universe from oneself and that the second is the idea that dream objects are an illusion in contradistinction to those seen while awake. This is compared to the illusion that a dreamer mistakes the dream-rope for a dream-serpent. (The dream is itself an illusion and the mistake is an illusion in the illusion.)

60-70. "Consider the dream as a dreamer would and tell me whether the trees do not afford shade to the pedestrians, and bear fruits for the use of others. Is the dream realized to be untrue and evanescent in the dream itself?

"Do you mean to say that the dream is rendered false after waking from it? Is not the waking world similarly rendered false in your dream or deep sleep?

"Do you contend that the waking state is not so because there is continuity in it after you wake up? Is there no continuity in your dreams from day to day?

"If you say that it is not evident, tell me whether the continuity in the wakeful world is not broken up every moment of your life.

"Do you suggest that the hills, the seas and the earth itself are really permanent phenomena, in spite of the fact that their appearance is constantly changing? Is not the dream-world also similarly continuous with its earth, mountains, rivers, friends and relatives?

"Do you still doubt its abiding nature? Then extend the same reasoning to the nature of the wakeful world and know it to be equally evanescent.

"The ever-changing objects like the body, trees, rivers, and islands are easily found to be transitory. Even mountains are not immutable, for their contours change owing to the erosion of waterfalls and mountain torrents; ravages by men, boars and wild animals, insects; thunder; lightning and storms; and so on. You will observe similar change in the seas and on earth.

"Therefore I tell you that you should investigate the matter closely. (You will probably argue as follows:)

71-76. "Dream and wakefulness resemble each other in their discontinuous harmony (like a chain made up of links). There is no unbroken continuity in any object because every new appearance implies a later disappearance. But continuity cannot be denied in the fundamentals underlying the objects!

"Because a dream creation is obliterated and rendered false by present experience—what distinction will you draw between the fundamentals underlying the dream objects and the present objects?

"If you say that the dream is an illusion and its fundamentals are equally so, whereas the present creation is not so obliterated and its fundamentals must therefore be true, I ask you what illusion is. It is determined by the transitory nature, which is nothing but appearance to, and disappearance from, our senses.

"Is not everything obliterated in deep sleep? If you maintain however, that mutual contradiction is unreliable as evidence and so proves nothing, it amounts to saying that self-evident sight alone furnishes the best proof. Quite so, people like you do not have a true insight into the nature of things.

77-79. "Therefore, take my word for it, the present world is only similar to the dream world. Long periods pass in dreams also. Therefore, purposefulness and enduring nature are in every way similar to both states. Just as you are obviously aware in your waking state, so also you are in your dream state.

80. "These two states being so similar, why do you not mourn the loss of your dream relations?

81. "The wakeful universe appears so real to all only by force of habit. If the same be imagined vacuous it will melt away into the void.

82-83. "One starts imagining something; then contemplates it; and by continuous or repeated association resolves that it is true unless contradicted. In that way, the world appears real in the manner one is used to it. My world that you visited furnishes the proof thereof; come now, let us go round the hill and see."

85. Saying so, the sage's son took the king, and went round the hill and returned to the former spot.

86-87. Then he continued: "Look, O King! the circuit of the hill is hardly two miles and a half and yet you have seen a universe within it. Is it real or false? Is it a dream or otherwise? What has passed as a day in that land, has counted for twelve thousand years here, which is correct? Think, and tell me. Obviously you cannot distinguish this from a dream and cannot help concluding that the world is nothing but imagination. My world will disappear instantly if I cease contemplating it.

"Therefore convince yourself of the dream-like nature of the world and do not indulge in grief at your brother's death.

90. "Just as the dream creations are pictures moving on the mind screens, so also this world including yourself is the obverse of the picture depicted by pure intelligence and it is nothing more than an image in a mirror. See how you will feel after this conviction. Will you be elated by the accession of a dominion or depressed by the death of a relative in your dream?

91. "Realize that the Self is the self-contained mirror projecting and manifesting this world. The Self is pure unblemished consciousness. Be quick! Realize it quickly and gain transcendental happiness!"

Thus ends the Chapter on the Vision of the Hill City in *Tripura Rahasya*.

Chapter XIV

How the Universe Is Mere Imagination; How to Gain That Strong Will Which Can Create It; and the Highest Truth

1-6. Having heard the sage's son, Mahasena began to think clearly and seriously; he concluded the world to be dream-like and overcame his grief. Growing strong in mind, he was not perturbed. Then he asked his companion: "Great and wise saint! You know this world and beyond. I do not believe that there is anything that you do not know. Please answer me now: How can you say that the whole is pure imagination? However much I may imagine, my imagination does not materialise. But you have created a universe by the force of your will. And yet, how do time and space differ in these creations? Please tell me." On being thus asked, the sage's son replied:

7. "The will conceives either effectively or ineffectively according as it is uniform or broken up by indecision.

8. "Do you not know this world to be the result of Brahmâ's desire? This looks real and permanent because the original desire is so powerful.

9. "Whereas the world of your creation no one takes seriously, and your own mistrust makes it useless.

10-15. "Conceptions materialise for various reasons as follows: by virtue of the natural function as with Brahmâ, the Creator; by the possession of live-gems as with *Yakshas* and *Rakshasas* (classes of celestial beings); by the use of herbs as with Gods (nectar is reputed to contain the extracts of superb herbs); by the practice of *yoga* as with yogis; by the miraculous power of incantations as with a few *siddhas;* by the force of penance as with some sages; and by virtue of boons as with the Architect of the universe *(Viswakarma).*

85

"One should forget the old associations in order to make one's new conception effective and this endures only so long as it is not obstructed by the old one. A conception is forceful unless obstructed by an antecedent one and thus destroyed. It is effective only when forceful; in that way even great things may be achieved.

16. "Your conceptions do not materialise for the aforesaid reason. Therefore you must practise focussing of thought if you desire your own creations to endure.

17-23. "I shall tell you now about the difference in time and space. You are not proficient in the affairs of the world, and therefore you are mystified. I shall now make it clear how these differences appear. The Sun helps all to see but blinds the owls; water is the abode of fishes but drowns man; fire burns a man but is food to *tittiri* (a species of bird); fire is ordinarily put out by water but it flourishes in the middle of ocean at the time of dissolution. Similar discrepancies are evident elsewhere. Men and animals engage in activities with their limbs and senses, whereas spirits do so with bodies of others. Instances like these are innumerable. Their explanation is as follows:

24-25. "Sight is of the eye and cannot be without it. A jaundiced eye sees everything yellow and myopia produces the double image of a single object.

26-32. "Abnormal visions are thus the direct result of abnormal eyes. The Karandakas, in an Eastern island, are said to see everything red; so also the inhabitants of Ramanaka isle see everything upside down. One hears many more strange stories of the kind, all of which are based on abnormalities of vision. They can all be remedied by proper treatment. The same applies to other senses including the mind. The relation between space and objects and between time and events is according to your estimate of them; there is no intrinsic relationship between them.

33. "(Having so far proved the objects and events to be only within, he proceeds to establish that there is no 'exterior' to the self.) 'What is designated as exterior' by people, is simply the origin and prop of the universe like the screen with relation to the picture on it.

34-40. "There could be nothing external to that 'exterior' except it be one's own body. How can that be externalised from the 'exterior'? For example, when you say 'outside the hill' the hill is withdrawn from the space beyond; it is not included in it. But the body is seen in space just as a pot is seen.

"The body must therefore be external to the seer. What is visible lies within the range of illumination: if without, it cannot be seen. Therefore the illumined objects must be within the vision of the illuminant. The body, etc., are the illumined, because they are themselves objectified. The illumined and the illuminant cannot be identical.

"Again the illuminant cannot be objectified; for who is the seer apart from it? and how can the illumination by which he sees be apart from him? That the illuminant affords the light and serves as an object standing apart from the seer, is impossible to maintain. Therefore the illuminant cannot admit of any foreign admixture in it, and he is the illumination in perfection—only one, and the *being* of all.

41. "He extends as time and space; they are infinite and perfect, being involved as the illuminant, illumination and the illumined.

42. "As regards *within* or *without,* everything is included in illumination. How can then anything be 'outer' unless it is like a peak on a mountain?

43. "The whole universe is thus in the illumination which shines self-sufficient, by itself, everywhere, and at all times.

44-45. "Such illumination is Her Transcendental Majesty Tripura, the Supreme. She is called Brahmâ in the Vedas, Vishnu by the Vaishnavites, Siva by the Saivites, and Sakti by the Saktas. There is indeed nothing but She.

46. "She holds everything by Her prowess as a mirror does its images. She is the illuminant in relation to the illumined.

47-49. "The object is sunk in illumination like the image of a city in a mirror. Just as the city is not apart from the mirror, so also the universe is not apart from consciousness. Just as the image is part and parcel of the clear, smooth, compact and one mirror, so also the universe is part and parcel of the perfect, solid and unitary consciousness, namely the Self.

50. "The world cannot be demonstrably ascertained. Space is simply void serving for the location of materials.

51. "The universe is, always and all-through, a phenomenon in the Self. The question then arises how consciousness, being void, is dense at the same time.

52. "Just as a mirror, though, dense and impenetrable, contains the image, so also pure consciousness is dense and impenetrable and yet displays the universe by virtue of its self-sufficiency.

53. "Though consciousness is all-pervading, dense and single, it still holds the mobile and immobile creation within it, wonderful in its variety, with no immediate or ultimate cause for it.

54-55. "Just as the mirror remains unaffected by the passage of different images and yet continues to reflect as clearly as before, so also the one consciousness illumines the waking and dream states which can be verified by proper meditation.

56. "O King! Examine again your day-dreams and mental imagery. Though they are perfect in detail, yet they are no less mental.

57. "Consciousness permeating them obviously remains unblemished before creation or after dissolution of the world; even during the existence of the world, it remains unaffected as the mirror by the images.

58. "Though unperturbed, unblemished, thick, dense and single the absolute consciousness being self-sufficient manifests within itself what looks 'exterior,' just like a mirror reflecting space as external to itself.

59-60. "This is the first step in creation; it is called ignorance or darkness; starting as an infinitesimal fraction of the whole, it manifests as though external to its origin, and is a property of the ego-sense. The alienation is on account of the latent tendencies to be manifested later. Because of its non-identity with the original consciousness, it is now simple, insentient energy."

Note: The *commentary* has it: What is absolute consciousness goes under the name of *Mâyâ* just before creation, and is later called *Avidya* (or ignorance) with the manifestation of the ego. The agitation in the quietness is due to subtle time fructifying the latent tendencies of the ego which had not merged in the primordial state at the time of the dissolution of the Universe.

61. "That consciousness which illumines the 'exterior' is called *Sivatattva,* whereas the individual feeling as 'I' is *Saktitattva.*

Note: Siva is awareness of the 'exterior'; *Sakti* is the dynamic force operating the potential tendencies in the individual self.

62. "When the awareness of the 'exterior,' combined with the 'I,' encompasses the entire imagined space as 'I' it is called *sadâ-siva-tattva.*

63. "When, later, discarding the abstraction of the Self and the exterior, clear identification with the insentient space takes place, it is called *isvara-tattva.* The investigation of the last two steps is pure *vidyâ* (knowledge).

64. "All these five *tattvas* are pure because they relate to an as-yet-undifferentiated condition like potentialities in a seed.

65. "After the differentiation is made manifest by will-force the insentient part predominates over the other, as opposed to the contrary condition before.

66. "That insentient predominance is called *Mâyâ Shakti* after differentiation is clearly established, like the sprout from a seed.

67-69. "The sentient phase is now engaged, being relegated to a minor position, and takes on the name of *Purusha* being covered by five sheaths, namely *kalâ* (something of doership), *vidya* (some knowledge), *raga* (desire), *kâla* (time—allotted life) and *niyati* (fixed order of things).

70. "Anamnesis of individuals made up of the proclivities acquired as a result of engaging in diverse actions in previous births, is now supported by intelligence and remains as *prakriti* (nature).

71. "This *prakriti* is tripartite because the fruits of actions are of three kinds; She manifests as the three states of life wakefulness, dream and deep sleep, She then assumes the name, *chitta* (mind).

72. "The anamnesis goes by the name of *Prakriti* in dreamless slumber, and *Chitta* in the other states. It is always comprised

of the insentient phase of the proclivities of the mind and the
sentient phase of intelligence.

73. "When the proclivities still remain in abeyance without
being used up, its totality is called *avyakta* (unmanifested); differences arise only in *chitta*, there is no difference among individuals in sleep and so it is *prakriti*, the same assuming the name
of *chitta* when differences manifest.

Note: Sleep is characterized by undifferentiation and so it is
the same for all, irrespective of propensities of the mind.
Simultaneous with the awareness of the body the other states
manifest. Individual enjoyments—pleasure and pain—lie only
in the wakeful and dream states, according as the innate tendencies of the mind mature and yield fruits. When one crop is
over sleep supervenes, then there is no enjoyment and no distinction according to crops. As the anamnesis is ready with the
next crop, sleep is shaken off and differences arise. So it is clear
how the one undifferentiated condition manifests as the universe in all its diversity and resolves into itself periodically.

75. "Therefore the mind *(chitta)* is *purusha* (the individual)
when the sentient phase is assertive, and the same is *ayakta*
(unmanifest) when *prakriti* (nature), the insentient phase, is
assertive.

76. "That *chitta* is tripartite according to its functions,
namely, ego, intellect and mind.

77. "When influenced by the three qualities, it manifests in
greater details as follows: by *satva* (brightness), it becomes the
five senses, hearing, sight, touch, taste and smell; by *rajas*
(activity) speech, hands, feet, organs of excretion and of pro-
creation; by *tamas* (darkness) earth, air, fire, water and ether.

78. "The supreme intelligence coquets with the universe in
this manner, remaining all the time unaffected, a witness of its
own creation.

79. "The present creation is the mental product of Brahmâ
or Hiranyagarbha, appointed creator by the will-force of the
Primal Being, Sri Tripura.

80. "The cognition 'you' and 'I' is the essence of any kind of
creation; such cognition is the manifestation of transcendental

consciousness; there cannot be any difference (just as there is no difference in space, bounded by a pot or not bounded by it).

81. "The diversities in creation are solely due to qualifications limiting the consciousness; these qualifications (*i.e.,* body, limiting of age) are the mental imagery of the creator (consistent with the individual's past merits); when the creative will-force wears away there is dissolution and complete undifferentiation results.

82. "As for your will-power, it is overpowered by the creator when that impediment is surmounted by the methods already mentioned, your will-power will also become effective.

83. "Time, space, gross creations, etc., appear in it according to the imagery of the agent.

84-86. "A certain period is only one day according to my calculation whereas it is twelve thousand years according to Brahmâ: the space covered by about two miles and a half of Brahmâ is infinite according to me and covers a whole universe. In this way, both are true and untrue at the same time.

87-88. "Similarly also, imagine a hill within you, and also time in a subtle sense. Then contemplate a whole creation in them; they will endure as long as your concentration endures— even to eternity for all practical purposes, if your will-power be strong enough.

"Therefore I say that this world is a mere figment of imagination.

89. "O King! it shines in the manifest conscious Self within. Therefore what looks like the external world is really an image on the screen of the mind.

90. "Consciousness is thus the screen and the image, and so *yogis* are enabled to see long distances of space and realize long intervals of time.

91. "They can traverse all distance in a moment and can perceive everything as readily as a gooseberry in the hollow of one's palm.

92. "Therefore recognise the fact that the world is simply an image on the mirror of consciousness and cultivate the contemplation of 'I am,' abide as pure being and thus give up this delusion of the reality of the world.

93-97. "Then you will become like myself one in being self-sufficient."

Dattatreya continued:

"On hearing this discourse of the sage's son, the king overcame his delusion; his intellect became purified and he understood the ultimate goal. Then he practised *samâdhi,* and became self-contained, without depending on any external agency, and led a long and happy life. He ceased to identify himself with the body, and became absolute as transcendental space until he was finally liberated. So you see, Bhârgava, that the universe is only mental image, just as firm as one's will-power, and no more. It is not independent of the Self. Investigate the matter yourself, and your delusion will gradually lose hold of you and pass off."

Thus ends the Chapter XIV on the story of the Hill City in *Tripura Rahasya.*

Chapter XV

On What Need Be Known and Need Not Be Known and on the Nature of the Self

1. On hearing Dattareya relate the wonderful story of the Hill City, Parasurâma marvelled more and more.

2. He, with a clear mind, pondered over the teachings of his Master, and then returned to him and asked him again:

3. "Lord, I have considered the purport of your teachings in the shape of the magnificent stories you told me.

4. "I understand that intelligence alone is real and single, and that objects are only unreal images like a city reflected in a mirror.

5. "Her Transcendental Majesty, the Maheswari, is that consciousness manifesting as Intelligence cognisant of the whole range of phenomena beginning from the unmanifest state of sleep and ending with this world passing in quick succession within itself.

6. "All these are apparently due to the self-sufficiency of that consciousness and they come into being without any immediate cause. This much I have understood after deep consideration.

7. "But this intelligence is said to be beyond cognition because it always remains as pure knowledge itself.

8. "I do not see how it can be realized if it surpasses knowledge. The goal is not achieved without realizing it.

9. "The goal is liberation. What is its nature? If one can be liberated while alive, still how is the course of his emancipated life regulated, if that is at all possible?

10. "There are sages who are active. What is the relation between the world of action and their pure conscious being?

11. "How can they engage in action while all the time they inhere in absolute consciousness? Such consciousness can be of only one kind, and liberation also can be only one in order to be effective.

12-17. "How then are these differences noticed in the lives of the jnanis? Some of them are active; some teach scriptures; some worship deities; some abstract themselves into *samâdhi;* some lead an austere life and emaciate themselves; some give clear instructions to their disciples; some rule kingdom quite justly; some openly hold disputations with other schools of thought; some write down their teachings and experiences; others simulate ignorance; a few even conduct reprehensible and loathsome actions; but all of them are famous as wise men in the world.

18. "How can there be such differences in their lives when there can be no difference in the state of liberation common to all? Or are there grades in knowledge and liberation?

19. "Kindly enlighten me on these points, because I am eager to learn the truth and submit to you as my sole Teacher."

20. Thus requested, Dattatreya appeared pleased with the questions and answered the worthy disciple as follows:

21. "Worthy Rama! You are indeed fit to reach that goal because you have now turned towards the right way of investigation.

22. "This is due to the Grace of God which puts you in the right way of investigation. Who can attain anything worthy, without divine Grace?

23. "The beneficent work of the self-inhering divine Grace is finished when the inward turning of one's mind increases in strength day by day.

24-25. "What you have said so far is quite true; you have rightly understood the nature of consciousness but have not realized it. A knowledge of the property of a thing without actual experience of the thing itself is as useless as no knowledge.

26. "True experience of the Self is the unawareness of even 'I am.' Can the world persist after such unawareness? Secondhand knowledge is no better than the recollection of a dream.

27. "Just as the accession of treasure in a dream is useless, so also is secondhand knowledge.

28. "I shall illustrate it with a very ancient story. There was formerly a very virtuous king ruling over Videha.

29. "He was Janaka by name, very wise and conversant with both this world and beyond. At one time he worshipped with sacrificial rites the Goddess, inhering as the Self.

30. "There came for the occasion, all the Brahmins, pandits, hermits, critics, those versed in the Vedas, those accustomed to share in sacrificial rites and sacrifices, etc.

31. "At the same time, Varuna, the God of waters, wanted to perform a similar sacrifice, but worthy men did not accept the invitation.

32-37. "For they were pleased with Janaka who respected them duly.

"Then Varuna's son, who was a great dialectician, came to them. He disguised himself as a Brahmin, in order to decoy the Brahmin guests. On entering the royal chamber he duly blessed the king and addressed him thus before all the assembly. 'O King, your assembly is not as good as it should be. It looks like a lovely lake of lotuses ravaged by crows, jackdaws and herons; it would be better without this medley of incompetents. I do not find a single individual here who will be an ornament to a great assembly like a swan to a lovely lake of lotuses. May God bless you! I shall have nothing to do with this multitude of fools.'

38-41. "Being thus insulted by Varuna's son, the whole assembly stood up to a man and said in anger: 'You charlatan of a Brahmin! How dare you insult everybody here? What learning have you which is wanting in us? Wicked man that you are, you are only a bluffer! You shall not leave this place until you have proved your superiority over us. There are great *pandits* assembled here from all over the world. Do you hope to subdue all of them by your learning? Tell us your special subject in which you imagine yourself more proficient than us!'

Thus challenged, Varun's son replied:

42-43. "I will in a minute outdo you all in debate; but that shall be only on the condition that if I am defeated, you will throw me into the sea; and if you are defeated, I will consign you to the sea, one after another. If you agree to this condition, let us have a debate.

44-45. "They consented and the debate began in right earnest. The *pandits* were shortly defeated by the fallacious logic of the opponent and they were sunk in the sea by hundreds.

46. "Varuna's followers then took away the sunken *pandits* to his sacrifice where they were received with respect which much pleased them.

47. "There was one by name Kahoela, among those who were thus sunk. His son Ashtavakra, having heard of his father's fate, hastened to Janaka's court and challenged the debater skilled in fallacy. The masquerader was now defeated and straightaway condemned to the sea by the young avenger. Then Varun's son threw off his mask in the court and restored back all the men formerly drowned in the sea. Kahoela's son was now puffed with pride and behaved offensively before the assembled court. The *pandits* were made to feel mortified before the youth.

51-52. "Just then, a female ascetic appeared in their midst, to whom the offended assembly looked for help. Encouraging them in their hopes, the charming maiden with matted locks and hermit's clothes was highly honored by the king and she spoke in sweet and yet firm tone's:

53. "'Oh child! Son of Kahoela! You are indeed very accomplished, for these Brahmins have been rescued by you after you defeated Varun's son in debate.

54-56. "'I want to ask of you a short question, to which please give a straight answer, explicit and unreserved. What is that condition reaching which there will be all-round immortality: knowing which all doubts and uncertainties will disappear; and established in which all desires will vanish? If you have realized that unbounded state, please tell me directly.'

"Being approached by the ascetic, the son of Kahoela replied with confidence:

57-58. "'I know it. Listen to what I say. There is nothing in the world not known to me. I have studied all the sacred literature with great care. Therefore hear my answer.

59-63. "What you ask is the primal and efficient cause of the universe, being itself without beginning, middle or end, and unaffected by time and space. It is pure, unbroken, single Consciousness. The whole world is manifested in it like a city in a mirror. Such is that transcendental state. On realizing it, one becomes immortal; there is no place for doubts and uncertainties, as there is no more reason for ignorance as at the sight of innumerable reflected images; and there will be no more room for desire, because transcendence is then experienced.

"It is also unknowable because there is no one to know it, besides itself.

"Ascetic! I have now told you the truth as contained in the Scriptures.'

64-71. "After Ashtavakra had finished, the hermit spoke again: 'Young sage! What you say, is rightly said and accepted by all. But I draw your attention to that part of your answer where you admitted its unknowability for want of a knower outside of consciousness; and also that its knowledge confers immortality and perfection. How are these two statements to be reconciled? Either admit that consciousness is unknowable, is not known to you, and thus conclude its non-existence; or say that it is, and that you know it—and therefore it is not unknowable.

"You evidently speak from secondhand knowledge, gathered from the scriptures. Clearly, you have not realized it and so your knowledge is not personal.

"Think now—your words amount to this—you have a personal knowledge of the images but not of the mirror. How can that be?

"Tell me now if you are not ashamed of this prevarication before King Janaka and his assembly.'

"Being thus reprimanded by the ascetic, he could not speak for some time because he felt mortified and ashamed; so he remained with bent head thinking it over.

72-73. "However, the Brahmin youth could not find any satisfactory answer to her question, so he submitted to her in great humility: 'O ascetic! Truly I cannot find the answer to your question. I submit to you as your disciple. Pray tell me how the two scriptural statements are to be reconciled. But I assure you that I have not told a deliberate lie, for I know that any merits a liar may have are counteracted by his lies so that he is condemned as unworthy.'

74. "Thus requested, the ascetic was pleased with Ashtavakra's sincerity and said to him in the hearing of the assembly.

75-84. "'Child, there are many who being ignorant of this sublime truth, live in a state of delusion. Dry polemics will not help one to Reality for it is well guarded on all sides. Of all the people now assembled here, no one has experienced Reality, except the king and myself. It is not a subject for discussion. The most brilliant logic can only approach it but never attain it. Although unaffected by logic coupled with a keen intellect, it can however be realized by service to one's *Guru* and the grace of God.

"O thou who art thyself the Son of a Sage, listen to me carefully, for this is hard to understand even when hearing it explained. Hearing it a thousand times over will be useless unless one verifies the teachings by means of investigation into the Self with a concentrated mind. Just as a prince labors under a misapprehension that the string of pearls still clinging to his neck has been stolen away by another and is not persuaded to the contrary by mere words but only believes when he finds it around his neck by his own effort so also, O youth, however clever a man may be, he will never know his own self by the mere teaching of others unless he realizes it for himself. Otherwise he can never realize the Self if his mind is turned outward.

85. "A lamp illumines all around but does not illumine itself or another light. It shines of itself without other sources of light. Things shine in sunlight without the necessity for any other kind of illumination. Because lights do not require to be illumined, do we say that they are not known or that they do not exist?

"Therefore, as it is thus with lights and things made aware by the conscious self, what doubt can you have regarding abstract consciousness, namely the Self?

"Lights and things being insentient, cannot be self-aware. Still, their existence or manifestation is under no doubt. That means they are self-luminous. Can you not similarly investigate with an inward mind in order to find out if the all-comprehending Self is conscious or not conscious?

"That Consciousness is absolute and transcends the three states (wakefulness, dream and slumber) and comprises all the universe making it manifest. Nothing can be apprehended without its light.

"Will anything be apparent to you, if there be no consciousness? Even to say that nothing is apparent to you (as in sleep) requires the light of consciousness. Is not your awareness of your unawareness (in sleep) due to consciousness?

"If you infer its eternal light, then closely investigate whether the light is of itself or not. Everybody falls in this investigation however learned and proficient he may be, because his mind is not bent inward but restlessly moves outward. As long as thoughts crop up, so long has the turning inward of the mind not been accomplished. As long as the mind is not inward, so long the Self cannot be realized. Turning inward means absence of desire. How can the mind be fixed within if desires are not given up?

"Therefore become dispassionate and inhere as the Self. Such inherence is spontaneous (no effort is needed to inhere as the Self). It is realized after thoughts are eliminated and investigation ceases. Recapitulate your state after you break off from it, and then will know all and the significance of its being knowable and unknowable at the same time. Thus realizing the unknowable, one abides in immortality for ever and ever.

"I have now finished. Salutations to you! Farewell!

"But you have not yet understood my words because this is the first time you hear the truth. This king, the wisest among men, can make you understand. So ask him again and he will clear your doubts."

"When she had finished, she was honored by the king and the whole assembly, and then she instantly dissolved in air and disappeared from human sight.

"I have now related to you, O Rama, the method of Self-Realization."

Thus ends the Chapter XV on Ashtavakra Section in *Tripura Rahasya*.

Chapter XVI

On Consciousness; Control of Mind; and Sleep

1. When Parasurâma had heard the story, he marvelled greatly and requested his Master to continue.

2-5. "Lord, this ancient legend is marvellous. Please tell me what Ashtavakra asked the king next, and the instructions he received. I had not hitherto heard this story full of sublime truths. Please continue the story. Master, I am anxious to hear it in full."

Being so requested, Dattatreya, the great sage and Master, continued the holy narrative. "Listen, O Bhargava, to the discourse with Janaka.

6-7. "On the departure of the holy ascetic from vision, Ashtavakra, the son of a sage, asked Janaka who was surrounded by a whole group of *pandits,* the full explanation of the ascetic's brief but recondite speech. I shall now tell you Janaka's reply, to which listen attentively.

8-9. "Ashtavakra asked, 'O King of Videha, I have not clearly understood the teaching of the ascetic because of its brevity. Please explain to me then, Lord of mercy, how I shall know the unknowable.'

Being thus asked, Janaka, as if surprised, replied:

10-13. "O thou son of a sage, listen to me! It is neither unknowable nor remains unknown at any moment. Tell me how even the ablest of Masters can guide one to something which always remains unknown. If a Guru can teach, it means that he knows what he says. This transcendental state is quite easy or may be well-nigh impossible according as one's mind is inward bent in peace or out-moving in restlessness. It cannot be taught if it always remains unknown.

14. "The fact that the Vedas point to it only indirectly as 'not this—not this' shows that the knowledge can be imparted to others.

"Whatever you see becomes known by the very abstract intelligence.

15-19. "Now carefully analyze the underlying consciousness which, though abstract and apart from material objects, yet illumines them all the same. Know it to be the truth. O sage! What is not self-luminous can only fall within the orbit of intelligence and cannot be Intelligence itself. Intelligence is that by which objects are known; it cannot be what it is if it becomes the object of knowledge. What is intelligible must always be different from intelligence itself, or else it could not be made known by it. Intelligence in the abstract cannot admit of parts, which is the characteristic of objects. Therefore objects take on shapes. Carefully watch absolute Intelligence after eliminating all else from it.

20. "Just as a mirror takes on the hues of the images, so also the abstract Intelligence assumes the different shapes of objects by virtue of its holding them within itself.

21. "Abstract Intelligence can thus be made manifest by eliminating from it all that can be known. It cannot be known as such and such, for it is the supporter of one and all.

22. "This, being the Self of the seeker, is not cognisable. Investigate your true Self in the aforesaid manner.

Note: There is no other agent to know the Self nor light by which to know it.

23. "You are not the body, nor the senses, nor the mind, because they are all transient. The body is composed of food, so how can you be the body?

24. "For the sense of 'I' (ego) surpasses the body, the senses and the mind, at the time of the cognition of objects.

Commentary: The Self always flashes as 'I' due to its self-luminosity. The body and such things do not. The 'I' surpasses the body, etc., simultaneously with the perception of objects, for the bodily conception does not exist with the perception of objects. Otherwise the two perceptions must be coeval.

"The contention may be set out that the eternal flash of the Self as 'I' is not apparent at the time of the perception of objects. If 'I' did not shine forth at the time, the objects would not be perceived just as they are invisible in the absence of light.

Why is not the flash apparent? Perceptibility is always associated with insentient matter. Who else could see the self-luminosity of the Self? It cannot shine in absolute singleness and purity. However it is there as 'I.'

"Moreover everyone feels 'I see the objects.' If it were not for the eternal being of 'I,' there would always arise the doubt *if I am* or *if I am not*—which is absurd.

"Nor should it be supposed that 'I' is of the body, at the time of perception of objects. For, perception implies the assumption of that shape by the intellect, as is evident when identifying the body with the Self?

"Nor again should it be said that at the time of perception 'I am so and so, Chaitra,'—the Chaitra sense over-reaches the 'I' sense, but the 'I' sense is never lost by the Chaitra sense.

"There is the continuity of 'I' in deep slumber and in *samâdhi*. Otherwise after sleep a man would get up as somebody else.

"The concentration is possible that in deep sleep and *samâdhi,* the Self remains unqualified and therefore is not identical with the limited consciousness of the ego, 'I,' in the wakeful state. The answer is as follows: 'I', is of two kinds—qualified and unqualified. Qualification implies limitations whereas its absence implies its unlimited nature.

'I' is associated with limitations in dream and wake: full states, and it is free from them in deep slumber and *samâdhi* states.

"In that case is the 'I' in *samâdhi* or sleep associated with trifold division of subject, object and their relation? No! Being pure and single, it is unblemished and persists as 'I-I,' and nothing else. The same is Perfection.

25. "Whereas Her Majesty the Absolute Intelligence is ever resplendent as 'I,' therefore She is all and ever-knowing. You are She, in the abstract.

26. "Realize it yourself by turning your *sight* inward. You are only pure abstract Consciousness. Realize it this instant, for procrastination is not worthy of a good disciple. He should realize the Self at the moment of instruction.

102

27. "Your eyes are not meant by the aforesaid word *sight*. The mental eye is meant, for it is the eye of the eye, as is clear in dreams.

28. "To say that the sight is turned inward is appropriate because perception is possible only when the sight is turned towards the object.

29-31. "The sight must be turned away from other objects and fixed on a particular object in order to see it. Otherwise that object will not be perceived in entirety. The fact that the sight is not fixed on it is the same as not seeing it. Similarly is it with hearing, touch, etc.

32. "The same applies to the mind in its sensations of pain and pleasure, which are not felt if the mind is otherwise engaged.

33. "The other perceptions require the two conditions, namely, elimination of others and concentration on the one. But Self-Realization differs from them in that it requires only one condition: *elimination of all perceptions.*

34. "I shall tell you the reason for this. Although consciousness is unknowable, it is still realizable by pure mind.

35-45. "Even the learned are perplexed on this point. External perceptions of the mind are dependent on two conditions.

"The first is elimination of other perceptions and the second is fixation on the particular item of perception. If the mind is simply turned away from other perceptions, the mind is in an indifferent state, where there is absence of any kind of perception. Therefore concentration on a particular item is necessary for the perception of external things. But since consciousness is the Self and not apart from the mind, concentration on it is not necessary for its realization. It is enough that other perceptions (namely, thoughts) should be eliminated from the mind and then the Self will be realized.

"If a man wants to pick out one particular image among a series of images passing in front of him as reflections on a mirror, he must turn his attention away from the rest of the pictures and fix it on that particular one.

"If on the other hand, he wants to see the space reflected it is enough that he turns away his attention from the pictures and the space manifests without any attention on his part, for, space is immanent everywhere and is already reflected there. However it has remained unnoticed because the interspatial images dominated the scene.

"Space being the supporter of all and immanent in all, becomes manifest if only the attention is diverted from the panorama. In the same way, consciousness is the supporter of all and is immanent in all and always remains perfect like space pervading the mind also. Diversion of attention from other items is all that is necessary for Self-Realization. Or do you say that the Self-illuminant can ever be absent from any nook or corner?

46. "There can indeed be no moment or spot from which consciousness is absent. Its absence means their absence also. Therefore consciousness of the Self becomes manifest by mere diversion of attention from things or thoughts.

47. "Realization of Self requires absolute purity only and no concentration of mind. For this reason, the Self is said to be unknowable (meaning not objectively knowable).

48. "Therefore it was also said that the sole necessity for Self-Realization is purity of mind. The only impurity of the mind is thought. To make it thought-free is to keep it pure.

49. "It must now be clear to you why purity of mind is insisted upon for Realization of Self. How can the Self be realized in its absence?

50-51. "Or, how is it possible for the Self not to be found gleaming in the pure mind? All the injunctions in the scriptures are directed towards this end alone. For instance, unselfish action, devotion, and dispassion have no other purpose in view.

52. "Because, transcendental consciousness, *viz.*, the Self, is manifest only in the stain-free mind."

After Janaka had spoken thus, Ashtavakra continued to ask:

53-54. "O King, if it is as you say that the mind made passive by elimination of thoughts is quite pure and capable of manifesting Supreme Consciousness, then sleep will do it by itself, since it satisfies your condition and there is no need for any kind of effort."

55. Thus questioned by the Brahmin youth, the King replied, "I will satisfy you on this point. Listen carefully.

56-63. "The mind is truly abstracted in sleep. But then its light is screened by darkness, so how can it manifest its true nature? A mirror covered with tar does not reflect images but can it reflect space either? Is it enough, in that case, that images are eliminated in order to reveal the space reflected in the mirror? In the same manner, the mind is veiled by the darkness of sleep and rendered unfit for illumining thoughts. Would such eclipse of the mind reveal the glimmer of consciousness?

"Would a chip of wood held in front of a single object to the exclusion of all others reflect the object simply because all others are excluded? Reflection can only be on a reflecting surface and not on all surfaces. Similarly also, realization of the Self can only be with an alert mind and not with a stupefied one. New-born babes have no realization of the Self for want of alertness.

"Moreover pursue the analogy of a tarred mirror. The tar may prevent the images from being seen, but the quality of the mirror is not affected, for the outer coating of tar must be reflected in the interior of the mirror. So also the mind, though diverted from dreams and wakefulness, is still in the grip of dark sleep and not free from qualities. This is evident by the recollection of the dark ignorance of sleep when one wakes.

64. "I will now tell you the distinction between sleep and *samâdhi*. Listen attentively:

"There are two states of mind:

(1) Illumination and (2) Consideration.

65. "The first of them is association of the mind with external objects and the second is deliberation on the object seen.

66. "Illumination is unqualified by the limitations of objects: deliberation is qualified by the limitations pertaining to the objects seen, and it is the forerunner of their clear definition.

Note: The mind first notes a thing in its extended vision. The impression is received only after noting the thing in its non-extensive nature, and becomes deeper on musing over the first impression.

67. "There is no distinction noted in the preliminary stage of simple illumination. The thing itself is not yet defined, so illumination is said to be unqualified.

68. "The thing becomes defined later on and is said to be such and such, and so and so. That is the perception of the thing after deliberation.

69-70. "Deliberation is again of two kinds: the one is the actual experience and is said to be fresh, whereas the other is cogitation over the former and is called *memory*. The mind always functions in these two ways."

71-72. "Dreamless slumber is characterised by the illumination of sleep alone, and the experience continues unbroken for a time, whereas the wakeful state is characterised by deliberation repeatedly broken up by thoughts and therefore it is said not to be ignorance.

"Sleep is a state of nescience though it consists of illumination alone yet it is said to be ignorance for the same reason as a light though luminous is said to be insentient.

Commentary: Pure intelligence is made up of luminosity, but is not insentient like a flame. It is gleaming with consciousness, thus differing from the flame. For intellect is evidence as thinking principle. Therefore it is called Absolute Consciousness, active principle, vibratory movement, all-embracing Self, or God. Because of these potentialities it creates the universe.

"Sri *Shankara* has said in *Soundarya Lahàri* 'Siva owes his prowess to *Shakti*; He cannot even stir in Her absence.' Siva should not therefore be considered to be mere inexpressible entity depending for His movements upon *Mâyâ* (like a man on his car). Sri *Shankara* continues, 'Siva is yoked by Thee, Oh *Shakti*, to His true being. Therefore a blessed few worship Thee as the endless series of waves of bliss, as the underlying basis of all that is, as the Supreme Force, maintaining the Universe, and as the Consort of Transcendence.' Thus the identity of Siva and *Shakti* with each other or with Transcendence is evident.

"The argument that the universe is illusory, being a figment of imagination like a hare's born, is extended further by the statement that the creation leading up to it must be equally illusory. Then the co-existence of Siva and *Shakti* is useless; and Siva being incomprehensible without *Shakti*, the idea of God-head falls to pieces. But the scriptures point to God as the primal essence from which the world has sprung, in which it exists, and into which it resolves. That statement will then be meaningless. Why should the other scriptural statement 'There is no more than One' alone be true? Is it to lend support to the argument of illusion? The proper course will be to look for harmony in these statements in order to understand them aright.

"Their true significance lies in the fact that the universe exists, but not separately from the primal Reality—God. Wisdom lies in realizing everything as Siva and not treating it as void.

"The truth is that there is one Reality which is consciousness in the abstract and also transcendental, irradiating the whole universe in all its diversity from its own being, by virtue of its self-sufficiency, which we call *mâyâ* or *shakti* or Energy. Ignorance lies in the feeling of differentiation of the creatures from the Creator. The individuals are only details in the same Reality.

"In sleep, the insentient phase of stupor overpowers the sentient phase of deliberation. But the factor of illumination is ever present and that alone cannot become apparent to men, in the absence of deliberation. Therefore, sleep is said to be the state of ignorance, as distinguished from wakefulness which is conceded to be knowledge.

73. "This conclusion is admitted by the wise also. Sleep is the first born from Transcendence also called the *unmanifest*, the *exterior*, or the *great void*.

74-76. "The state prevailing in sleep is the feeling 'There is naught.' This also prevails in wakefulness, although things are visible. But this ignorance is shattered by the repeated upspring of thoughts. The wise say that the mind is submerged in sleep because it is illumining the unmanifest condition. The submersion of mind is not, however, peculiar to sleep for it happens also at the instant of cognition of things.

77. "I shall now talk to you from my own experience. This subject is perplexing for the most accomplished persons.

78. "All these three states, namely, *samâdhi,* sleep and the instant of cognition of objects, are characterised by absence of perturbation.

79. "Their difference lies in the later recapitulation of the respective states which illumine different perceptions.

80. "Absolute Reality is manifest in *samâdhi;* a void or unmanifest condition distinguishes sleep and diversity is the characteristic of cognition in wakefulness.

81. "The illuminant is however the same all through and is always unblemished. Therefore it is said to be abstract intelligence.

82. *"Samâdhi* and sleep are obvious because their experience remains unbroken for some appreciable period and can be recapitulated after waking up.

83. "That of cognition remains unrecognised because of its fleeting nature. But *samâdhi* and sleep cannot be recognised when they are only fleeting.

84. "The wakeful state is iridescent with fleeting *samâdhi* and sleep. Men when they are awake can detect fleeting sleep because they are already conversant with its nature.

85-86. "But fleeting *samâdhi* goes undetected because people are not so conversant with it. O Brahmin! fleeting *samâdhi* is indeed being experienced by all, even in their busy moments; but it passes unnoticed by them, for want of acquaintance with it. Every instant free from thoughts and musings in the wakeful state is the condition of *samâdhi.*

87. *"Samâdhi* is simply absence of thoughts. Such a state prevails in sleep and at odd moments of wakefulness.

88. "Yet, it is not called *samâdhi* proper, because all the proclivities of the mind are still there latent, ready to manifest the next instant.

89. "The infinitesimal moment of seeing an object is not tainted by deliberation on its qualities and is exactly like *samâdhi.* I will tell you further, listen!

90-93. "The unmanifest state, the first-born of abstract Intelligence revealing 'There is not anything' is the state of abstraction full of light; it is, however, called sleep because it is the insentient phase of consciousness. Nothing is revealed because there is nothing to be revealed. Sleep is therefore the manifestation of the insentient state.

"But in *samâdhi,* Brahman, the Supreme Consciousness, is continuously glowing. She is the engulfer of time and space, the destroyer of void, and the pure *being (Jehovah*—I AM). How can She be the ignorance of sleep?

94. "Therefore sleep is not the end-all and the be-all."

Thus did Janaka teach Ashtavakra.

Thus ends the chapter on the discourse of Janaka to Ashtavakra in *Tripura Rahasya.*

Chapter XVII

On the Uselessness of Fleeting Samadhis and the Way to Wisdom

1. "O Bhargava! I shall now tell you what further conversation took place between Janaka and Ashtavakra.

2-3. Ashtavakra asked, "King! please tell me in greater detail what you call fleeting *samâdhi* in the wakeful state, so that I may follow it up in order to achieve enduring *samâdhi.*"

Thus requested, Janaka replied:

4-11. "Listen, O Brahmin! the following are instances of that state: when a man remains unaware of 'in and out' for a short interval and is not overpowered by the ignorance of sleep; the infinitesimal time when one is beside one-self with joy; when embraced by one's beloved in all purity; when a thing is gained which was intensely longed for but given up in despair; when a lonely traveller moving with the utmost confidence is suddenly confronted with the utmost danger; when one hears of the sudden death of one's only son, who was in the best of health, in the prime of life, and at the apex of his glory.

Note: They are examples of *samâdhi* in raptures of happiness or of pleasure and in spasms of fear or of sorrow.

12-14. "There are also intervals of *samâdhi,* namely the interim period between the waking, dream and sleep states; at the time of sighting a distant object, the mind holding the body at one end projects itself into space until it holds the object at the other end, just as a worm prolongs itself at the time of leaving one hold to catch another hold. Carefully watch the state of mind in the interval.

15-18. "Why dilate on these intervals? All happening will be brought to a standstill if intelligence be homogeneous. They are made possible when a certain harmony reigns in intelligence which ordinarily is repeatedly broken.

"Therefore the great founders of different systems of philosophy have said that the difference between the Self *(i.e.,* abstract intelligence) and intellect (individualistic) lies only in their continuity. Sugata *(i.e.,* Buddha) considers the Self to be the stream of Intelligence broken up, of course, at short intervals; Kanada says that it is intellect which is characteristic of the Self.

"Anyway when once interruptions in the stream of Intelligence are admitted, it follows that these intervals between the various modifications of the intellect into objects, would represent its unmodified, original state. O son of Kahoela, know that if one can become aware of these broken *samadhis* no other *samâdhi* need attract one."

19-23. The Brahmin youth asked further, "O King, why are not all liberated if their lives are so iridescent with momentary *samâdhi,* if it be the enlightener of the unmanifest void in sleep? Liberation is the direct result of unqualified *samâdhi.* The Self being pure intelligence, why does it not recognise itself and remain always liberated?

"Ignorance is dispelled by pure intelligence, which is *samâdhi,* and this is the immediate cause of salvation.

"Please tell me, so that all my doubts may be set at rest."

The King replied as follows:

24-26. "I will tell you the secret. The cycle of births and deaths is from time immemorial caused by ignorance which displays itself as pleasure and pain and yet is only a dream and unreal. Being so, the wise say that it can be ended by knowledge. By what kind of knowledge? Wisdom born of realization: *viz.,* "I am That.""

Commentary: An aspirant for wisdom first turns away from the pleasures of life and absorbs himself in the search for knowledge, which he learns from a master. This is hearsay knowledge. In order to experience it, he ponders over it and clears his doubts. Then he applies the knowledge to himself and tries to feel his immortal being transcending the body, mind, etc., he succeeds in feeling his Self within. Later he remembers the Vedic teaching imparted by his Guru that the Self being unqualified, cannot be differentiated from God and experiences his unity with the Universal Self. This is in short the course of wisdom and liberation.

27-29. "Ignorance cannot be expelled by the mere experience of an unqualified expanse of intelligence as in *nirvikalpa samâdhi*. For such expanse is in harmony with everything (including ignorance). It is like the canvas used in painting; the canvas remains the same whatever picture may be painted on it. Unqualified knowledge is simple light; the objects are manifest by and in it.

Commentary: The mirror is clear and uniform when there are no objects to reflect; the same appears variegated by images reflected in it. So also the Self is pure intelligence and clear when not contaminated by thoughts; this state is called *nirvikalpa*. When soiled by thoughts, it is *savikalpa*.

30. "But ignorance or delusion should not be confounded with the *savikalpa* state—for ignorance is only the original contamination (*i.e.,* cause) continuing as effect.

Commentary: Pure intelligence (God) in His insentient aspect functions as *Mâyâ* or the self-contained entity projecting ignorance as creation.

31-34. "The original cause lies in the knowledge of perfection in the Self.

Note: One expects the contrary. The apparent contradiction is explained further on.

"The idea of perfection is due to absence of parts. Parts can appear only with time, space and form. However, the sense of completeness appears without these agencies, implying a yearning for them—thus giving rise to the sense of want. Then and there limitations come into being, and the fundamental cause of ignorance manifests as 'I am.' That is the embryonic seed from which shoots forth the sprout of the body as the individualised self (growing up to the gigantic tree of the cycle of births and deaths). The cycle of births and deaths does not end unless ignorance is put an end to. This can happen only with a perfect knowledge of the self, not otherwise.

35-38. "Such wisdom as can destroy ignorance is clearly of two sorts: indirect and direct. Knowledge is first acquired from a Master and through him from the scriptures. Such indirect knowledge cannot fulfil the object in view. Because theoretical knowledge alone does not bear fruit; practical knowledge is necessary which comes through *samādhi* alone. Knowledge born of *nirvikalpa samādhi* generates wisdom by the eradication of ignorance and objective knowledge.

39-47. "Similarly, experience of casual *samādhi* in the absence of theoretical knowledge does not serve the purpose either. Just as a man, ignorant of the qualities of an emerald, cannot recognise it by the mere sight of it in the treasury, nor can another recognise it if he has not seen it before, although he is full of theoretical knowledge on the subject, in the same way theory must be supplemented with practice in order that a man might become an expert. Ignorance cannot be eradicated by mere theory or by the casual *samādhi* of an ignorant man.

"Again want of attention is a serious obstacle; for a man looking up to the sky cannot identify the individual constellations. Even a learned scholar is no better than a fool, if he does not pay attention when a thing is explained to him. On the other hand, a man though not a scholar but yet attentive having heard all about the planet Venus, goes out in confidence to look for it, knowing how to identify it, and finally discovers it, and so is able to recognise the same whenever he sees it again. Inattentive people are simply fools who cannot understand the ever-recurring *samadhis* in their lives. They are like a man ignorant of the treasure under the floor of his house who begs for his daily food.

48. "So you see that *samādhi* is useless to such people. The intellect of babes is always unmodified and yet they do not realize the self.

49. *"Nirvikalpa samādhi* clearly will never eradicate ignorance. Therefore in order to destroy it *savikalpa samādhi* must be sought.

50-52. "This alone can do it. God inherent as the self is pleased by meritorious actions which are continued through several births after which the desire for liberation dawns and not otherwise, even though millions of births may be experienced. Of all things in creation, to be born a sentient being requires good luck; even so to acquire a human body requires considerable merit; while it is out of the ordinary for human beings to be endowed with both virtuous tendencies and sharp intellect.

53-60. "Observe, O Brahmin, that the mobile creation is a very small fraction of the immobile and that human beings form but a small fraction of the mobile, while most human beings are little more than animals, being ignorant of good and bad, and of right and wrong. Of sensible people, the best part runs after the pleasures of life seeking to fulfil their desire. A few learned people are stained with the longing for heaven after death. Of the remaining few, most of them have their intellects bedimmed by *Mâyâ* and cannot comprehend the oneness of all (the Creator and creation). How can these poor folk, held in the grip of *Mâyâ,* extend their weak sight to the sublime Truth of Oneness? People blinded by *Mâyâ* cannot see this truth. Even when some people rise so high in the scale as to understand the theory, misfortune prevents their being convinced of it (for their desires sway them to and fro with force greater than the acquired, puny, theoretical knowledge, which if strictly followed should put an end to such desires, which flourish on the denial of oneness). They try to justify their practical actions by fallacious arguments which are simply a waste of time.

"Inscrutable are the ways of *Mâyâ* which denies the highest Realization to them, it is as if they threw away the live gem in their hands thinking it to be a mere pebble.

61. "Only those transcend *Mâyâ* with whose devotion the Goddess of the Self is pleased; such can discern well and happily.

62. "Being by the grace of God endowed with proper discernment and right-earnestness, they become established in transcendental Oneness and become absorbed.

"I shall now tell you the scheme of liberation.

63. "One learns true devotion to God after a meritorious life continued in several births, and then worships Him for a long time with intense devotion.

64. "Dispassion for the pleasures of life arises in a devotee who gradually begins to long for knowledge of the truth and becomes absorbed in the search for it.

114

65. "He then finds his gracious Master and learns from him all about the transcendental state. He has now gained theoretical knowledge.

Note: This is *sravana.*

66. "After this he is impelled to revolve the whole matter in his mind until he is satisfied from his own practical knowledge with the harmony of the scriptural injunctions and the teachings of his Master. He is able to ascertain the highest truth with clearness and certitude.

Note: This is *manana.*

67. "The ascertained knowledge of the Oneness of the Self must afterwards be brought into practice, even forcibly, if necessary, until the experience of the truth occurs to him.

Note: This is *nidhidhyasana.*

68. "After experiencing the Inner Self, he will be able to identify the Self with the Supreme and thus destroy the root of ignorance. There is no doubt of it.

69. "The inner Self is realized in advanced contemplation and that state of realization is called *nirvikalpa samâdhi.*

"Memory of that realization enables one to identify the Inner Self with the Universal Self (as "I am That").

Note: This is *pratyabhina jnana.*

Commentary: Contemplation is designated in its progressive stages, as *savikalpa samâdhi* (qualified *samâdhi*) and *nirvikalpa samâdhi* (unqualified *samâdhi*). *Dhyana* (contemplation) leads to the repose consequent on the resolve that the mind in its absolute purity is only the Self. There are interruptions by thought obtruding in the earlier stages. Then the practice goes by the name of *dhyana.* When the repose remains smooth and uninterrupted for some appreciable time, it is called *savikalpa samâdhi.* If by its constant practice, the repose ensues without any previous resolve *(i.e.,* effortlessly) and continues uninterrupted for some time, it is called *nirvikalpa samâdhi.* The Inner Self glows in all its purity, in the last stage.

After rising from it, the memory of the uncommon experience of the Self remains; it enables him to identify the transcendence of the one with that same One which is in all. (This is the *sahaja state,* as is often said by Sri Ramana. Translator.)

70. "That is the Oneness of the Self, the same as the identification of the transcendence of the one with that same one in all the diversities of the world apparent to each individual. This destroys the root of ignorance, instantly and completely.

71. *"Dhyana* has been said to develop into *nirvikalpa samâdhi.* Whereas modifications signify the many-sidedness of consciousness, *nirvikalpa* signifies its unitary nature.

72. "When the mind does not create pictures due to thoughts it is the unmodified state which is its primal and pure condition.

73. "When the pictures on a wall are erased, the original wall remains. No other work is necessary to restore its original condition.

74. "Similarly, the mind remains pure when thoughts are eliminated. Therefore the unqualified state is restored if the present disturbance is ended.

75. "There is indeed nothing more to be done for the most holy condition to be maintained. Nevertheless, even *pandits* are deluded in this matter, owing to the bane of *Mâyâ.*

76. "The acutely intelligent can accomplish the purpose in a trice. Aspirants may be divided into three groups: (1) the best, (2) the middle class, and (3) the lowest.

77. "Of these, the best class realize at the very moment of hearing the truth. Their ascertainment of truth and contemplation thereon are simultaneous with their learning.

78-92. "Realization of truth requires no effort on their part. Take my case for instance. On a moonlit summer night, I was lying drunkenly on a downy bed in my pleasure garden in the loving embrace of my beloved. I suddenly heard the sweet nectar-like songs of invisible aerial beings who taught me the oneness of the Self of which I was unaware till that moment. I instantly thought over it, meditated on it, and realized it in less than an hour. For about an hour and a half I remained in *samâdhi*-the state of supreme bliss.

"I regained consciousness and began to muse over my experience 'Oh wonderful! How full of bliss I was! It was extraordinary. Let me return to it. The happiness of the king of the Gods cannot equal even to a fraction of my bliss.

"Not even the Creator, Brahmâ, could have that bliss; my life had been wasted in other pursuits. Just as a man ignores the fact that he holds *chintamani* (the celestial gem capable of fulfilling one's desires) in his hands, and goes begging food, so also people ignorant of the fount of bliss within themselves, waste their lives seeking external pleasures! For me such hankerings are done with! Let me always abide in the eternal, infinite source of bliss within me! Enough of such foolish activities! They are shades of darkness and vain repetitions of useless labor. Be they delicious dishes, perfumed garlands, downy beds, rich ornaments or vivacious damsels—they are mere repetitions, with no novelty or originality in them. Disgust for them had not arisen in me before because I had been foolishly treading the way of the world.

"As soon as I had decided on and attempted to turn my mind inward, another bright idea struck me:

93-95. "What confusion I am in! Although I am always in the perfection of Bliss, what is it I want to do? What more can I acquire? What do I lack? When and whence can I get anything? Even if there were anything new to be gained, would it endure? How can I who am Infinite Consciousness-Bliss know effort?

96-98. "Individual bodies, their senses, minds, etc., are similar to visions in a dream; they are projected from me. Control of one mind leaves all other minds as they are. So what is the use of controlling my mind? Minds, controlled or uncontrolled, appear only to my mental eye.

99. "Again, even if all minds are controlled, mine remains free. For my mind is like infinite space, the receptacle of all things. Who is to control it and how?

100. "How can *samâdhi* be brought about when I am already in the perfection of bliss, for the Self is Bliss-Consciousness, even more perfect than infinite space?

101. "My own light manifests diverse activities all about the world which is again my own manifestation.

102. "What matters it if one should manifest as action or inaction? Where is the gain or loss in such manifestation?

103. "Similarly what matters it for the perfect blissful Self if it fall into *nirvikalpa samâdhi? Samâdhi* or no *samâdhi,* I am the same Perfection and eternal Peace.

104-105. "Let the body do what it likes. Thinking thus I always abide in my own Self as the Perfect fountain-head of Bliss and pure uninterrupted consciousness. I am therefore in the state of perfection and remain unblemished.

"My experience is typical of the best aspirants.

106-107. "Wisdom is achieved in the course of many births by the lowest aspirants. As for the middle class, wisdom is gained in the same birth—but slowly and gradually according to the aforesaid scheme of (1) learning the truth, (2) conviction of the same, (3) meditation—qualified *samâdhi* and unqualified *samâdhi,* and (4) finally *sahaja samâdhi* (to be unattached even while engaged in the activities of the world). This last state is very rarely found.

108. "Why fall into *nirvikalpa samâdhi,* without gaining the fruit of its wisdom! Even if he should experience it a hundred times it will not liberate the individual. Therefore I tell you that momentary *samadhis* in the waking state are fruitless.

109. "Unless a man live the ordinary life and check every incident as the projection of the Self, not swerving from the Self in any circumstances, he cannot be said to be free from the handicap of ignorance.

110. "*Nirvikalpa samâdhi* is characterised by the experience of the true Self alone, namely, Pure Intelligence. Though eternal and resplendent even ordinarily, this Abstract Intelligence is as if it did not exist.

111-112. "Abstract Intelligence is the background on which the phenomena are displayed, and it must certainly manifest itself in all its purity, in their absence, although its appearance may look new at first. It remains unrecognised because it is not distinguished from the phenomena displayed by it. On their being eliminated it becomes apparent.

"This in short is the method of Self-Realization.

113. "O Brahmin! Think over what you have now learnt, and you will realize. With the wisdom born of your realization, you will inhere as the Self and be eternally free. "

Dattatreya said:

114-15. "After giving these instructions to Ashtavakra, Janaka sent him away. Ashtavakra reached his own place and put the lessons into practice. Very soon he too became a *jivanmukta* (liberated while yet alive)."

Thus ends the seventeenth chapter.

Chapter XVIII

1. Dattatreya continued: "Thus pure intelligence, free from objective knowledge, has been proved to exist; it can be felt on many occasions in ordinary life.

2. "However, it goes undetected because people are in the meshes of *Mâyâ* and not conversant with it. Alertness alone will reveal it.

3-5. "Why say so much about it? The long and short of it is this. Objective knowledge is gained by the mind; the mind cannot be objectified. Still it follows that there must be mind even in the absence of objects. Such pure mind entirely divested of all objective knowledge (or thoughts) is pure intelligence. Awareness is its nature. Therefore it is always realized, for no other knower beside itself can ever be admitted.

6-7. "Do you think, O Bhargava, that the Self is not aware when objects are seen? If not aware, the Self cannot be. If the Self is not, how can you raise this question! Can you seek any good for yourself if the Self be a myth like a flower in the sky? How can I establish the Self for you? Consider and tell me.

8-9. "Or do you mean to say that there is ordinarily an awareness of the Self but it cannot be particularised? If so, know it to be the unending awareness which is perpetually existing. That is your Self. The Self is free from particulars. How strange that knowing it, you are still ignorant!

10. "At the time of cognising of an object, the pure intellect assumes its shape and manifests as such. Of itself it is pure and has no form. Objective knowledge is thus a particularised section of pure intelligence. The Self is ever-shining, unparticularised, unblemished, ordinary existence—self-aware and self-sufficient.

11-13. "If you say that the body, etc., usually appear as the Self, I tell you that they are only the play of thoughts and nothing more. For, think well and observe carefully. When you see a pot, are you aware that it is your Self like the body? (No, your body is no less a thought and appearance in consciousness, than the pot.) Then why should the body alone be confused with the Self?

"If you argue that there is no harm or mistake in identifying the body with the Self, because it is no worse than glorifying a part instead of the whole. I tell you: Do not confine such glorification to one part only to the exclusion of all others. Extend it right through and glorify the whole universe as the Self.

14. "In that case, there will be no confusion of the object with the subject, and you will always remain as the subject.

15. "For the Self is always self-resplendent and one without a second, and it displays diversities of phenomena as a mirror its reflections.

16. "Therefore rule out creation as a mere thought or series of thoughts and realize the non-dual, residual, pure intelligence as the Self.

17. "If the body and creation are transcended and the Self realized even once, there ensues that wisdom which will eradicate ignorance and override the cycle of births and deaths.

18. "*Moksha* (liberation) is not to be sought in heavens or on earth or in the nether regions. It is synonymous with Self-Realization.

19. "*Moksha* is not any thing to be got afresh for it is already there, only to be realized. Such realization arises with the elimination of ignorance. Absolutely nothing more is required to achieve the *aim* of life.

20. "*Moksha* must not be thought to be different from the Self. If it is a thing to be acquired, its absence before attainment is implied. If it can be absent even once why should not its absence recur? The *moksha* will be found to be impermanent and so not worth while striving for.

"Again if it can be acquired, acquisition implies non-self. What is non-self is only a myth like a hare growing horns.

Note: Sri Ramana says that *moksha* is another name for 'I' or 'Self.'

21. "The Self is on the other hand all-round Perfection. So where else can *moksha* be located? If it were so, *moksha* would be like a reflection in a mirror.

22-27. "Even the popular idea is that *moksha* is release from bondage, meaning destruction of ignorance. Ignorance is itself a form of thought: destruction is its absence; to bring about its absence is only another form of thought. So then on investigation the whole statement gets involved and becomes meaningless. For a thought cannot be destroyed and be a thought still. Dream is said to be real as well as unreal (in experience and in substance, respectively). Really speaking, dream too is not unreal. For, what is unreality? Impermanency. This again is recognised by the thought of the non-continuity of the dream, which implies the thought content to be dream. Is it truly non-continuous then? The intellect being always continuous, there cannot be a moment of the non-existence of anything. So then, even at the moment of thinking the absence of a thing, that thing really exists in the mind and so it is real and not unreal. All objects are, however, non-existent when not contemplated by the mind. But reality is determined by the being or non-being which cannot be ascertained by the mind because its denial implies the formation of the mental image of the denied thing and it is absurd to deny its existence. In the absence of denial, the thing must be and so *everything* is.

"Thus the existence of pure intelligence is proved by its manifestation, as all else, and thus *moksha* cannot be exterior to the Self, anything to be gathered, acquired or assimilated.

28. "*Moksha* is defined as the steady glow of the Self in perfection. (The question arises whether the Self is imperfect at one time, *i.e.*, in ignorance and perfect at another time, *i.e.*, in *moksha.*) The non-modification of abstract intelligence into the objective phenomena is said to be the state of perfection. (So there is no contradiction.)

29. "Abstract Intelligence contracts at the stimuli to modification and becomes limited. Otherwise, it is infinite and unbroken.

30. "If you mean to suggest that such intelligence is broken up into segments by time, etc.—tell me whether the disintegrating influences are within the Self or without.

31-32. "If beyond consciousness, they cannot be proved to exist; if within, consciousness pervades them and is not divided.

The breaking up at intervals as seen in the world is perceived by consciousness as events (the broken parts) and time (the disintegrator), both of which are pervaded by consciousness. The consciousness is itself the time and the events.

33-34. "If time be not pervaded by consciousness, how do intervals become evident? In the universal pervasiveness of consciousness, how is it to be considered broken up? Breaking up must be brought about by the agency of something external. But anything beyond the pale of consciousness cannot be even maintained or discussed.

35. "Nor can it be granted the disintegrating factor is made visible by its effects of division, while it still evades intelligence, in its entirety. For that is to say that it exists so far as its effect is concerned and does not exist in other ways—which is absurd.

36. "Therefore even the concept of *exterior* must lie within the bounds of consciousness (*cf., avyakta* in sleep or *exterior* in the scheme of creation). Similarly, all that is known and knowable must also lie within.

37. "In view of this conclusion, how can the container be split up by the contained? Investigate the truth on these lines, Rama!

38-41. "Being within, the universe cannot be different from consciousness. For you know that two things cannot co-exist within the same limits. If they do, intermingling is the result. However, the universe maintains its distinctness because it is like a reflection in the mirror of consciousness.

"As regards the appearance of *avyakta,* or *exterior* in the scheme of creation which was traced to the root-cause of ignorance, how can manifestation in it be real? Their reality must be associated with the fact of their being of the nature of Consciousness, *i.e.,* the Self. It is therefore proper to conclude that the Self is alone and single and there is nothing beyond."
When Dattatreya had finished, Parasurâma asked further:

42-43. "O Lord, I find it difficult to follow your reasoning when you say that Abstract Intelligence, being only one, yet manifests as the diverse objects of creation. The two entities, the cogniser and the cognised object, are distinct and separate. Of these, the cogniser, namely consciousness, may be self-luminous illumining the objects.

44. "Just as objects stand apart from light so the universe seems apart from the Intelligent Principle.

45. "Experience does not reveal the identity of the two. Furthermore, you are confirming the statement of Janaka as regards *samâdhi*.

46. "Janaka has said: 'Mind divested of thoughts becomes pure and is identical with the Self and further, that alone destroys ignorance.'

47. "How can that be the Self? Mind is always taken to be a faculty with which the Self functions in the supra-material planes.

48. "The Self would be no better than insentient but for the mind, which characterises it as different from the insentient world.

49. "Further, even the scriptures admit that liberation and bondage are only attitudes of the mind according as it is unmodified or modified, respectively.

50. "How can the mind be the Self as well as its faculty? Again, granting that the world is an image on the mirror of consciousness, the fact of its perfection is there, so the non-duality of consciousness does not follow.

51. "There are hallucinations known, like a rope mistaken for a serpent. Hallucination is not correct knowledge; but it does not end the duality attendant on its perception.

52. "Still again, unreal images cannot serve any useful purpose, whereas the universe is enduring and full of purpose.

53. "Tell me how you assert it to be unreal, thus establishing the non-duality of the Supreme.

"Furthermore, if the world itself is unreal, how does that unreality happen to distinguish between fact and hallucination in the affairs of life.

54. "Still more, how does everybody happen to have the same hallucination of mistaking the unreal phenomena for reality.

"All these doubts are troubling me. Please clear them for me."

55. Dattatreya, the omniscient, heard these questions and was pleased with them. Then he proceeded to answer:

56. "You have done well, Parasurâma, to ask these questions although not for the first time. They must be examined until one is thoroughly convinced.

57. "How can the Guru himself anticipate all the doubts of the disciple unless he states them clearly? There are different grades of mind and different temperaments too.

58. "How can clear knowledge be gained if one's doubts are not raised to be met? The student with an analytical turn of mind gains deep-seated knowledge. His questions help towards depth of knowledge.

59-61. "The unquestioning student is of no use. The earnest student is recognised by his questions.

"Consciousness is one and non-dual, but shines as if diversified like the clean surface of a mirror reflecting variegated colors.

"Note how the mind unmodified in sleep, remaining single and blank, is later modified by dream and manifests as the dream world. Similarly, the One Consciousness—Sri Tripura—flashes forth as the various phenomena of the universe.

62. "The cogniser and the cognised objects are seen in dream also. Even a blind man, without sight, perceives objects.

63. "How does he do so unless by mental perception? Can anything be known at any time or place in the absence of the light of the mind?

64. "There can be no images in the absence of a mirror, for the images are not apart from the mirror.

65. "Similarly, nothing is cognisable if it lies beyond the pale of the cognising principle. For the same reason I say that the mind cannot lie apart from intelligence in the abstract.

66. "Just as the cogniser, cognition and the cognised are identified with the mind in dream, so also the seer, the sight and the phenomena are identical with the mind in the wakeful state.

67-71. "Just as an axe was created in the dream for felling a tree, which is the thing for which it was designed, so is the mind said to be the faculty for giving perception.

"But, Rama, the faculty can be only of the same degree of reality as the action itself. For was anyone injured at any time by a human horn? The action and the instrument must clearly be of the same degree of truth. Since the action itself is unreal, can the mind, the faculty, be real? So, Rama, there is no faculty known as the mind. Mind is only surmised for the location of the dream subject, dream vision and dream objects. Its reality is of the same order as that of a dream.

"Pure intelligence is quite unblemished; mind and other faculties are mere fabrications for enabling transactions to continue, which, however go on because the Absolute is self-sufficient and manifests as subject and objects. The same is often pure and unqualified, as in the aforesaid momentary *samâdhi*.

"I shall explain to you further:

72-79. "Absolute Consciousness and space resemble each other in being perfect, infinite, subtle, pure, unbounded, formless, immanent in all, yet undefiled within and without but space differs from the other, in being insentient.

"In fact, the conscious Self is space. This being so, they are not different from one other. Space is Self; and Self is space. It is the ignorant who see the Self as space alone owing to their delusion, just as the owls find darkness in dazzling sunlight. The wise however find in space the Self, the Abstract Intelligence.

"Her Transcendental Majesty, stainless and self-contained, irradiates diversity in Her Self like an individual in the state of dream. This diversity in the shape of men, animals and other phenomena, does not delude the Self in its purity, but does delude aberrations of the Self, namely, the individual egos.

80-81. "Her Majesty, the Absolute, remains always aware of Her Perfection and Oneness. Though Herself immutable, She appears mutable to Her own creatures just as a magician beguiles the audience with his tricks but remains himself undeceived.

82. "She is light—One without a second; and yet She appears divided to Her Own creatures, because of the veil of illusion.

83. "Just as the magician's tricks delude the audience alone and not himself, so also the veiling of *Mâyâ,* affects the creatures

and not the creator; when the individuals held in the meshes of *Mâyâ*, see diversity and also discuss *Mâyâ*.

84-85. "This Mâyâ is the dynamic aspect of the latent self-sufficiency of the Supreme and is unfailing. See how yogis, charmers and magicians remain confident and sure, without revealing themselves, and yet play upon the imagination of others seeking to achieve the impossible.

86. "Division in the Absolute amounts to contraction within particular limits under the guise of the ego which is usually termed imperfection, or ignorance.

87. "In this manner, Bhargava, has the Absolute invested its own pure and independent Self with ignorance and seems to be iridescent with its different entities.

88. "Hence the identity of space with the Self is not apparent to the learned, because they are incapable of investigating the Self with a steady mind, for that is diverted by its inherent disposition to go outward.

89-90. "Second-hand knowledge of the Self gathered from books or *gurus* can never emancipate a man until its truth is rightly investigated and applied to himself; direct Realization alone will do that. Therefore, follow my advice and realize yourself, turning the mind inward.

91. "She who is the Transcendental Consciousness, creating all and comprising their essence, is Pure Radiance and therefore devoid of anything insentient.

92. "She reposes in Her own Self undefiled by the ego. The insentient cannot exist of themselves but depend on Intelligence for their recognition and definition.

93-94. "They cannot shine by their own merit and reveal their own existence. Their imbecility and their dependence on consciousness betrays their imperfection.

"But pure Intelligence is absolute, shines by itself and feels its own existence, without any extraneous aids. Since it is self-radiant, it is self-contained. Such is the Perfect 'I'—the transcendental 'I'—totally absent from and unassociated with insentient creation.

95. "Because the aggregate of all phenomena is of Pure Intelligence—the Supreme—and there is nothing beyond Her

orbit, there cannot possibly be anything to divide Her into sectors and so She is unbroken and continuous like mirror reflecting images.

96-97. "How are divisor and division possible for the Absolute. Such freedom from disintegration is Perfection; and the Self-radiance of such Perfectness is the unbroken 'I-I' consciousness—known as Self-repose; the eternal, immanent, unique and homogeneous essence.

98-99. "Though descriptions of and statements about the Supreme differ according to the aspects emphasised, yet She is simply self-sufficiency, energy, and abstract, unbroken, single essential Being—all unified into One, just as light and heat go to make fire, yet the three factors are discussed and described separately in practical life.

100-01. "Such is the Power called *Mâyâ*, capable of accomplishing the impossible, and remaining undefiled, notwithstanding Her manifested diversity as phenomena resembling a mirror and its images. She is the eternal, single, unbroken 'I'-ness running through all manifestations.

102-03. "These seeming breaks in the continuum are said to be non-self—the same as ignorance, insentience, void, Nature, non-existence of things, space, darkness, or the first step in creation, all of which represent nothing but the first scission in pure intelligence.

104. "The passage from the infinite absolute to a limited nature is influenced by *Mâyâ* and the transition is called *space*.

105. "But this is as yet undistinguishable from the Self owing to the non-development or absence of the ego, which is the seed of the cycles of births and deaths.

106-113. "Diversity is visible only in space, and this space is in the Self, which in turn projects it at the moment when differentiation starts although it is not then clear. Rama! Look within. What you perceive as space within is the expanse wherein all creatures exist, and it forms their Self or consciousness. What they look upon as space is your Self. Thus, the Self in one is space in another, and *vice versa*. The same thing cannot differ in its nature. Therefore there is no difference between space and Self—which is full and perfect Bliss-Consciousness.

"However space implies sections. Each section of intelligence is called mind. Can it be different from the Self? Pure Intelligence contaminated with inanimate excrescences is called *jiva* or the individual, whose faculty for discrimination is consistent with its self-imposed limitations and is called mind.

"Thus in the transition from the Absolute to the individual, space is the first veil cast off. The clear, concentrated Self becomes pure, tenuous, susceptible space in which hard, dense, crowded, or slender things are conceived. They manifest as the five elements of which the body is composed. The individual then encases himself in the body like a silkworm in its cocoon. Thus the Absolute shines as awareness in the body (namely, 'I am the body')—just as a candle lights the covering globe. The individual consciousness is thus found to be only the radiance of the Self reflected in the body, which it illumines like an enclosed lamp illumining the interior of its cover.

114. "Just as the light of the lamp spreads out through holes made in the cover, so also the light of Intelligence extends from within through the senses to the external world.

115-16. "Consciousness, being absolute and all-pervading like space, cannot go out through the senses; but still its light extending as space presents certain phenomena; and this cognition amounts to lifting the veil of darkness to that extent. This is said to be the function of mind.

Note: The rays of light are imperceptible in ether but when they impinge on matter the objects become visible by the reflection of the light rays on their surface. Similarly, consciousness appears to disclose the presence of objects in space by unveiling them from the ignorance surrounding them.

117. "Therefore, I tell you that mind is no other than consciousness. The difference lies in the fact that the mind is restless and the Self is always peaceful.

118-20. "Realization of the Self subdues the restless mind which is the dynamic aspect of consciousness. On this being subdued, there gleams out the peace-filled, perfect, intelligent bliss which is synonymous with emancipation. Be assured of this. Do not think that an interlude of blank or veil of nescience will supervene after the cessation of thoughts. For, there is no such factor as a blank or veil of nescience. It is simply a figment of the imagination.

121-22. "If in a day-dream a man imagines himself taken, harassed and beaten by an enemy he will suffer from the effects until and unless he dismisses the day-dream. Will he continue to be bound by the enemy after the dream is dismissed with the enemy and his body? So it is with the veil of nescience.

123. "O Rama! Even from the very beginning there has really been no bondage or tie to the cycle of births and deaths. Only do not be deluded by identifying yourself with insentient matter but enquire: What is this bondage?

124. "The strongest fetter is the certainty that one is bound. It is as false as the fearful hallucinations of a frightened child.

125. "Even the best of men cannot find release by any amount of efforts unless his sense of bondage is destroyed.

126. "What is this bondage? How can the pure uncontaminated Absolute Self be shackled by what look like images in the mirror of the Self?

127-30. "To imagine that the Self is shackled by mental projections is to imagine that the fire reflected in a mirror can burn it. There is absolutely no bondage beyond the foolish certainty that you are bound and the difference of entity created by mind. Until these two blemishes are washed away by the holy waters of investigation into the Self, neither I, nor Brahmâ the Creator, nor Vishnu, nor Siva, nor even Sri Tripura the Goddess of Wisdom, can help that person to be emancipated. Therefore, Rama, surmount these two hurdles and remain eternally happy.

131. "The mind will shine as the Self if the mind be denuded of those thoughts now crowding it, and then all sense of duality will cease to exist.

132. "Mind is nothing but sectional knowledge as *this* and *that*. Eliminate such, and then pure knowledge will alone remain. This is the Self.

133. "As for the well-known example of the hallucination of a snake in a coil of rope the rope is real and the snake is unreal.

134-35. "Even after the true state of affairs is known and the hallucination of a snake dismissed, there is still the reality of the rope (which contains the potentiality of the recurrence of the same hallucination in the same person or in others). The danger is always there until the rope is recognised to be of and in the Self.

136. "Then objectivity totally ceases, and pure knowledge alone remains. There is thus a complete annihilation of duality.

137. "The sense of duality persists because there is the conviction of the purposefulness of the objective world. But such purposefulness and even durability is experienced even in dreams.

138-44. "The difference between dreams and the wakeful state lies in the fact that in the waking state the dream is determined to be false, whereas in the dream the waking state is not so determined. Therefore the waking state is universally taken to be real. But this is wrong. For, do you not experience the same extent of permanency and purposefulness in dreams as in the wakeful state?

"Wakeful consciousness does not intervene in dreams nor does dream-consciousness intervene in the wakeful state, while the two factors—enduring nature and purposefulness—are common to both.

"Examine your past dreams and past waking experiences in the light of these facts and see for yourself.

"Again, note the appearance of reality in magical phenomena and the seeming purposeful actions of magical creations. Does reality rest on the slender basis of such appearances?

"The confusion is due to want of discrimination between the real and the unreal among ignorant folk. Ignorantly indeed do they say that the wakeful universe is real.

145-48. "*Reality must endure for ever and ever.* 'Consciousness either *is* or *is not.*' In the former case, it is obvious and in the latter it is implied, for the conception of its absence implies consciousness. (Therefore consciousness cannot be established to be transitory. It is permanent and therefore real.)

"Insentient matter is diverse in nature and its impermanency obvious. For, one object excludes all others.

"But can you conceive the absence of consciousness anywhere or at any time? If you say that there is no awareness in your sleep, tell me how you know that period or again how you know that you were not aware. If absolutely unaware, you would not now be able to say, 'I was not aware.' How was this unawareness illumined for you? Therefore you cannot escape the conclusion that there must be consciousness even to know its unawareness also. So, there is no moment when consciousness is not.

"I shall now tell you briefly the difference between reality and unreality.

149. "Reality is that whose existence is self-evident and does not require other aids to reveal it. Unreality is the contrary.

"If you say, however, that a thing is real until and unless its existence is contradicted, consider the example of a coil of rope being mistaken for a snake. The fancied snake would according to you be *real* in the interval antecedent to correct knowledge but that is absurd.

150-51. "Furthermore, if contradiction means nonexistence, the mental image of the thing contradicted must be admitted, and that means the thing verbally denied is mentally admitted. Therefore contradiction leads one nowhere and does not determine the unreality of a thing; nor does the appearance of a thing determine its reality. Appearance and contradiction are both intermediate.

152-54. "(According to me), there is nothing beyond the range of consciousness; also nothing certainly cannot indeed be; therefore he who denies consciousness, must be nothing but a dry logician. He may as well deny himself and say, 'I am not.' Then who speaks and what does he say? If he who denies himself out of incompetence and stupidity, can teach others and remove their ignorance by the force of his logic, then this rock before me could equally do the same.

155. "Therefore the appearance of a thing and its utility do not determine the reality of a thing or otherwise.

"All knowledge is secondary and unreliable. There is no doubt about it.

156-59. "The greatest of all delusions is the conviction that knowledge is not a delusion.

"A hallucination holds the field in the interval antecedent to correct knowledge in the same way as it does when we mistake a shining mother-of-pearl for a piece of silver. So also the mistake of the reality of the universe persists until primary and basic Self-knowledge is realized. This false sense is universal like the blue color of the sky and it will end simultaneously with the realization of Pure Intelligence.

160. "I have now answered your questions. Do not waver but make up your mind at once.

161. "I shall enlighten you further on the point you raised with regard to the activities of *jnanis* (sages).

162-65. "*Jnanis* may be classified as (1) the best, (2) the middle class and (3) the lowest. Of these, the last know the Self and yet are influenced by the pleasures and pains accruing to them according to their *prarabdha* (past *karma)*. *Jnanis* of the higher order even while reaping the fruits of their past *karma* are however firmer in their internal happiness like men inebriated with drink. *Jnanis* of the highest order are never detached from the enjoyment of their bliss even if confronted with a million times more *prarabdha;* they are not surprised at the most unnatural and miraculous happenings; they are not elated by the greatest pleasures, nor depressed by the worst miseries. They are always peaceful and calm within, although they appear to act like common folk.

"These differences are due to the differences in their intellects and to the degrees of development of *jnana* (wisdom).

166. "Their activities depend on their predispositions as determined by their past *karma*. But all their actions are like those of a drunken man.

Thus ends the Eighteenth Chapter in *Tripura Rahasya.*

Chapter XIX

1. After having heard Sri Dattatreya say so, Parasurâma asked him further regarding the conduct and activities of the *jnanis.*

2-4. "Lord, please tell me clearly how intellects differ according to the stages of *jnana* (wisdom). Is not wisdom of one kind alone, being simply the revelation of the Self? *Moksha* (emancipation) is the simple unfolding of the Self and is alone to be sought. How can it be dependent on stages of development according to mental predispositions? Do the methods also differ in the same way?"

5. Thus asked again, Sri Datta, the Ocean of Mercy, began to answer his questions.

6. "I shall now tell you the secret of it all. There is no difference in the methods, nor does *jnana* differ in fact.

7. "The fruits differ according to the grades of accomplishment. The same extends through several births and on its completion, *jnana* easily unfolds itself.

8. "The degree of efforts is according to the stage of incompleteness brought over from past births. However, *jnana* is eternal and no effort is really needed.

9. "Because it is already there and needs no accomplishment, *jnana* is pure intelligence, the same as consciousness which is ever self-radiant.

10-13. "What kind of effort can avail to disclose the eternally self-resplendent consciousness? Being coated with a thick crust of infinite *vasanas* (dispositions), it is not easily perceived. The incrustation must first be soaked in the running steam of mind control and carefully scraped off with the sharp chisel of investigation. Then one must turn the closed urn of crystal quartz—namely, the mind cleaned in the aforesaid manner—on the grinding wheel of alertness and finally open the lid with the lever of discrimination.

"Lo! the *gem* enclosed within is now reached and that is all!

"Thus you see, Rama, that all efforts are directed to cleaning up the Augean stables of predispositions.

14-15. "Intellects are the cumulative effects of the predispositions acquired by *karma.* Effort is necessary so long as the predispositions continue to sway the intellect.

"The dispositions are countless but I shall enumerate a few of the most important.

16. "They are roughly classified into three groups, namely, (1) *Aparadha* (fault), (2) *Karma* (action) and (3) *Kama* (desire).

17-29. "The disposition typical of the first group is diffidence in the teachings of the Guru and the holy books which is the surest way to degeneration. Misunderstanding of the teachings, due to assertiveness or pride is a phase of diffidence and stands in the way of realization for learned *pandits* and others.

"Association with the wise and the study of holy books cannot remove this misunderstanding. They maintain that there is no reality transcending the world; even if there were, it cannot be known; if one claims to know it, it is an illusion of the mind; for how can knowledge make a person free from misery or help his emancipation? They have many more doubts and wrong notions. So much about the first group.

"There are many more persons who cannot, however well-taught, grasp the teachings; their minds are too much cramped with predispositions to be susceptible to subtle truths. They form the second group—the victims of past actions, unable to enter the stage of contemplation necessary for annihilating the *vasanas.*

"The third group is the most common, consisting of the victims of desire who are always obsessed with the sense of duty *(i.e.,* the desire to work for some ends). Desires are too numerous to count, since they rise up endlessly like waves in the ocean. Even if the stars are numbered, desires are not. The desires of even a single individual are countless—and what about the *totality* of them? Each desire is too vast to be satisfied, because it is insatiable; too strong to be resisted; and too subtle to be eluded. So the world, being in the grip of this demon, behaves madly and groans with pain and misery, consequent on its own misdeeds. That person who is shielded by desirelessness (dispassion) and safe from the wiles of the monster of desire, can alone rise to happiness.

"A person affected by one or more of the above said three dispositions cannot get at the truth although it is self-evident.

30-33. "Therefore I tell you that all efforts are directed towards the eradication of these innate tendencies.

"The first of them (*i.e.,* fault) comes to an end on respectfully placing one's faith in holy books and the master. The second (*i.e.,* action) may be ended only by divine grace, which may descend on the person in this birth or in any later incarnation. There is no other hope for it. The third must be gradually dealt with by dispassion, discrimination, worship of God, study of holy scriptures, learning from the wise, investigation into the Self and so on.

34. "Efforts to overcome these obstacles are more or less according as the obstacles are greater or lesser.

35-37. "The most important of the qualifications is the desire for emancipation. Nothing can be achieved without it. Study of philosophy and discussion on the subject with others are thoroughly useless, being no better than the study of arts. For the matter of that, one might as well hope for salvation by a study of sculpture and the practice of that art. The study of philosophy in the absence of a longing for salvation, is like dressing up a corpse.

38-40. "Again, Rama, a casual desire for emancipation is also vain. Such desire often manifests on learning of the magnificence of the emancipated state. It is common to all but never brings about any abiding results. Therefore a passing desire is worthless.

"The desire must be strong and abiding, in order that it may bear fruit. The effects are in proportion to the intensity and duration of the desire.

41-43. "The desire must be accompanied by efforts for the accomplishment of the purpose. Then only will there be concerted effort. Just as a man scalded by fire runs immediately in search of soothing unguents and does not waste his time in other pursuits, so also must the aspirant run after emancipation to the exclusion of all other pursuits. Such an effort is fruitful and is preceded by indifference to all other attainments.

44-46. "Starting by discarding pleasures as being impediments to progress he develops dispassion and then the desire for emancipation, which grows in strength. This makes a man engage in the right efforts in which he becomes thoroughly engrossed. After these stages are passed, the most unique consummation takes place."

When Dattatreya finished, Parasurâma was completely bewildered and asked him further:

47-49. "Lord, You said earlier that association with the wise, divine grace and dispassion are the prime factors for attaining the highest aim of life. Please tell me which is the most essential and how it can be accomplished. For nothing happens without an antecedent cause. This is certain. What is the root cause of the fundamental requisite? Or is it only accidental?"

50. Thus asked, Dattatreya answered him as follows:
"I shall tell you the root-cause of it all. Listen!

51-61. "Her transcendental Majesty, the absolute-Consciousness, being self-contained, originally pictured the whole universe in Her being, like images in a mirror. She took on the individuality, named *Hiranyagarbha* (the Creator), and considering the predispositions of the egos enclosed in that egg *(Hiranyagarbha),* She unfolded the Scriptures—the reservoir of sublime truths—for the fulfilment of desires. Since the embryonic individuals were full of unfulfilled desires *Hiranyagarbha* began to think out the means of their fulfilment. He elaborated a scheme of cause and effect, of actions and fruits, and consequently the individuals born later on to revolve in that wheel of cause and effect. They take different shapes and are placed in different environments consistent with their predispositions. After passing through innumerable species, the individual evolves as a human being owing to the merit he has accumulated. At first he will take to selfish pursuits. With growing desire, he will seek the unobstructed fulfilment of mighty ambitions. But in due course the methods advocated in holy books will be adopted. Failures are inevitable everywhere. Disappointments result. Expert advice is sought. Such advice will be forthcoming only from a man living in unbroken beatitude. Such a sage will, in due course, initiate the seeker in divine magnificence. The initiate's accumulated merits, reinforced by association with the wise and by divine grace, make him persist in the course, and gradually take him step by step to the highest pinnacle of happiness.

62-64. "Now you see how association with the wise is said to be the root-cause of all that is good. This happens partly through the accumulated merits of the person and partly through his unselfish devotion to God, but always as if by accident like a fruit which has suddenly fallen from the void. Therefore the goal of life being dependent on so many causes, there is variety in its attainment, either according to the intellect or the predispositions of the person. The state of the *jnani* also differs, according as his efforts have been great or less.

65-66. "Proportionately slight effort is enough for erasing slight *vasanas*. He whose mind has been made pure by good deeds in successive past incarnations, gains supreme results quite out of proportion to the little effort he may make (as with Janaka).

67-68. "The glimpse of *jnana* (realization) gained by one whose mind is crowded with dense *vasanas* accumulated in past incarnations, does not suffice to over-ride one's deep-rooted ignorance. Such a one is obliged to practise *samādhi (nidhid-hyasana* or control of mind and contemplation) in successive births for effective and final realization.

"Thus there are seen to be different classes of sages.

69. "O Scion of Bhrgu's lineage! there are differences in states of *jnana* characterised by the aspects and attitudes of intellect and the varieties in its activities.

70-77. "Such differences are quite obvious in Brahmā (the Creator), Vishnu (the Preserver) and Siva (the Destroyer) who are *jnanis* by nature. That does not mean that *jnana* (realization) admits of variety. These attitudes depend on their *vasanas* (dispositions) and environments. They are Lords of the universe and all-knowing. Their *jnana* is pure and uncontaminated by what they do. Whether a *jnani* is fair or dark in complexion, his *jnana* neither shares these qualities nor the qualities of the mind. See the difference in the three sons of Atri, namely, Durvasa (said to be of the aspect of Siva, and reputed to be exceedingly irritable), Chandra (the moon, of the aspect of Brahmâ and reputed to be the husband of the twenty-seven constellations who are in their turn daughters of Daksha) and myself (Dattatreya, of the aspect of Sriman Narayana or Visnu, reputed to be the ideal of saints, roaming nude in the forests, etc.). Vasishta (one of the greatest *rishis,* well-known as the family preceptor of the Solar line of kings) never fails in the strictest adherence to duty as prescribed by the Scriptures; whereas, Sanaka, Sanandana, Sanatsujata and Sanatkumara (four sons born of Brahmâ's volition and instructed by Narada) are types of ascetics totally indifferent to any action including religious rites; Narada is the ideal of *bhakti* (devotion to God); Bhargava (Sukra, the well-known preceptor of Asuras, who incessantly *fight* against the gods) supports the enemies of the gods whereas the equally great sage Brihaspati (Jupiter, the preceptor of gods) supports the gods against their enemies; Vyasa is ever busy codifying the Vedas, and is propagating their truth in the shape of the *Mahabharata,* the *Puranas* and the *Upapuranas;* Janaka famous as the ascetic-king; Bharata looking like an idiot; and many others.

Note: Bharata was a great king who, according to the custom of the great Kshatriya emperors, abdicated his throne in favor of his son when he attained his majority and retired into the forest to do penance. On one occasion, hearing the roar of a lion, a deer in an advanced state of pregnancy took fright and leapt across the stream. Her womb was disturbed and she landed on the other shore with her young one in placenta and dropped dead. The royal hermit took pity on the little thing, washed it, took it in his hands and returned to the hermitage. The baby-deer was carefully tended and remained always by its master's side. The hermit and the deer grew fond of each other.

After some time, the hermit knew that he was dying and became anxious about the safety of the deer in the forest after his own death. He died with that thought and consequently re-incarnated as a deer. Being a sage with pious disposition, the re-incarnated deer was placed in a holy environment, retaining knowledge of its past. So it did not associate with its species but remained close to a hermitage listening to the chant of the

Vedas and discussions on philosophy. When it died it was reborn as a boy in a pious Brahmin family.

The parents died while he was still young. The boy was always helping others but never took to any definite work. He was healthy, strong and free from care. The neighborhood put him down as an idiot, and so he appeared as he loafed about.

One night, the ruling chief of Savvira, passed in a palanquin; he was in haste to reach a renowned sage who lived in another province. One of his bearers took ill on the way; so his men looked about for a substitute; on finding this Brahmin boy 'idiot,' they impressed him for the work; and he took his place as a bearer of the palanquin.

The chief was irritated at the slow pace of the bearers and reprimanded them. Even after repeated warnings, the pace continued to be slow and the chief was wild with rage. He alighted from the palanquin and found the new recruit to be the culprit who was thrashed and ordered to hasten.

Still there was no improvement and the chief chided him again, but could make no impression on the 'idiot.' The chief was exasperated, got down and remonstrated with him. But he received a reply which astonished him and further conversation convinced the chief of the idiot's greatness. So the chief became the disciple of Bharata, the idiot.

78. "There are so many others with individual characteristics such as Chyavana, Yajnavalkya, Visva-mitra, etc. The secret is this.

Note: Chyavana: A king once went with the royal family and retinue for a pleasure trip into a forest which was famous as the habitation of a remarkable sage, Chyavana by name. The young princess was playing with her companion. She came across what looked like an ant-hill and put a spike into one of its holes. Blood came out. She took fright, and returned to the elder members of the family, but did not disclose her prank to any of them.

When they had all returned home the king and many others fell ill. They suspected some involuntary evil had been perpetrated on Chyavana. When an envoy arrived in the forest praying for his blessings, the sage was found hurt in the eyes and he sent word to the king as follows:

"Your daughter hurt my eyes by driving a spike into the ant-hill which had grown over me while I was in *samâdhi*. I am now old and helpless. Send the mischief maker here to make amends for her mischief by becoming my helpmate."

When the envoy communicated the message to the king, he spoke to the princess, who readily acceded to the wishes of the saint. So she lived in the forest with her aged consort and carefully attended to his comforts. She used to bring water from a neighboring spring. One day the twin gods, known as Asvins, came there and admiring her loyalty to her aged husband, revealed themselves to her and offered to rejuvenate her ancient husband. She took her husband to the spring and awaited the miracle. They asked the saint to dive into the water. They too dived simultaneously. All three emerged like one another. The girl was asked to pick out her husband. She prayed to God and was enabled to identify him. The saint promised in return to include the twin benefactors among the gods eligible for sacrificial propitiation. He invited his father-in-law to arrange for a sacrifice and called on the names of the Asvins. Indra—the chief of the gods—was angry and threatened to spoil the sacrifice if innovations of the kind contemplated by Chyavana were introduced. Chyavana easily incapacitated Indra by virtue of his penance and kept his promise to his benefactors. In the meantime, Indra apologised, and was pardoned and restored to his former state.

Yagnavalkya is the sage of sages mentioned in *Brihadaranyaka Upanishad. Visvamitra* is too well known to be described here. He was the grand-uncle of Parasurâma.]

79. "Of the three typical *vasanas* mentioned that one of action is the most potent and is said to be ignorance.

80-83. "Those are the best who are free from all of the *vasanas*, and particularly from the least trace of that of action. If free from the fault of mistrust of the teachings of the master, the *vasana* due to desire, which is not a very serious obstruction to realization, is destroyed by the practice of contemplation. Dispassion need not be very marked in this case. Such people need not repeatedly engage in the study of Scriptures or the receiving of instructions from the Master, but straightaway pass into meditation and fall into *samâdhi*, the consummation of the highest good. They live evermore as *Jivanmuktas* (emancipated even while alive).

84-86. "Sages with subtle and clear intellect have not considered it worthwhile to eradicate their desire etc., by forcing other thoughts to take their place *because desires do not obstruct realization*. Therefore their desires continue to manifest even after realization as before it. Neither are they tainted by such *vasanas*. They are said to be emancipated and diverse-minded. They are also reputed to be the best class of *jnanis*.

87-90. "Rama, he whose mind clings to the ignorance of the necessity of work cannot hope for realization even if Siva offers to instruct him. Similarly also the person who has the fault of marked indifference to or misunderstanding of the teachings cannot attain. On the other hand, a man only slightly affected by these two *vasanas*, and much more so by desires or ambitions, will by repeated hearing of the holy truth, discussion of the same, and contemplation on it, surely reach the goal though only with considerable difficulty and after a long lapse of time. Such a sage's activities will be small because he is entirely engrossed in his efforts for realization.

Note: His activities will be confined to the indispensable necessities of life.

91. "A sage of this class has by his long practice and rigorous discipline controlled his mind so well that predispositions are totally eradicated and the mind is as if dead. He belongs to the middle class in the scheme of classification of sages and is said to be a sage without mind.

92-94. "The last class and the least among the sages are those whose practice and discipline are not perfect enough to destroy mental predispositions. Their minds are still active and the sages are said to be associated with their minds. They are barely *jnanis* and not *jivanmuktas* as are the other two classes. They appear to share the pleasures and pains of life like any other man and will continue to do so till the end of their lives. They will be emancipated after death.

95-96. *"Prarabdha* (past *karma)* is totally powerless with the middle class, who have destroyed their minds by continued practice.

"The mind is the soil in which the seed namely *prarabdha* sprouts (into pleasures and pains of life). If the soil is barren, the seed loses its sprouting power by long storage, and becomes useless.

97-103. "There are men in the world who can carefully attend to different functions at the same time and are famous as extraordinarily skilful; again some people attend to work as they are walking and conversing; while a teacher has an eye upon each student in the class-room and exercises control over them all; or you yourself knew *Kartaviryarjuna,* who wielded different weapons in his thousand hands and fought with you using all of them skilfully and simultaneously. In all these cases, a single mind assumes different shapes to suit the different functions at the same time. Similarly the mind of the best among *jnanis* is only the Self and yet manifests as all without suffering any change in its eternal blissful nature as the Self. They are therefore many-minded.

Note: Kartaviryarjuna was the chief of the Haihayas who were the sworn enemies of Parasurâma. He was himself a devotee of Sri Dattatreya and had received the most wonderful boon from his Master, namely, that his name should be transmitted to posterity as that of an ideal king unparalleled in legend or history. His reign was indeed remarkable and his prowess was unequalled, much less excelled. Still, as destiny would have it, he was challenged by Parasurâma and killed in battle.

104-05. "The *prarabdha* of *jnanis* is still active and sprouts in the mind but only to be burnt up by the steady flame of *jnana.* Pleasure or pain is due to the dwelling of the mind on occurrences. But if these are scorched at their source, how can there be pain or pleasure?

106-08. *"Jnanis* of the highest order, however, are seen to be active because they voluntarily bring out the *vasanas* from the depth of the mind and allow them to run out. Their action is similar to that of a father sporting with his child, moving its dolls, laughing at the imagined success of one doll over another, and appearing to grieve over the injury to another, and so on; or like a man showing sympathy for his neighbor on the occasion of a gain or loss.

109-12. "The *vasanas* not inimical to realization are not weeded out by the best class of *jnanis* because they cannot seek new ones to crowd the old out. Therefore the old ones continue until they are exhausted and thus you find among them some highly irritable, some lustful and others pious and dutiful, and so on.

"Now the lowest *order* of *jnanis* still under the influence of their minds know that there is no truth in the objective universe. Their *samâdhi* is not different from that of the rest.

113. "What is *samâdhi*? *Samâdhi* is being aware of the Self, and nothing else—that is to say—it should not be confounded with the *nirvikalpa* (undifferentiated) state, for this state is very common and frequent as has been pointed out in the case of momentary *samadhis*.

114-15. "Every one is experiencing the *nirvikalpa* state, though unknowingly. But what is the use of such unrecognised *samadhis*? A similar state becomes possible to the *hatha yogis* also. This experience alone does not confer any lasting benefit. But one may apply the experience to the practical affairs of life. *Samâdhi* can only be such and such alone. (*Sahaja samâdhi* is meant here.)

Commentary: Samâdhi: Aspirants may be *jnana yogis* or *hatha yogis*. The former learn the truth from the scriptures and a *Guru:* cogitate and understand it clearly. Later they contemplate the truth and gain *samâdhi*.

The wise say that *samâdhi* is the control resulting from the application of the experienced truth (*i.e.,* the awareness of the Self) to the practical affairs of life. This *samâdhi* is possible only for *jnana yogis*.

The *hatha yogis* are of two kinds: the one intent on eliminating all perturbations of the mind, starts with the elimination of the non-self and gradually of all mental vacillations. This requires very long and determined practice which becomes his second nature and the *yogi* remains perfectly unagitated. The other practises the six preliminary exercises and then controls the breath *(prânâyâma)* until he can make the air enter the *sushumna nadi.* Since the earlier effort is considerable owing to control of breath, there is a heavy strain which is suddenly relieved by the entry of air in *sushumna.* The resulting happiness is comparable to that of a man suddenly relieved of a pressing load on his back. His mind is similar to that of man in a swoon or a state of intoxication. Both classes of *hatha yogis* experience a happiness similar to that of deep slumber.

A *jnana yogi,* on the other hand, has theoretical knowledge of the Self, for he has heard it from the *Guru* and learnt it from the *Sastras,* and has further cogitated upon the teachings. Therefore, the veil of ignorance is drawn off from him even before the consummation of *samâdhi.* The substratum of consciousness free from thoughts of external phenomena is distinguished by him like a mirror reflecting images. Furthermore in the earlier stage of *samâdhi,* he is capable of remaining aware as absolute consciousness quite free from all blemishes of thought.

"Whereas a *hatha yogi* cannot remain in such a state. In the *jnani's samâdhi,* both the veil of ignorance and perturbation of thoughts are removed. In the *hatha yogi's samâdhi,* though the Self is *naturally* free from the two obstacles, yet it remains hidden by the veil of ignorance. The same is torn off by the *jnani* in the process of his contemplation.

"If asked what difference there is between the *samâdhi* of a *hatha yogi* and sleep, it must be said that the mind overpowered by deep ignorance is covered by dense darkness in sleep whereas the mind being associated with *satva* (quality of brightness) acts in *samâdhi* as a thin veil for the self-effulgent principle. The Self may be compared to the Sun obstructed by dark and dense clouds in sleep, and by light mist in *samâdhi.* For a *jnani,* the Self shines in its full effulgence like the Sun unobstructed in the heavens.

"This is how the sages describe *samâdhi.* "

116-17. (Having spoken of the *jnani's samâdhi* as approved by the sages, Dattatreya proceeds to prove its unbroken nature). "What is *samâdhi*? *Samâdhi* is absolute knowledge uncontaminated by objects. Such is the state of the best *jnanis* even when they take part in the affairs of the world.

"The blue color of the sky is known to be an unreal phenomenon and yet it appears the same to both the knowing and the unknowing, but with this difference that the one is misled by the appearance and the other is not.

118. "Just as the false perception does not mislead the man who knows, so also all that is perceived which is known to the wise to be false will never mislead them.

119. "Since the middle class of *jnanis* have already destroyed their minds, there are no objects for them. Their state is known as the supramental one.

120. "The mind is agitated when it assumes the shape of those objects which it mistakes for real; and unagitated otherwise. Therefore the latter state alone is supramental.

Note: The mind of the highest order of *jnanis* though associated with objects, knows them to be unreal and therefore is not agitated as is the case with the ignorant.

121. "Since a *jnani* of the highest order can engage in several actions at the same time and yet remain unaffected, he is always many-minded and yet remains in unbroken *samādhi*. His is absolute knowledge free from objects.

"I have now told you all that you want to know."

Thus ends the Chapter XIX on the different states of *jnanis* in *Tripura Rahasya*.

Chapter XX

Vidya Gita

1-20. "I shall now relate to you an ancient sacred story. On one occasion very long ago there was a very distinguished gathering of holy saints collected in the abode of Brahmâ, the Creator, when a very subtle and sublime disputation took place. Among those present were Sanaka, Sanandana, Sanatkumara and Sanatsujata, Vasistha, Pulastya, Pulaha, Kratu, Brighu, Atri, Angiras, Pracheta, Narada, Chyavana, Vamadeva, Visvamitra, Gautama, Suka, Parasara, Vyasa, Kanva, Kasyapa, Daksha, Sumanta, Sanka, Likhita, Devala and other celestial and royal sages. Each one of them spoke of his own system with courage and conviction and maintained that it was better than all the rest. But they could reach no conclusion and so asked Brahmâ: 'Lord! We are sages who know all about the world and beyond, but each one's way of life differs from that of the others because the dispositions of our minds differ. Some of us are always in *nirvikalpa samâdhi,* some engaged in philosophical discussions, some sunk in devotion, some have taken to work, and others seem exactly like men of the world. Which is the best among us? Please tell us. We cannot decide ourselves because each thinks that his way is the best.'

"Thus requested, Brahmâ seeing their perplexity answered: 'Best of saints! I also would like to know. There is Parameswara who is the All-knower. Let us go and ask him.' Collecting Vishnu on their way, they went to Siva. There the leader of the deputation, Brahmâ, asked Siva about the matter. Having heard Brahmâ, Siva divined the mind of Brahmâ and understood that the *rishis* were wanting in confidence and so that any words of his would be useless. He then said to them, 'Hear me, *Rishis!* Neither do I clearly see which is the method. Let us meditate on the Goddess—Her Majesty Unconditioned Knowledge—we shall then be able to understand even the subtlest of truths by

147

Her Grace.' On hearing these words of Siva, all of them, including Siva, Vishnu and Brahmâ, meditated on Her Divine Majesty, the Transcendental Consciousness pervading the three states of life (waking, dream and sleep). Thus invoked, She manifested in Her glory as the Transcendental Voice in the expanse of pure consciousness.

"They heard the Voice speak like thunder from the skies, 'Speak out your minds, O *Rishis*! Be quick, the desires of my devotees will always be fulfilled immediately.'

21-28. "Hearing the Voice, the exalted *rishis* prostrated and Brahmâ and the others praised the Goddess—namely Absolute Consciousness pervading the three states of life.

"Salutations to Thee! the Greatest! the Best! the Most Auspicious! the Absolute Knowledge! the Consciousness of the three states! the Creatrix! the Protectress! the Dissolver in the Self! the Supreme One transcending all! Salutations again!

"There was no time when Thou wert not, because Thou art unborn! Thou art ever fresh and hence Thou never growest old. Thou art all; the essence of all, the knower of all, the delighter of all. Thou art not all. Thou art nowhere, with no core in Thee, unaware of anything, and delighting no one.

"O Supreme Being! Salutations to Thee, over and over again, before and behind, above and below, on all sides and everywhere.

"Kindly tell us of Thy relative form and Thy transcendental state, Thy prowess, and Thy identity with *jnana*. What is the proper and perfect means for attaining Thee, the nature and the result of such attainment? What is the utmost finality of accomplishment, beyond which there remains nothing to be accomplished? Who is the best among the accomplished sages? Salutations again to Thee!

29. "Thus besought, the Goddess of ultimate knowledge began with great kindness to explain it clearly to the sages:

30. "Listen, sages! I shall categorically explain to you all that you ask. I shall give you the nectar drawn out as the essence from the unending accumulation of sacred literature.

31-40. "I am the abstract intelligence wherefrom the cosmos originates, whereon it flourishes, and wherein it resolves, like the images in a mirror. The ignorant know me as the gross universe, whereas the wise feel me as their own pure being eternally glowing as 'I-I' within. This realization is possible only in the deep stillness of thought-free consciousness similar to that of the deep sea free from waves. The most earnest of devotees worship me spontaneously and with the greatest sincerity which is due to their love of me. Although they know that I am their own non-dual Self, yet the habit of loving devotion which is deep-rooted in them makes them conceive their own Self as ME and worship ME as the life-current pervading their bodies, senses and mind without which nothing could exist and which forms the sole purport of the holy scriptures. Such is my Transcendental State.

"My concrete form is the eternal couple—the Supreme Lord and Energy—always in undivided union and abiding as the eternal consciousness pervading the three phenomenal states of waking, dream and sleep, and reclining on the cot whose four legs are Brahmâ (the Creator), Vishnu (the Protector), Siva (the Destroyer) and Isvara (Disappearance) and whose surface is Sadasiva (Grace) which is contained in the mansion known as 'fulfilment of purpose' enclosed by the garden of '*Kadamba*' trees in the jewel island situated in the wide ocean of nectar surrounding the cosmos and extending beyond.

'Brahmâ, Vishnu, Siva, Isvara, Sadasiva, Ganesa, Skanda, the gods of the eight quarters, their energies of her gods, celestials, serpents and other superhuman beings all manifestations of myself. However, people do not know ME because their intellect is shrouded in ignorance.

41. "I grant boons to those who worship ME. There is no one besides ME worthy of worship or capable of fulfilling all desires.

Commentary: All deities who receive worship and all conceptions of God are My manifestations, because I am pure intelligence which cannot under any circumstances be transcended.

42. "The fruits of worship are put forth by Me according to the mode of worship and the nature of individual desires. I am indivisible and interminable.

43. "Being non-dual and abstract intelligence I spontaneously manifest even as the smallest detail *in* the universe and *as* the universe.

44. "Though I manifest in diverse ways, I still remain unblemished because absoluteness is My being. This is My chief power, which is somewhat hard to fully understand.

45. "Therefore, O *Rishis!* consider this with the keenest of intellect. Though I am the abode of all and immanent in all I remain pure.

46-49. "Although I am not involved in any manner and am always free, I wield My power—called *Mâyâ;* become covered with ignorance, appear full of desires, seek their fulfilment, grow restless, project favorable and unfavorable environments, am born and reborn as individuals, until growing wiser I seek a teacher and sage, learn the truth from him, put it in practice and finally become absolved. All this goes on in My pure, uncontaminated, ever free absolute intelligence. This manifestation of the ignorant and the free, and of others, is called My creation which is however, without any accessories—My power is too vast to be described. I shall tell you something of it in brief. It is that the cosmos is only the obverse of the many details in them leading up to different results.

50. "Knowledge relating to me is complex but it can be dealt with under the two categories, dual and non-dual, of which the former relates to worship and the latter to realization. On account of their intricacies, there are many details in them leading up to different results.

51. "Dual knowledge is manifold because it depends on the concept of duality and manifests as worship, prayer, incantation, meditation, etc., all of which are due to nothing more than mental imagery.

52-53. "Even so, they are efficacious in contradistinction to daydreams, for the law of nature provides for it. There are degrees in the efficacy of the methods, of which the most important concerns the aspect mentioned before (Note: see above the concrete form of Devi). The ultimate goal of all is certainly non-dual realization.

Commentary: Mental imagery cannot put forth tangible results either directly or in successive stages. But the one relating to God differs from ordinary daydreams in that it purifies and strengthens the mind in order to make it fit to realize the Self. Again the most efficacious among the concepts of God is the one already mentioned, namely, the eternal couple. Although it will not directly remove ignorance yet it will help its removal for the resurrection of the man as a full blown *jnani.*

54. "Worship of Abstract Intelligence in a concrete form is not only useful but essential for non-dual realization. For how can one be made fit for it, without Her benediction?

55. "Non-dual realization is the same as pure Intelligence, absolutely void of objective knowledge. Such realization nullifies all objective knowledge, revealing it in all its nakedness to be as harmless as a picture of a pouncing tiger or of an enraged serpent.

56. "When the mind has completely resolved into the Self, that state is called *nirvikalpa samâdhi* (the undifferentiated peaceful state). After waking up from it, the person is overpowered by the memory of his experience as the one, undivided, infinite, pure Self and he knows 'I am That' as opposed to the puerile I-thought of the ignorant. That is Supreme Knowledge (*vijnana* or *pratyabhijna jnana*).

Note: The advanced state of meditation is *savikalpa samâdhi,* where the person is aware that he has turned away from objectivity towards subjectivity and feels his proximity to the state of Self-Realization. When he actually sinks within the Self, there is no knowledge apart from the simple awareness of blissful existence. This is *nirvikalpa samâdhi.* Waking up, he sees the world just as any other man does but his outlook has become different. He is now able to know his pure Self and no longer confounds himself with the ego. That is the acme of Realization.

57. "Theoretical knowledge consists in differentiating between the Self and the non-Self through a study of the Scriptures, or the teachings of a Master, or by one's own deliberation.

58-62. "Supreme wisdom is that which puts an end to the sense of non-Self once and for all. Non-dual realization admits nothing unknown or unknowable and pervades everything in entirety so that it cannot in any way be transcended (e.g., a mirror and the images). When that is accomplished, the intellect becomes quite clear because all doubts have been destroyed; (doubts are usually with regard to creation, the identity of the Self and their mutual relationship) and then the predispositions of the mind (e.g., lust, greed, anger, etc.) are destroyed, though any remnants of these that may remain are as harmless as a fangless viper.

63. "The fruit of Self-Realization is the end of all misery here and hereafter and absolute fearlessness. That is called Emancipation.

Note: There is an end of misery in sleep; but the potentiality of misery is not ended. Realization destroys the cause of misery and sets the man free for ever.

64-65. "Fear implies the existence of something, apart from oneself. Can the sense of duality persist after non-dual Realization, or can there be darkness after sun-rise?

"O *Rishis!* There will be no fear in the absence of duality. On the other hand, fear will not cease so long as there is the sense of duality.

66. "What is perceived in the world as being apart from the Self is also clearly seen to be perishable. What is perishable must certainly involve fear of loss.

67. "Union implies separation; so also acquisition implies loss.

68-70. "If emancipation be external to the Self, it implies fear of loss, and is therefore not worth aspiring to. On the other hand, *moksha* is fearlessness and not external to the Self.

"When the knower, knowledge and the known merge into unity that state is totally free from fear and hence *moksha* results.

"*Jnana* (Supreme Wisdom) is the state devoid of thoughts, will and desire, and is unimpeded by ignorance.

71. "It is certainly the primal state of the knower, but remains unrecognised for want of acquaintance with it. The *Guru* and *sastras* alone can make the individual acquainted with the Self.

72-77. "The Self is abstract intelligence free from thought. The knower, knowledge and the known are not real as different entities. When differentiation among them is destroyed, their true nature is evident in the resulting non-dual consciousness, which is also the state of emancipation.

"There is in fact no differentiation among the knower, etc. The differences are simply conventions retained for the smooth working of earthly life. Emancipation is eternal and, therefore, here and now, it is nothing to be acquired. The Self manifests as the knower, knowledge and the known; the cycle of births and deaths endures with all the apparent reality of a mountain so long as this manifestation lasts. As soon as the manifestation is realized to consist of the Self alone without any admixture of non-self, the cycle of births and deaths comes to a standstill, and is broken down to fragments like clouds dispersed by strong winds.

78. "Thus you find that earnestness is the only requisite for emancipation. No other requisite is needed if the longing for emancipation is intense and unwavering.

79. "What is the use of hundreds of efforts in the absence of a real and unswerving desire for emancipation? That is the sole requisite and nothing else.

80-81. "Intense devotion signifies mental abstraction as the devotee loses himself in the desired object. In this particular instance, it will mean emancipation itself. For such unwavering devotion must certainly succeed and success is only a question of time—which may be days, months, years, or even the next birth, according as the predispositions are light or dense.

82-83. "The intellect is ordinarily befouled by evil propensities and so nothing good flourishes there. Consequently, the people are boiled in the seething cauldron of births and deaths. Of these evil propensities, the first is want of faith in the revelations made by the *Guru* and in the *sastras;* the second is addiction to desires; and the third is dullness (*i.e.,* inability to understand the revealed truth). This is a brief statement of them.

84-85. "Of these, want of faith is betrayed by one's doubts regarding the truth of the statements and by failure to understand them. The doubt arises whether there is *moksha;* and later misunderstanding leads to its denial. These two are sure obstacles to any sincere efforts being made for realization.

86. "All obstacles are set at nought by a determined belief in the contrary; that is to say—determined belief regarding the existence of *moksha* will destroy both uncertainty and misunderstanding.

"But the question arises how this determined belief will be possible when faith is wanting. Therefore cut at its root. What is its root?

87-88. "Want of faith has its root in unfavorable logic. Give it up and take to approved logic as found in holy books and expounded by a *Guru*. Then enlightenment becomes possible and faith results. Thus ends the first evil propensity.

89-95. "The second propensity, namely desire, prevents the intellect from following the right pursuit. For, the mind engrossed in desire, cannot engage in a spiritual pursuit. The abstraction of a lover is well known to all; he can hear or see nothing in front of him. Anything said in his hearing is as good as not said. Desire must therefore be first overcome before aspiring for spiritual attainment. That can be done only by dispassion. The propensity is manifold, being the forms of love, anger, greed, pride, jealously, etc. The worst of them is pursuit of pleasure which, if destroyed destroys all else. Pleasure may be subtle or gross. Neither of these must be indulged in, even in thought. As soon as the thought of pleasure arises, it must be dismissed by the will-power developed by dispassion.

96-99. "In this way, the second evil propensity is overcome. The third, known as dullness resulting from innumerable wicked actions in preceding births, is the worst of the series and hardest to overcome by one's own efforts. Concentration of mind and understanding of truth are not possible when dullness prevails.

"There is no remedy for it other than worship of the Goddess of the Self (adoration, prayer, meditation, etc.). I remove the devotee's dullness according to his worship, quickly, or gradually, or in the succeeding birth.

100-102. "He who unreservedly surrenders himself to Me with devotion, is endowed with all the requisites necessary for Self-Realization. He who worships Me, easily overcomes all obstacles to Self-Realization. On the other hand, he, who being stuck up, does not take refuge in Me—the pure intelligence manipulating the person—is repeatedly upset by difficulties so that his success is very doubtful.

103-104. "Therefore, O *Rishis*! the chief requisite is one-pointed devotion to God. The devotee is the best of aspirants. The one devoted to abstract consciousness excels every other seeker. Consummation lies in the discernment of the Self as distinguished from the non-Self.

105-112. "The Self is at present confounded with the body, etc., such confusion must cease and awareness of the Self must result as opposed to nescience in sleep.

"The Self is experienced even now; but it is not discerned rightly, for it is identified with the body, etc., there is therefore endless suffering. The Self is not hidden indeed; it is always gleaming out as 'I,' but this 'I,' is mistaken for the body, owing to ignorance. On this ignorance ceasing, the 'I' is ascertained to be the true consciousness alone; and that sets all doubts at rest. This and nothing else has been ascertained by the sages to be finality. Thaumaturgic powers such as flying in space, etc., are all fragmentary and not worth a particle of Self-Realization. For this is the unbroken and immortal bliss of the Self in which all else is included.

"Thaumaturgic powers are also hindrance to Self-Realization. Of what use are they? They are but simple acrobatic tricks. The Creator's status appears to a Self-Realized man to be only a trifle. What use are these powers, unless for wasting one's time?

113. "There is no accomplishment equal to Self-Realization which is alone capable of ending all misery because it is the state of eternal Bliss.

114. "Self-Realization differs from all accomplishments in that the fear of death is destroyed once for all.

115. "Realization differs according to the antecedent practice and, commensurate with the degree of purity of mind, may be perfect, middling or dull.

Note: Realization of the Self and eternal inherence as unbroken 'I-I' in all surroundings are the practices and the fruit.

116-119. "You have seen great *pandits* well versed in the Vedas and capable of chanting them quite correctly amidst any amount of distractions. They are the best. Those who are capable businessmen, repeat the Vedas quite correctly when they engage in chanting them without other distractions. These are the middle class.

"Whereas others are constantly chanting them and do it well. Such are of the lowest order among *pandits.* Similarly there are distinctions among the sages also.

120-121. "Some sages abide as the Self even while engaged in complex duties, such as ruling a kingdom *(e.g.,* King Janaka); others can do so in intervals of work; still others can do so by constant practice alone. They are respectively of the highest, the middle and the lowest order. Of these, the highest order represents the utmost limit of realization.

122. "Unbroken supreme awareness even in dream is the mark of the highest order.

123. "The Person who is not involuntarily made the tool of his mental predispositions but who invokes them at his will, is of the highest order.

124. "He who abides in the Self as 'I-I,' as spontaneously and continuously as the ignorant man does in the body, is again of the highest order.

125. "He who, though engaged in work, does not look upon anything as non-self, is a perfect sage.

126. "He who even while doing his work remains as in a sleep is a perfect sage.

127. "Thus the best among the sages are never out of *samadhi,* be they working or idle.

128-133. "He who is from his own experience capable of appreciating the states of other *jnanis* including the best among them, is certainly a perfect sage. He who is not influenced by happiness or misery, by pleasure or pain, by desires, doubts or fear, is a perfect sage. He who realizes pleasure, pain and every other phenomenon to be in and of the Self, is a perfect sage. He who feels himself pervading all—be they ignorant or emancipated—is a perfect sage. He who knowing the trammels of bondage, does not seek release from them and remains in peace, is a perfect sage.

"The perfect among the sages is identical with Me. There is absolutely no difference between us.

134. "I have now told you all these in answer to your questions. You need no longer be perplexed with doubts.

135. "Having said so, Transcendental Intelligence became silent.

"Then all the *Rishis* saluted Siva and the other Gods and returned to their own abodes.

"I have now told you the sacred *Gita* of pure knowledge, which destroys all sins and purifies the mind. This *Gita* is the best among *Gitas* because it has proceeded from Abstract Intelligence Herself and it leads one to emancipation on being attentively heard and cogitated upon.

"This *Gita* is the raft to save one from sinking in the ocean of *samsara* (cycle of births and deaths), and so it must be read or repeated every day with love and care."

Thus ends the chapter of *Vidya Gita* in *Tripura Rahasya*.

Chapter XXI

On the Accomplishment of Wisdom, Its Nature and Scriptural Lore

1. After Parasurâma heard this from Sri Dattatreya he felt as if released from the meshes of ignorance.

2-8. He again saluted Sri Datta and asked him with great devotion: "Lord! please tell me exactly how wisdom can be accomplished. I want to hear the essence of it in brief. The method should also be easy and at the same time efficient. Please also tell me the characteristics of the sages, so that I may readily recognise them. What is their state with or without the body? How can they be unattached though active? Kindly tell me all this."

Thus requested, the son of Atri spoke to him with pleasure: "Listen! Rama, I am now telling you the secret of accomplishment. Of all the requisites for wisdom, Divine Grace is the most important. He who has entirely surrendered himself to the Goddess is sure to gain wisdom readily. Rama! this is the best of all the methods.

9-17. "This method does not require other aids to reinforce its efficiency, as other methods do for accomplishing the end. There is a reason for it. Pure Intelligence illumining all has cast a veil of ignorance of Her own over all. Her true nature is evident only after removing this veil by discrimination. This is hard for those whose minds are directed outward; and it is easy, sure and quick for devotees engrossed in the Goddess of the Self to the exclusion of all else.

"An intense devotee, though endowed with only a little discipline of other kinds (e.g., dispassion), can readily understand the truth though only theoretically, and expound it to others. Such exposition helps him to imbue those ideas and so he absorbs the truth. This ultimately leads him to identify all individuals with Siva and he is no longer affected by pleasure or pain. All-round identification with Siva makes him the best of *jnanis* and a *jivanmukta* (emancipated here and now). Therefore *bhakti yoga* (way of devotion) is the best of all and excels all else.

18-24. "The characteristics of a *jnani* are hard to understand, because they are inscrutable and inexpressible. For instance, a *pandit* cannot be adequately described except by his appearance, gait and dress because his feelings, depth of knowledge, etc., are known to himself alone; while the flavor of a particular dish cannot be exactly conveyed by word to one who has not tasted it; but a *pandit* can be understood only by another *pandit* by his method of expression. A bird alone can follow the track of another bird.

"There are of course some traits which are obvious, and others which are subtle and inscrutable. Those which are obvious are their speech, language, postures of meditation, signs of worship, dispassion, etc., which can however be imitated by non-sages.

25. "What are accomplishments to others to the accompaniment of dispassion, meditation, prayer, etc., remain natural to the sage whose mind is pure and unsophisticated.

26. "He whom honor and insult, loss or gain, cannot affect, is a sage of the best class.

27. "The best among sages can, without hesitation give complete answers on matters relating to Realization and the sublimest truths.

28. "He seems to be spontaneously animated when discussing matters pertaining to *jnana* (realization) and is never tired of their exposition.

29. "His nature is to remain without efforts. Contentment and purity abide in him. Even the most critical situations do not disturb his peace of mind.

30. "These are qualities which must be tried for oneself and verified; they are of no value as tests applied to others, for they may be genuine or spurious.

31. "An aspirant must first apply the tests to himself and always prove his own worth; he can then judge others.

32-33. "How can the repeated testing of oneself fail to improve one? Let one not spend one's time judging others; but let one judge oneself. Thus one becomes perfect.

34-38. "What have here been called the traits of a *jnani* are meant for one's own use and not for testing others, because they admit of many modifications according to circumstances. For instance, a *jnani* who has realized the Self with the least effort may continue in his old ways although his mind is unassailable. He looks like a man of the world for all practical purposes. How then can he be judged by others? Nevertheless, one *jnani* will know another at sight just as an expert can appraise precious stones at a glance.

"The *jnanis* of the lowest order behave like ignorant men in their care for their bodies.

39-54. "They have not attained *sahaja samâdhi (samâdhi* unbroken even while engaged in work, etc.). They are in the state of Perfection only when they are calm or composed. They have as much of the body-sense and enjoy pleasure and pain with as much zest as any animal when they are not engaged in the investigation of the Self.

"Though they are not always inquiring into the Self, yet there are periods of the perfect state owing to their previous practice and experience. All the same, they are emancipated because the animal-sense is only an aberration during interludes of imperfection and does not always leave any mark of them. Their aberration is similar to the ashy skeleton of a piece of burnt cloth which, though retaining the old shape, is useless. Again, the intervals of Realization have an abiding effect on their lives, so that the world does not continue to enthral them as heretofore. A dye applied to the border of a cloth 'creeps' and shades the body of the cloth also.

"The middle class of *jnanis* are never deluded by their bodies. Delusion is the false identification of 'I' with the body; this never arises with the more advanced *jnanis,* namely the middle class among them. Identification of the Self with the body is attachment to the body. The middle class of *jnanis* are never attached to the body. Their minds are mostly dead because of their long practice and continued austerities. They are not engaged in work because they are entirely self-possessed. Just as a man moves or speaks in sleep without being aware of his actions, so also this class of *yogi* does enough work for his minimum requirements without being aware of it. Having transcended the world, he behaves like a drunken man. But he is aware of his actions. His body continues on account of his *vasanas* (predispositions) and destiny. *Jnanis* of the highest class do not identify the Self with the body but remain completely detached from their bodies. Their work is like that of a charioteer driving the chariot, who never identifies himself with the chariot. Similarly the *jnani* is not the body nor the actor; he is pure intelligence. Though entirely detached from action within, to the spectator he seems to be active. He performs his part like an actor in a drama; and plays with the world as a parent does with a child.

55-56. "Of the two higher orders of *jnanis,* the one remains steadfast through his sustained practice and control of mind, whereas the other is so on account of the force of his discrimination and investigation. The difference lies in the merits of their intellect, I shall now relate to you a story in this connection.

57-79. "There was formerly a king by name Ratnangada ruling in the City of Amrita on the banks of the Vipasa. He had two sons Rukmangada and Hemangada—both wise and good and dearly loved of their father. Of them Rukmangada was well versed in the *Sastras* and Hemangada was a *jnani* of the highest order. On one occasion both of them went out on a hunting expedition into a dense forest, followed by their retinue. They accounted for many a deer, tigers, hares, bisons, etc., and being thoroughly exhausted, they rested beside a spring. Rukmangada was informed by some persons that there was a *Brahmarakshas* (a species of ghoulish spirit of a learned but degenerate Brahmin) close by, who was very learned, accustomed to challenge *pandits* for discussion, vanquish them and then eat them. Since Rukmangada loved learned disputations, he went with his brother to the ghoul and engaged him in argument. He was however defeated in the debate and so the ghoul caught hold of him to devour him. Seeing it, Hemangada said to the ghoul, 'O

Brahmarakshas, do not eat him yet! I am his younger brother. Defeat me also in argument so that you may eat us both together.' The ghoul answered, I have long been without food. Let me first finish this long-wished for prey, and then I shall defeat you in debate and complete my meal with you. I hope to make a hearty meal of you both.

"Once I used to catch any passerby and eat him. A disciple of Vasishta, by name Devarata, once came this way and he cursed me, saying, 'May your mouth be burnt if you indulge in human prey any more.' I prayed to him with great humility and he condescended to modify his curse thus: 'You may eat such as are defeated by you in debate.' Since then I have been adhering to his words. I have now waited so long for prey that this is very dear to me. I shall deal with you after finishing this.'

"Saying so, he was about to eat the brother; but Hemangada again interceded, saying, 'O *Brahmarakshas,* I pray you kindly accede to my request. Tell me if you would relinquish my brother if other food were found for you. I will redeem my brother in that way if you will allow it.' But the ghoul replied, saying, 'Listen, King! there is no such price for redemption. I will not give him up. Does a man let his long-wished for food slip away from his hold? However I shall tell you now a vow which I have taken. There are many questions deeply afflicting my mind. If you can answer them satisfactorily, I shall release your brother.' Then Hemangada asked the ghoul to mention the questions so that he might answer them. The ghoul then put him the following very subtle questions which I shall repeat to you, Parasurâma! They are:

80. "What is more extensive than space and more subtle than the subtlest? What is its nature? Where does it abide? Tell me, Prince."

81. "Listen, Spirit! Abstract Intelligence is wider than space and subtler than the subtlest. Its nature is to glow and it abides as the Self."

82. "How can it be wider than space, being single? or how is it subtler than the subtlest? What is that glow? and what is that Self? Tell me, Prince."

83. "Listen, Spirit! Being the material cause of all, intelligence is extensive though single; being impalpable, it is subtle. Glowing obviously implies consciousness and that is the Self."

84. Spirit: "Where and how is *Chit* (Abstract Intelligence) to be realized and what is the effect?"

85. Prince: "The intellectual sheath must be probed for its realization. One-pointed search for it reveals its existence. Rebirth is overcome by such realization."

86. Spirit: "What is that sheath and what is concentration of mind? Again what is birth?"

87. Prince: "The intellectual sheath is the veil drawn over Pure Intelligence; it is inert by itself. One-pointedness is abiding as the Self. Birth is the false identification of the Self with the body."

88. Spirit: "Why is that Abstract Intelligence which is ever shining not realized? What is the means by which it can be realized? Why did birth take place at all?"

89. Prince: "Ignorance is the cause of non-realization. Self realizes the Self; there is no external aid possible. Birth originated through the sense of doership."

90. Spirit: "What is that ignorance of which you speak? What is again the Self? Whose is the sense of doership?"

91. Prince: "Ignorance is the sense of separateness from consciousness and false identification with the nonself. As for the Self, the question must be referred to the Self in you. The ego or the 'I-thought' is the root of action.

92. Spirit: "By what means is ignorance to be destroyed? How is the means acquired? What leads to such means?"

93. Prince: "Investigation cuts at the root of ignorance. Dispassion develops investigation. Disgust of the pleasures of life generates dispassion towards them."

94. Spirit: "What is investigation, dispassion or disgust in pleasures?

95. Prince: "Investigation is analysis conducted within oneself, discriminating the non-self from the Self, stimulated by a stern, strong and sincere desire to realize the Self. Dispassion is non-attachment to surroundings. This results if the misery consequent on attachment is kept in mind."

96. Spirit: "What is the root cause of the whole series of these requirements?"

97. Prince: "Divine Grace is the root cause of all that is good. Devotion to God alone can bring down His Grace. This devotion is produced and developed by association with the wise. That is the prime cause of all."

98. Spirit: "Who is that God? What is devotion to Him? Who are the wise?"

99. Prince: "God is the master of the Cosmos. Devotion is unwavering love for Him. The wise are those who abide in Supreme Peace and melt with love for all."

100. Spirit: "Who is always in the grip of fear, Who of misery, Who of poverty?"

101. Prince: "Fear holds a man possessed of enormous wealth; misery, of large family; and poverty, of insatiable desires."

102. Spirit: "Who is fearless? Who is free from misery? Who is never needy?"

103. Prince: "The man with no attachments is free from fear; the one with controlled mind is free from misery; the Self-Realized man is never needy."

104. Spirit: "Who is he that passes men's understanding and is visible though without a body? What is the action of the inactive?"

105. Prince: "The man emancipated here and now passes men's understanding; he is seen though he does not identify himself with the body; his actions are those of the inactive."

106. Spirit: "What is real? What is unreal? What is inappropriate? Answer these questions and redeem your brother."

107. Prince: "The subject (*i.e.,* the Self) is real; the object (*i.e.,* the non-self) is unreal; worldly transactions are inappropriate.

"I have now answered your questions. Please release my brother at once."

108. "When the Prince had finished, the ghoul released Rukmangada with pleasure and himself appeared metamorphosed as a Brahmin.

109. "Seeing the figure of the Brahmin full of courage and *tapas* (penance), the two princes asked him who he was.

110-112. "'I was formerly a Brahmin of Magadha. My name is Vasuman. I was famous for my learning and known as an invincible debator. I was proud of myself and sought the assembly of those learned *pandits* who collected in my country under royal patronage. There was among them a great saint, perfect in wisdom and entirely Self-possessed. He was known as Ashtaka. I went there for love of debate. Though I was a mere logician, I argued against his statement on Self-Realization, by sheer force of logic. He backed his arguments by profuse quotations from the holy scriptures. Since I was out to win laurels, I continued to refute him. Finding me incorrigible, he kept silent. However, one of his disciples, descendant of Kasyapa lineage, was enraged at my audacity and cursed me before the king, saying: 'You chip of a Brahmin! How dare you refute my Master without first understanding his statements? May you at once become a ghoul and remain so for a long time.'"

"'I shook with fear at the imprecation and took refuge at the feet of the sage Ashtaka. Being always Self-possessed, he took pity on me though I had figured as his opponent just before; and he modified his disciple's curse by pronouncing an end to it as follows: 'May you resume your old shape as soon as a wise man furnishes appropriate answers to all the questions which were raised here by you, answered by me but refuted by your polemics.'

"O Prince! You have now released me from that curse. I therefore consider you as the best among men, knowing all that pertains to life here and beyond."

"The princes were astonished at that story of his life.

123-124. "The Brahmin asked Hemangada further questions and became further enlightened. Then the princes returned to their city after saluting the Brahmin.

"I have now told you everything, O Bhargava!"

Thus ends the chapter on the Episode of the Ghoul in *Tripura Rahasya*.

Chapter XXII

The Conclusion

1-4. After Sri Dattatreya had finished, Parasurâma asked again respectfully: "Lord, what further did that Brahmin ask Hemangada and how did the latter enlighten him? The account is very interesting and I desire to hear it in full." Then Sri Datta, the Lord of Mercy, continued the story: Vasuman asked Hemangada as follows:

5-8. "Prince! I shall ask you a question. Please answer me. I learnt about the Supreme Truth from Ashtaka and later from you. You are a sage; but still, how is it that you go out hunting? How can a sage be engaged in work? Work implies duality; wisdom is non-duality; the two are thus opposed to each other. Please clear this doubt of mine."

Thus requested, Hemangada told the Brahmin as follows:

9-14. "O Brahmin! Your confusion owing to ignorance has not yet been cleared up. Wisdom is eternal and natural. How can it be contradicted by work? Should work make wisdom ineffective, how can wisdom be useful any more than a dream? No eternal good is possible in that case. All this work is dependent on Self-awareness (*i.e.*, wisdom). Being so, can work destroy wisdom and yet remain in its absence? Wisdom is that consciousness in which this world with all its phenomena and activities is known to be as an image or series of images; duality essential for work is also a phenomenon in that non-dual awareness.

"There is no doubt that a man realizes the Self only after purging himself of all thoughts, and that he is then released from bondage, once for all. Your question has thus no basis and cannot be expected of the wise."

Then the Brahmin continued further:

15-16. "True, O Prince! I have also concluded that the Self is pure, unblemished Intelligence. But how can it remain unblemished when *will* arises in it? *Will* is modification of the Self, giving rise to confusion similar to that of a snake in a coil of rope."

17-26. "Listen, O Brahmin! You do not yet clearly distinguish confusion from clarity. The sky appears blue to all alike whether they know that space is colorless or not. Even the one who knows speaks of the 'blue sky' but is not himself confused. The ignorant man is confused whereas the man who knows is not. The latter's seeming confusion is harmless like a snake that is dead. His work is like images in a mirror. There lies the difference between a sage and an ignorant man. The former has accurate knowledge and unerring judgment, whereas the latter has a blurred conception and his judgment is warped. Knowledge of Truth never forsakes a sage although he is immersed in work. All his activities are like reflections in a mirror for, being Self-Realized, ignorance can no longer touch him.

"Wrong knowledge due to sheer ignorance can be corrected by true knowledge; but wrong knowledge due to fault cannot be so easily corrected. So long as there is myopia, the eyesight will be blurred and many images of a single object will be seen. Similarly, so long as there is the *prarabdha* (residual past *karma*) unaccounted for, the manifestation of the world will continue for the *jnani*, though only as a phenomenon. This will also vanish as soon as the *prarabdha* has played itself out and then pure, unblemished Intelligence alone will remain. Therefore I tell you, there is no blemish attached to a *jnani* though he appears active and engaged in worldly duties."

Having heard this, the Brahmin continued to ask:

27. "O Prince! How can there be any residue of past *karma* in a *jnani*? Does not *jnana* burn away all *karma* as fire does a heap of camphor?"

28-29. Then Hemangada replied: "Listen Brahmin! The three kinds of *karma* (1) mature (*prarabdha*), (2) pending (*agami*) and (3) in store (*sancita*) are common to all—not excluding the *jnani*. The first of these alone remains for the *jnani* and the other two are burnt away.

30. "*Karma* matures by the agency of time; such is divine law. When mature, it is bound to yield its fruits.

31. "The *karma* of the one who is active after Self-Realization, is rendered ineffective by his wisdom.

32. "*Karma* already mature and now yielding results is called *prarabdha*: it is like an arrow already shot from a bow which must run its course until its momentum is lost."

Note: Prarabdha must bear fruits and cannot be checked by realization of the Self. But there is no enjoyment of its fruits by the realized sage.

33-35. "Environments are only a result of *prarabdha*: notwith-standing they seem the same for all, *jnanis* react to them differently according to their own stages of realization.

"Pleasure and pain are apparent to the least among the sages, but do not leave any mark on them as they do on the ignorant; pleasure and pain operate on the middle class of sages in the same way; however, they react only indistinctly to their surroundings, as a man in sleep does to a gentle breeze or to an insect creeping over him; pleasure and pain are again apparent to the highest among the sages, who however look upon them as unreal like a hare growing horns.

36. "The ignorant anticipate pleasure and pain before enjoyment, recapitulate them after enjoyment, and reflect over them, so that they leave a strong impression on their minds.

37. "*Jnanis* of the lowest order also enjoy pleasure and pain like the ignorant, but their remembrance of such experiences is frequently broken up by intervals of realization. Thus the worldly enjoyments do not leave an impression on their minds.

38. "*Jnanis* of the middle class, accustomed to control their minds by long-continued austerities, keep their minds in check even while enjoying pleasure and pain, and thus their response to the world is as indistinct as that of a man in sleep to a gentle breeze playing on him or an ant creeping over his body.

39-41. "*Jnanis* of the highest order are left untouched for they always remain as the burnt skeleton of a cloth (retaining its old shape but useless) after their realization. Just as an actor is not really affected by the passions which he displays on the stage, so also this *jnani*, always aware of his perfection, is not affected by the seeming pleasures and pains which he regards as a mere illusion like the horns of a hare.

42. "The ignorant are not aware of the pure Self; they see it always blemished and hence they believe in the reality of objective knowledge and are therefore affected by the pleasures and pains of life.

43-49. "As for the lowest order of *jnanis*, these realize the Self off and on, and spells of ignorance overtake them whenever overcome by their predispositions, they look upon the body as the Self and the world as real. They are often able to over-ride the old tendencies, and thus there is a struggle between wisdom and ignorance—each of them prevailing alternatively. The *jnani* ranges himself on the side of wisdom and fights against ignorance until falsity is thoroughly blown out, and truth prevails. Therefore *jnana* is indivisible.

50-57. "Forgetfulness of the Self never overtakes a middle class *jnani* and wrong knowledge never possesses him. However he of his own accord brings out some predispositions from his own depths in order to maintain his body according to *prarabdha*. This is the conduct of an accomplished *jnani*.

"As for the aspirant, there is no forgetfulness of the Self so long as he is engaged in practising *samâdhi*. But the accomplished *jnani* is always unforgetful of the Self and picks out his own predispositions according to his own choice.

"The highest *jnani* makes no difference between *samâdhi* and worldly transactions. He never finds anything apart from the Self and so there is no lapse for him.

"The middle order *jnani* is fond of *samâdhi* and voluntarily abides in it. There is accordingly a lapse, however slight, when he is engaged in worldly affairs, or even in the maintenance of his body.

"On the other hand, the *jnani* of the highest order involuntarily and naturally abides in *samâdhi* and any lapse is impossible for him under any circumstances.

"But the *jnani* of the middle order or of the highest order has no tinge of *karma* left in him because he is in perfection and does not perceive anything apart from the Self.

"How can there be anything of *karma* left when the wild fire of *jnana* is raging, consuming all in its way?

Commentary: Karma is inferred by the onlooker according to his own ideas of pleasure or pain-giving experiences for the *jnani,* hence the previous statement that *prarabdha* remains over without being destroyed by *jnana.* That holds true for the lowest order of *jnanis* and not to the rest. The fruit is that which is enjoyed; *jnanis* of the highest order do not partake of pleasure or pain. For they are in *samâdhi* and *that* does not admit of such enjoyments: when arisen from *samâdhi* the objects (*i.e.,* non-self) are known to be like images in a mirror, and the conscious principle of the seer and sight is equally known to be the Self. Just as the images are not apart from the mirror, so there is no non-Self apart from the Self; therefore pleasure and pain are not alien to the Self. That which is not alien need not be traced to another cause namely karma (*prarabdha*). The ideas of pleasure and pain in others need not be foisted on to *jnanis* and explanations sought—with the result of positing *prarabdha* in them. The *jnani* never says 'I am happy'; 'I am miserable'; then why should *prarabdha* be imagined in his case? The least among *jnanis* is apt to relax from the realization of the Self and then he gets mixed up with the world at intervals when he appropriates pleasure or pain. The conjecture of *prarabdha* is significant in his case but not in the case of other orders of *jnanis.*

The lowest state of *jnana* is open to the doubt whether such *jnana* as is obstructed off and on, betokens emancipation. Some agree that it does not. But realization of the Self occurs simultaneously with the raising of the veil of ignorance. This veil is destroyed whereas the outgoing tendency *viksepa* drags on a little longer. *Prarabdha* runs out after yielding its results. No residue is left for re-incarnation; nor are there the other stocks of *karma* to draw upon for perpetuating bewilderment. His mind perishes with the body as fire dies out for want of fuel. In the absence of a body the Realization of the Self must assert itself and emancipate the being.

There is still another class of men whose *jnana* is contradicted by worldly pursuits. That is no *jnana* in the true sense; it is only a semblance of it.

Difference among the different orders—*jnani*—simple and *jnanis*—*jivanmuktass*—is perceptible to onlookers in this life. The *jnanis* do not reincarnate.

Since they are found to be active sometimes or at all times, the onlooker requires an explanation and conjectures the residue of *prarabdha* as is the case with ordinary men. Otherwise their apparent pleasures and pains would be as if accidental, which is not acceptable to the philosopher. So, all this discussion about *prarabdha* to *jnanis*.

Srimad Bhagavad Gita no doubt says "One is reborn in environments consistent with the thought uppermost in one's mind while dying." The statement applies to others and not to *jnanis*. As for *jnanis*, the following are said in other scriptures.

1. *Jnani* has the root of misery cut off at the instant of realizing the Self. It is immaterial for him if he dies in a holy spot, or in foul surroundings, remaining aware, or overtaken by *coma*, just before death. He is emancipated all the same.

2. Unmistakably realizing Siva even once by a Master's advice, by scriptural statements or by inference, there could no longer remain any tinge of obligatory duty on his part because he is emancipated.

58. "Such *karma* is only a trick believed to be true by the onlooker. I shall explain this point further.

59-62. "The state of the *jnani* is said to be identical with that of Siva. There is not the least difference between them. Therefore *karma* cannot besmear a *jnani*."

"Vasuman had all his doubts cleared by this discourse of Hemangada. He had a clear understanding of true realization. Vasuman and the prince saluted each other and returned to their respective places."

Having heard all this, Parasurâma asked Sri Datta still further:

63-65. "Master! I have heard your holy words regarding Realization and Wisdom. My doubts are now cleared. I now understand the non-dual state of abstract consciousness pervading all and abiding in the Self. Nevertheless, kindly tell me the essence of the whole discourse in a few words so that I may always remember them."

66-68. Thus requested, Sri Datta again resumed:

"That which abides as the Self is Pure Intelligence Transcendental being comprised of the aggregate of all the egos in perfection. She is Self-contained, and fills the role of *Mâyâ* by virtue of Her own prowess. Being one without a second, She makes even the impossible happen and thus displays the Universe as a series of images in a mirror. I shall now tell you how.

Commentary: Perfect ego: Ego in Perfection: 'I-I' consciousness— Some distinctive characteristics have to be admitted in order to distinguish consciousness from inertia. Consciousness amounts to a flash of pure intelligence. It is of two kinds: (1) The subject and (2) the object. The latter of these is dependent on the former for its very existence; therefore the manifestation as 'I' is alone admissible. 'I' is imperfect when it is limited to the body or other similar entities, because time and space have their being in pure intelligence, or awareness as 'I-I,' which is thus perfect. Nothing can possibly surpass and yet it is all these; therefore it is the aggregate of all the egos. Nevertheless, consciousness is distinguished from inertia for the sake of preliminary instruction, so that the disciple may become conversant with the real nature of the Self. She is transcendental and also non-dual.

The self is the subject, and non-self is the object. She is also the individual egos falsely identified with bodies. She is Ego in perfection, while, abiding as pure Consciousness. This is the nature of Abstract Intelligence.

This unbroken 'I-I' consciousness remains before creation as *will,* self-sufficient and independent in nature and is also called *Svatantra*. She turns into action *(kriya)* during creation and is called *Mâyâ*.

Creation is not vibration or metamorphosis; it is a mere projection of images like those in a mirror. Because *Shakti* cannot be reached by time and much less broken up by it, she is eternal; so it follows that the universe has no origin.

69-71. "She who is transcendence, awareness, perfection and total-summation of all egos, of Her own Will divides Herself into two. Imperfection is concomitant with such scission; there is bound to be an insentient phase which represents the aforesaid *exterior* or *unmanifested void*. The sentient phase is *Sadasiva Tattva.*"

Note: This is called Isvara in the *Upanishads.*

72. "Now *Sadasiva,* also not being perfect, sees the unmanifest void *(i.e.,* the sentient phase becomes aware of the insentient phase) but yet knows it to be of Himself—feeling 'I am this also.'"

Note: The sentient phase is called *Isvara;* and the insentient phase is called *Mâyâ* or *Avidya,* in the *Upanishads.*

73-90. "Later *Sadasiva* identifies the insentient phase with His body at the time of starting Creation. Then he goes by the name *Isvara.* Now this contaminated Higher Ego, namely *Isvara,* divides Himself into the three aspects—*Rudra, Visnu* and *Brahmâ* (representing the modes of Ego associated with the three qualities darkness, brightness and activity) who in their turn manifest the cosmos consisting of many worlds. *Brahmas* are innumerable, all of whom are engaged in creating worlds; *Visnus* are equally taken up in protecting the worlds; and the *Rudras* in destroying them. This is the way of creation. But all of them are only images in the grand mirror of Abstract Consciousness.

"These are only manifest, but are not concrete, since they have never been created.

"The Supreme Being is always the sum-total of all the egos. Just as you fill the body and identify yourself with different senses and organs without deviating from the Ego, so does the transcendental Pure Intelligence similarly identify itself with all beginning from Sadasiva and ending with the minutest protoplasm, and yet remains single.

Again, just as you cannot taste anything without the aid of the tongue, nor apprehend other things without the aid of other senses or organs, so also the supreme Being *(Sadasiva)* acts and knows through the agency of *Brahmâ,* etc., and even of worms. Just as your conscious Self remains pure and unqualified although it forms the basis of all the activities of limbs, organs and senses, so also the Supreme Intelligence is unaffected though holding all the Egos within Herself. She is not aware of any distinctions in the vastness of the cosmos nor does She make difference among the Egos.

"In this manner, the Cosmos shines in Her like images in a mirror. The shining of the Cosmos is due to Her reflection. In the same way, the individuals in the world, namely you, I, and other seers are all flashes of Her consciousness. Since all are only phases of Supreme Intelligence, that alone will shine in purity bereft of taints or impediments in the shape of objects.

"Just as the shining mirror is clear when images no longer appear in it, and the same mirror remains untainted even when the images are reflected in it, so also Pure Intelligence subsists pure and untainted whether the world is seen or not.

91-92. "This untainted Supreme Intelligence is one without a second and filled with Bliss, because totally free from the least trace of unhappiness. The sum-total of all happiness of all the living beings has taken shape as the Supreme One because She is obviously desired by all; and she is no other than the Self, which consists of pure Bliss, because the Self is the most beloved of every being.

93. "For the sake of the Self people discipline their bodies and subdue their desires; all sensual pleasures are mere sparks of Bliss inherent in the Self.

Note: Spiritual men are known to lead abstemious lives, to deny ordinary comforts to their bodies and even to torture them, in order that they may secure a happy existence after death. Their actions clearly prove their love of the Self surviving the body, this life, etc. Their hope of future bliss further establishes the unique beatific nature of the Self, surpassing sensual pleasures which might be indulged in here and now.

94. "For sensual pleasures are similar to a sense of relief felt on unburdening oneself of a crushing load, or to the peace of sleep. Pure Intelligence is indeed Bliss because it is the only one sought for."

Commentary: Bliss is Self. Objects are thoughts taking concrete forms; thoughts arise from the thinker; the thinker connotes intelligence. If the thinker be purged of even the least trace of thought, individuality is lost and abstract intelligence alone is left. Nothing else is admissible in the circumstances.

Since it is ultimate reality, synonymous with emancipation or immortality, there must be beatitude in it in order that it may be sought. It, in fact, is compact with Bliss, yea, dense Bliss alone.

How? Because, the contrary, *(i.e.,* unhappiness) is associated with the exterior; it appears and disappears.

Such cannot be the case if unhappiness formed part of the Self. Pleasure might similarly be said to be associated with the body, the senses, possessions, etc. However a little thought will convince one that these so-called enjoyments are meant for the Self. So the Self is that which matters, and nothing else. But every little being always seeks pleasure. Thus pleasure is the Self.

But sensual pleasure is quite obvious; whereas the Bliss of Self is purely imaginary, because it is not similarly experienced. The scriptures must be cited against this contention. The Scriptures say that all the sensual pleasures do not together amount to a particle of the inherent bliss of Self. Just as unlimited space, or just as consciousness is unknown when pure, but becomes manifest in its associated state as objects around *e.g.,* a pot for fetching water—so also Bliss in purity is not enjoyable, but the same becomes enjoyable when broken up as sensual pleasures. This is the truth of the Scriptural statement.

One may contend that the Self is not Bliss but it seeks Bliss. If it were true, why should there be happiness in relieving oneself of a crushing load? This is perceptible at the instant of relief and similar happiness prevails in dreamless slumber. In these two instances, there are no positive sources of pleasure and yet there it is. This pleasure is however real since it is within one's experience and cannot also be avoided. Therefore it must be of the nature of Self. Still, this pleasure may be said to be relief from pain and not true pleasure. If so, why does a person awakened from sleep say "I slept happily"? The person has felt happiness in sleep. There are no happenings associated with that happiness; it is pure and must be of the nature of Self. Otherwise, even the worst savage of an animalcule would not relish sleep nor indeed long for it.

The question arises! If bliss be of the Self, why is it not always felt? The answer is that the inherent bliss is obstructed by desire, obligations and predispositions of the mind, just as the peren-

nial sound arising from within is not heard owing to the interference of external sounds but is perceived when the ears are
plugged. The pain of the load predominates for the time-being
over the other natural painful dispositions of the mind and disappears at the instant of unburdening. During the interval
before the other dispositions laying latent rise up to the surface,
there is peace for an infinitesimal moment and that is the true
Self coincide with pleasure. Other sensual pleasures are also to
be explained in the same way. There is an infinite variety of predispositions laying dormant in the heart, ready to spring up at
the right moment. They are always like thorns in the pillow.
When one of them sticks out, it predominates over the others
and grips the mind. Its manifestation takes the shape of an
intense desire. Its prevalence is painful in proportion to its
intensity. When that subsides on fulfillment, the pain disappears, and calm prevails for an infinitesimal period, until the
next predisposition appears. This interval represents the
pleasure associated with the fulfillment of desire. Thus every
one's rush for enjoyment betrays the search for Self—of course,
unawares and confused. If asked why no one seems to know the
real genesis of bliss, the answer is overwhelming ignorance born
of associating the pleasure with such incidents. The opinion
prevails that pleasure is caused by such and such, and is
destroyed on their disappearance. The fact is that pleasure is
simply the Self, and eternal.

95. "People do not recognise the Bliss inhering as their Self,
because of their ignorance. They always associate pleasure with
incidents.

96-98. "Furthermore, just as images in a mirror are associated with objects, ignoring the presence of the reflecting
surface, but after consideration are found to be dependent on
the mirror and not apart from it, and the mirror is found to be
untainted by the reflected images, so also the sages know the
Self alone to be unique, real and untainted by its own projections, namely, the world, etc.

99. "The relation of the Cosmos to Pure Intelligence, *i.e.,*
abstract Self, is like that of a pot to earth, or of an ornament to
gold, or of sculpture to the granite rock.

176

100. "O Parasurâma! Denial of the existence of the world does not amount to perfection. Denial is absurd. For, it implies intelligence, and intelligence displays itself as the universe.

101. "The intelligence denying or admitting the world is there shining over all! Can the world be erased out of existence by mere denial of it?"

Note: Here the point is that the Absolute is alone real and remains ever absolute, notwithstanding the concrete modifications which are no better than images in a mirror, not tainting it, nor existing apart from it. All are real, but real in their abstraction.

102. "Just as the images appear in a mirror and partake of its nature, so also the Cosmos is of and in the Self, and real inasmuch as it is the Self."

Note: The world is not real as an object and apart from the Self.

103-105. "This wisdom in perfection is the realization of all as the Self. Intelligence appears as objects by its own virtue, as a mirror appears as the images on it. This is the whole essence of the *Sastras*. There is no bondage, no liberation, no aspirant, no process of attainment. The transcendental Conscious Principle alone subsists in the three states of being. She remains as the one uniform, absolute being. She is ignorance; She is wisdom; She is bondage; She is liberation and She is the process therefore.

106. "This is all that need be known, understood and realized. There is nothing more. I have told you all in order."

The Sage Harithayana concluded:

107-111. "The man who knows it rightly will never be overtaken by misery. O Narada! Such is the section on Wisdom, recondite with reason, subtlety, and experience. Should any one not gain wisdom after hearing or reading it but continue to wallow in ignorance, he should be put down as nothing more than a stock or a stone. What hope is there for him?

"Hearing it even once must make a man truly wise; he is sure to become wise. Sin or obstruction to wisdom is destroyed by reading it; wisdom dawns on hearing it. Writing, appreciating and discussing its contents respectively destroys the sense of duality, purifies the mind and reveals the abiding Truth.

112. "She goes by the name of Emancipation when clearly and directly realized by investigation as the one undivided Self of all; otherwise, She goes by the name of Bondage. She is the one Consciousness threading the three states of being, but untainted and unbroken by them. She is the sound, word and the significance of *Hrim.*"

Thus ends the concluding Chapter in the most Sacred *Itihasa Tripura Rahasya.*

Appendix I

to Chapter V
Commentary Freely Rendered

The Story will be clear if recast as follows according to the commentator's foot-notes:

Before creation, my mother—namely, Pure Intelligence—gave me (the individual soul) a companion named Intellect (whose origin cannot be investigated but who yet remains as the subtle body enabling the individual to partake of pleasures and pains). Intellect is lost at death but reappears as if from nowhere at the time of rebirth. Intellect is bright and shining by nature and remains untainted. She is later associated with a wicked friend, *viz.* Ignorance, who made my friend wander away from me and be outward bent. The subtle intruder remained unnoticed by my mother (because intellect becoming outward turned, had forsaken Pure Intelligence). Intellect was enticed by ignorance and got entangled in objective phenomena. Discriminative faculty was at an ebb and the ego identified itself with intellectual activities. (Individuality disappears with the disappearance of Intellect. Hence they cannot remain without each other.) She by virtue of her innate purity held me in her grip. Therefore I could never forsake her. Intellect constantly associating with Ignorance (Avidya) came more and more under her sway until her friend of wonderful powers persuaded her to seek pleasures, celestial or otherwise (although foreign to oneself), so that she (Intellect) came under the influence of her (Ignorance) son—Delusion with whom she trysted in secret. She could not however elude my presence at any time (for Intellect shines only by individual Consciousness). I too became deluded on account of my friendship with her. My friend had in course of time borne a son who took after his father in every respect. His wicked nature developed in full as he grew up and he was marked by unsteadiness (that was Mind). He had extraordinary ability and was unchecked in his flights of passage. But his activities were only according to the qualities inherited from his father or paternal grandmother (*i.e.,* always ignorant and silly). Intellect was thus dragged by dark forces until she became clouded in darkness. She was gradually losing interest in me (pure Consciousness) who however loved her, altruistically and continued to do so. (That is to say consciousness is necessary for intellectual perceptions—be they ignorant or wise.) Because of my ceaseless company with Intellect, Delusion tried to overpower me, but I remained pure. Still, the phantasmagoria pertaining to Intellect were attributed to me— individual Consciousness. Such is the ignorance of common people. The mind became more and more associated with me as intellect almost totally ignored me and identified herself with delusion. As the mind grew up in company with Consciousness, his powers manifested more and more. He with his grand- mother's permission (*i.e.,* guided by ignorance) took Changeful for his wife. Mind enjoyed himself with her because she could satisfy him in every way. The five senses were born of this couple. These Senses, too, flourished on account of me (indi- vidual Consciousness) until they were able to stand on their own legs. The senses functioned in the sensory organ and their father—Mind—was able to project himself through them and enjoy himself thoroughly.

His enjoyments gave him pleasure just at the moment, and left their impressions on him, which he took with him in order to manifest them in dream and enjoy them secretly with his wife, unknown to the gross senses.

Desire possessed the mind and fed him to his entire satis- faction. His desire grew more and more until neither he nor all his associates could satisfy Desire. Constant association of Mind with Desire gave rise to Passion and Greed (the two sons of the second wife). Desire was exceedingly fond of her two sons. Mind was however tortured by these two sons.

Mind's misery was reflected in the Intellect. I (the individual Consciousness) was completely hidden behind the dark and active forces dragging the Intellect along and appeared mori- bund. Suffering thus for untold ages, the mind lost all initiative and was in the clutches of Desire. Then he gained at the time of creation, a city of ten gates—namely the body with ten outlets (two eyes, two ears, two nasal passages, mouth, and urinary and faecal passages and *brahmarandhra,* an opening in the skull). The same old story of misery was repeated in the new incarnation and was often worse. Intellect having in the meantime lost the *satvic* quality of brightness, did not shine well, and was torpid.

Mind continued to flourish in the company of Ignorance, Delusion and Desire, etc. Intellect could not eschew Mind on the one hand nor function in my absence. We all lived there together. Had I not been there, no one else could have lived in the city. I was protecting them all. On account of my intimacy with Intellect, I became nescient at times, foolish at others, unsteady, vacillating, angry, contemptible, etc. Therefore ignorant people put me down in the same category as Intellect. But the sages know that I have never been tainted. My genesis proves it. My mother is most virtuous, pure, not the least blemished, more extensive than space and subtler than even the subtlest, because she is immanent in all and sundry. Being omniscient, she is of limited knowledge also; that is to say, she is transcendental and individualised self; being omnipotent, she is fragile too; being the prop of all, she has no prop; being of all shapes, she has no shape (like a mirror reflecting forms); being all inclusive, she owns nothing; being the conscious Principle here and now, she is uncognisable; she has no lineage extending beyond Herself. Her daughters like me are too numerous to reckon.

My sisters are infinite in number, like waves on the sea. All of them are involved like myself in their companion's affairs. Though so enmeshed in Intellect, I am still equal to my mother in every respect because I possess the unique talisman to save me from being tainted.

To return to my life in the city, whenever Mind was fatigued, he used to sleep on his mother Intellect's lap. When he slept, none of his sons or others could be awake. The city was then guarded by his intimate friend, Breath. Then Intellect with all her family used to be clouded by Ignorance—her mother-in-law and then I (individual Consciousness) being free from all trammels used to repair to my mother (*i.e.,* Fulness) and remain in bliss. But I was obliged to come away as soon as the inhabitants of the city awoke.

Mind's friend—Breath—pervaded the whole city and protected all the citizens in every way. They would be scattered away if he were not there. He was the link between them and me. He derived his strength and powers from me. When that city fell to ruin, he would collect them all and pass with them to another city. Mind thus reigned in several places, with the aid of his friend (this refers to reincarnation).

Though befriended by Breath, though born of virtuous Intellect and though brought up by me, Mind was always wallowing in misery because he was wedded to his two incorrigible and insatiate wives, associated with the two wicked sons—Greed and Anger—and was swinging to and fro on account of the other five sons—the Senses. He could find no rest and was manipulated by them, so that he found himself in forests, in wilderness, in torrid heat or frigid cold, in cess-pools, in dark caverns, etc.—in short, in different kinds of hell.

His miseries reflected on Intellect; and I too being associated with her, was involved in their woes. Who can indeed avoid the evils of bad company?

On one occasion, Intellect sought my advice in secret (*i.e.,* when accidentally free from thoughts). I advised dispassionate conduct to her, by which she gained a good husband—Discrimination. She grew stronger, gathered courage to subdue to the Mind and kill Greed, Lust and Anger. The other five sons of his—namely, the Senses—were imprisoned. Soon after, she became loyal to me and finally united with me (*i.e.,* gained *nirvikalpa samâdhi*). Thus she reached my mother's place—Peace and Bliss.

This story illustrates that bondage and liberation are for Intellect only and not for the individual Consciousness, *i.e.,* the Self.

Appendix II

Siddha Gita from Yoga Vasishtha

Humble salutations to the Great Masters of all Ages!

Sri: Salutations to that Reality which inheres as the Self in all, from which all the creations are projected, in which they have their being and into which they are finally dissolved! Salutations to that Intelligence which inheres as the Self in all, from which the knower, knowledge and the known, the seer, sight and the seen, the doer, cause and deed, are manifested! Salutations to that Supreme Bliss which inheres as the Self in all, which constitutes the life of all and from whose unfathomable depths happiness is sprayed as fine particles in Heaven or on Earth (where on the sum-total of happiness is not equal to a particle of that unalloyed, natural Bliss). The *Siddhas* (invisible and immortal beings of the noblest order) proclaimed.

1. We adore that One which remains unfalteringly fixed, steady and eternal, which will not therefore admit of recurring births and deaths nor undergo modifications as this and that, and which is by unerring contemplation realized as one's own Self, from which certainly proceeds the chain of links of successive particles of happiness, seemingly derived from and wrongly associated with enjoyments, which are in their turn mere phenomena (*viz.*, the ego and the world, or subject and object) reflected as images on the non-dual, unique and abstract consciousness, because they are found on rightly discriminating investigation to merge into the Absolute Self.

Some other *Siddhas* bring it nearer home as follows:

2. We adore That which is realized as the Self originating, and yet remaining as the untainted witness of the birth of the Ego, its thoughts and the world around—by transcending the cogniser, cognition and the cognised objects pertaining to the wakeful and dream states as well as the ignorance pertaining to

dreamless slumber and made up of the latent tendencies of the mind.

Some other *Siddhas:*

3. We adore That which is realized as the Light inhering as the Self and illumining all, abiding always as the Consciousness in the believer and the non-believer alike—before creation and after dissolution of the Cosmos and is between them too—and lying hidden even in the successive links ceaselessly formulated as the original sources but rendered abortive by one conscious Self objectifying another in itself.

Note: Sloka 2 says the Reality is realized after eliminating all the triads. Some deny the same. There must be some conscious self to deny it. Again, if the original cause of creation be imagined to be as transient as the present creation, the enduring reality beyond the successive links cannot be denied. Or again, if a material cause be surmised, the efficient cause cannot be overlooked. The latter is imagined by the Self. The Self must be the ultimate reality.

4. We adore the Self as That in which all the worlds are fixed, of which they are, from which they emerge, for which they exist, by which all these are projected and for which they are in their being.

5. We adore the Self which shines formless as unbroken 'I-I' consciousness which transcends the ego, yet comprising all the Egos and entire knowledge. These after all make up the whole Cosmos.

6. Those who, ignoring the Lord of the Heart, go about seeking other gods, are like the fool who throws away from his hand the celestial gem *(kaustubha)* which fulfils all the desires of the possessor, and who then excavates the Earth in search of jewels.

Some *Siddhas* counsel Dispassion as follows:

7. The Lord of the Heart, who roots out the vigorously growing creeper bearing poisonous fruits of desires is gained after discarding everything as worthless.

8. That fool who, being aware of the evils of enjoyments, still runs after them, must not be deemed a man but be put down

for an ass. (The male ass runs after the female, even though kicked by her.)

9. The serpents under the cover of the senses must forcibly be laid, as often as they raise their hoods and hiss for prey, like mountains mercilessly hit by the thunderbolt of Indra (the God of rain, thunder and lightning).

The other *Siddhas* hit on the cardinal points as follows:

10. Acquire the bliss of peace by reining in the senses and stilling the mind. The mind does not, in its womb, hold seeds of pain as sensual pleasures do, but purges itself of impurities because it merges in its source as fire does when not fed with fuel. On the mind becoming still and disappearing into the primal source of bliss, there arises the Supreme Peace which holds out till final emancipation.

Appendix III

to Chapter IV

O people, turn away from sensual enjoyments and betake yourselves to contemplating your own selves (rather the Self), because sensual enjoyments end only in misery. What is meant by the Self? By Self is meant Consciousness as shown by the Mahâ Vâkya, 'Prajnânam Brahmâ.' The Prajnanam (Consciousness) must be worshipped. Here worship does not mean external or ritual worship. What is it then? To be unshakingly fixed in the intuition 'I am Brahman' in accordance with the Sutra, 'the state intuited as I.' *Objection:* It is in other words to annihilate the body and its associates. *Answer:* Rather it is, 'Contemplate Consciousness to the exclusion of objects illumined by it.' *Q:* How? It means all objects being illumined by Consciousness do not exist on their own merit. They are only fancied to be, like the horns of a hare. *Question:* If non-existent like the hare's horns, how do they appear to view at all? *Answer:* Only Consciousness shines forth and no other. *Q:* If there is only Chit and nothing beside, how does it shine forth as body, etc.? *A:* It is like images in a mirror. The real significance of the Agamâs (the tantric texts) is this:

Consciousness is truly the Self (Subjective Reality) because it cannot be referred to by the word 'this.' The non-self alone can thus be referred to. Only that can be Self (Subjective Reality) which itself being one, runs continuously through the realms of old recollections and ever-new thoughts. Being pure Consciousness by nature it cannot admit of differentiation and is the same whether in gods, asuras or men, etc. There cannot be the least doubt that time and space are not different from it since they remain immersed in it (that is, they cannot be conceived in the absence of Consciousness) and out of it they are non-existent like a hare's horn (that is, not existent).

Parama Siva spoken of in the *Sastras* is just this unbroken, uniform Consciousness, the Self. His own power known as *Mâyâ* which can make the impossible possible, hiding her real identity and manifesting her impurity as *avidyâ* (ignorance), produces duality. Of this duality the perceptible *(drisyam)* has not its origin in Siva, like a sprout in its seed; nor is it a modification *(parinâma)* because the material forming it is not continuous in its source, like clay in utensils of clay; nor is it a superimposition *(vivarta)* like a snake on a piece of rope because the duality of the perceiver and the perceived (is not acceptable). What then? Just as a mirror remaining unaffected presents within itself pictures owing to its clarity, so also *Chit* presents by its own power the objects illumined by itself within itself. Nor should the doubt arise that just as a mirror requires corresponding external objects for reflection in itself, there must be an external world to correspond to the reflection in *Chit.* For, the external object does not form the material for its reflection but only effects it, like the wheel and the stick being the effective causes for producing a pot. The accessories are variable because the wheel is rotated by hand. Similarly it is not improper to consider *Mâyâ, Chit*'s own power, to be the effective cause for producing the perceptible *(jagat)* in *Chit.* No other explanation but that of reflection fits in for appearance of the perceptible in *Chit.* There cannot be an object external to Consciousness for it cannot be illumined (in order to be reflected). Nor does the world appear owing to its relation to *Chit* because this will lead to *regressus ad infinitum.*

Also even in the absence of *Chit* the world must always be evident or not evident. All well-known objections have thus been refuted. For details consult *Pratyabhijna,* etc. Therefore this doctrine of reflection alone is valid.

to Chapter VII

Illusion can be overcome only by a sincere, earnest and constant devotion to God. But the atheists deny God and His creation of the universe. *Atheist:* How does it follow that Iswara is the creator of *jagat? Answer:* Because the *jagat* is seen to be a *kârya.* This is an artifact. *Q:* True, a pot, etc., are seen to be the products of work but not the mountains, oceans, etc. *A:* Because they consist of parts they must also have been made (created) by an unseen power. *(Yat Saavayavam tat karyam iti tarkena.)* This is according to the axiom: What is with parts must be *kârya.* Therefore the world, etc., are creations only. *Q: Paramânu* (the fundamental subtle primary particle) and *âkâsa* (ether) have no parts. So the *jagat* exclusive of these two must be taken to be *kârya. A:* No to both. They—that is, *Paramanu* and *âkâsa*—are *kârya* because they are perceptible (knowable). Their being *kârya* cannot be denied for the simple fact of their being impartible. They are known by inference. Many scriptural texts attest our position. They are (1) One God created the sky and the earth. (2) From the Self *âkâsa* came forth, etc. Here *âkâsa* implies other elements also. Owing to its knowability, the *jagat* must be a *kârya;* being a *kârya* there must be its *kartâ* (creator), and he must be now ascertained to be the creator of the universe. *Q:* This applies to a pot and the potter because both are seen. Not so in the other case. *A:* He is totally different from all other agents. For, the scripture says: "There was then (that is, before creation) neither *Sat* nor *asat* (anything nor nothing). There is no material with which to create this *jagat;* yet He did it; therefore He differs from all others. The Creator has now been established. *Q:* Should the reasoning based on the *agâmic* texts that the *jagat* is a *kârya* be upheld as impregnable, this should hold good for the reasoning based on *Barhaspatya Agarna* also which declares that the *loka* has no creator but appears solely according to nature. *A:* It is only a semblance of an agama. Here are some extracts from it:

Earth, air, fire and water are the four elements perceived (by the senses) and no fifth element is so perceived. The *loka* is composed of varying combinations of these four elements and is also changing every moment, so that each successive modification of this assemblage is similar to the previous one. The *loka* is only of the nature of these combinations and it rests in itself. Just as a solution of sugar acquires intoxicating power so also the mixture of ova and semen in the womb acquires intellectual power capable of action and cognition. Just as the intoxicating liquor is called wine, so also the intellect-united body is called a *purusha* (man). Pleasure is the goal of man and it forms heaven whereas pain is called hell; they are both natural. Mixtures of these two form the routine of life *(samsâra).* Just as the intoxication disappears after a time so also does the intellect; its total extinction is called *moksha* (liberation) by the wise. There is no heaven or hell to go to after death.

Such is the Charvaka doctrine which has already been refuted by all other schools of thought. It has been said to be a semblance of *agama* because it is opposed to *all* other *agamas.* Now it will be shown to be opposed to everyone's experience also. *Samsara* being an uninterrupted series of births, deaths, etc., is full of pain. Its root cause must be found and scotched. *Samsara* thus ending. Supreme Bliss ensues and this is the supreme goal of man. Such is the belief of the seekers of liberation; this is supported by holy texts and logic. Such being the case, to admit direct perception as the only valid proof and to assert on its basis that death is the only goal, show the *sastra* to be a so-called *sastra* only. Therefore that *agama* has not been admitted by wise men of discrimination to be helpful for gaining the supreme goal of man.

The Charvaka asserting only *svatmânasa* to the goal of man should be asked, "what is meant by *svatmânasa* which you say is the goal? Is it the momentary loss or the loss of the series or the ordinary loss as understood by all?" It cannot be the first since according to you the intellect that is the Self is momentary; the goal is attained every moment and no effort is needed to attain it. The other two are impossible (consistently with your views). For, at the time of the dissolution of one's own self *(svatmânasa)* there would remain nothing to say one's own *(svasya);* therefore the loss of one's own self is unattainable and this ends in no *purushârtha.* If you say this very unattainability is itself the *purushârtha,* then it may even result in the loss of another self (because there is no *syasya*)!

Again, about the *purushârtha* of the loss of one's self *(svatmânasa)* is it established on any *pramâna* or is it not? If you say "not," it is non-existent like a hare's horn. If you say it is—on what *prâmana?* You admit only direct perception as proof. For this the object must be present here now. The past or the future cannot be proved according to you. You who admit only direct perception as proof, to say that the intellect is an effect similar to the intoxicating power of a solution of sugar is like saying "I have no tongue." Your *sastra* was not given out by any all-knowing saint; it is dry and devoid of any reasoning. Having thus dealt with atheism, the *Sankhya* school of thought is next examined.

They are *parinama vadis, i.e.,* they assert that the *jagat* was originally contained in its source in a subtle manner; therefore it was before, it is now and it will be hereafter (this is *sad vada).* They say that the *jagat* was not created by an intelligent being; its source is the unintelligent principle, *prakrti,* in which its three constituent qualities—*satva, rajas* and *tamas* were in equipoise. It is itself devoid of intelligence, and cannot therefore do anything intelligently; it is inert *(jada).* However, it does not require an extraneous agent to modify itself into the *jagat* unlike clay requiring a potter to change it into a pot. By itself it is modified into *jagat* and thus it forms the source of the *jagat.* This is in brief the godless Sankhya doctrine.

Further on, in *prakrti's satva* (bright aspect) it is clear like a mirror; so it can take in reflections of *purusha,* the intelligent principle and the reflection of the universe, the inert nature of its *tâmasic* aspect. Owing to this union of the reflected seer and the seen, the *purusha* becomes associated with *aviveka* (the undiscriminating quality) of *prakrti;* so he feels 'I know the pot' *(i.e.,* any object); this forms his wrong identity and this is just his *samsâra.* If however, by *vichara* (investigation) he knows himself to be different from *prakrti, prakrti* abandons him at once like a thief who has been discovered; this is the end of his wrong identification and constitutes mukti. This is their belief.

According to their view the universe gets illumined by its relation to the *Chit (purusha)* reflected in *prakrti.* Regarding this reflected *Chit,* is it void of intelligence like its base *prakrti,* or is it intelligent by its own nature? In the former case, illumining the universe is impossible. If contended that even though inert it can still illumine, then the *satva* aspect of *prakrti* can serve the purpose and the reflected *Chit* is redundant. In the latter case there is no need for the reflected *Chit,* since direct relation with *Chit* itself will do. Nor can it be said that just as a mirror is unable by itself to illumine an object yet when sunlight is reflected on it, it illumines the object, so also the reflected *Chit* is needed; for, the sunlight does not require any medium as the mirror does for illumining objects. Nor can it be said that the reflected *Chit* partakes of the qualities of both *prakrti* and *Chit,* or is altogether different from either or from both of them. In the former case, it is impossible (like darkness and light being together) and in the latter case it is inconsistent with your doctrine *(apasiddhânta).* Furthermore, *prakrti* naturally active in the presence of *purusha* cannot cease to be so after the accession of discrimination *(viveka jnanottaram)* for one's own nature cannot change. Therefore bondage cannot be overcome (by adopting your system).

We see that a pot, etc., are formed by a potter, etc., endowed with intelligence, for it is done according to a plan—'I will make such a pot in this manner.' Since intelligence is required to make a pot, the *jagat* cannot be the production of an unintelligent principle—*prakrti.* The word 'unintelligent' is used deliberately to indicate that an image of a potter for instance—cannot make a pot. The *srutis* declare, "He (God) thought: I shall create the world"; I shall manifest names and forms, etc." The Original Being thought, and manifested the worlds with no constituent material at all, like a magician conjuring illusory objects. Hence the *anumâna* (inference) is perfectly valid; *jagat buddhimat kartrukam kâryatvat ghatadivat iti*—meaning the *jagat* has an intelligent maker because it is *karya,* as pot, etc. This means that only an intelligent being can be the creator of the *jagat* and not the unintelligent principle *prakrti.*

Still more, in order to establish the inert *prakrti* as the creator of the *jagat* the Sankhya cannot show any illustration as a valid proof.

Well, I admit the *jagat* has an intelligent being for its creator. Sure, a potter is necessary to make a pot; similarly the *jagat* must have a creator but he need not be Paramesvara, the Lord of All.

A: He must be Paramesvara because of the surpassing wonder that the earth stands amidst the water and these repose in empty space, etc. To accomplish such wonders the creator must have surpassingly wonderful powers. These powers must also be immeasurable and his capacity infinite. Therefore He must be different from any common artisan. We find each special work requires a specialist to do it. For the same reason the infinite universe should have one of infinite powers for its maker. Thus far, the existence of Iswara is established.

That He is the sole Refuge of all, will now be established. Surrender to Him whole-heartedly (without any other object but that of entrusting yourself to his care). If on the other hand there be any other desire, only half of your heart is with God and the other half with your desire. So it will be only half or part surrender which is not effective. Only surrender to Him body, heart and soul will lead to eternal Bliss. Iswara grants everything to His devotee.

Q: It is alright that persons in position being pleased with others' service, satisfy their wants to a limited extent. But Iswara being self-contained has no wants. And so He cannot be pleased with others' services. How then do you say that He is pleased and fulfils all the wants of devotees?

A: Because of His love of others' devotion, that is to say, others' devotion results in the reaction of God's love for them and the automatic fulfilment of all their desires. Moreover there is no certainty with worldly men in power whereas it is certain with God. Therefore the devotee is sure of his goal. *Q:* How is this assumption of certainty warranted? *A:* Otherwise God will be open to censure. Uncertainty in God's reaction or response means uncertainty in the results of everyday transactions of ours and untimely end of the *samsâra* projected by Him. You who desire the Supreme Goal need not engage in it nor seek it. But surrender yourself completely to God and He will establish you in the Supreme State.

Differences of opinion regarding the means of liberation and consequent doubts as to the means are thus resolved. *Q:* Which is God? Some say Siva, others Vishnu, or Indra or Ganesa etc. Who is supreme among them? *A:* No name and form attach to Him. He is none of them singly or He is all of them. He is not personal. He is pure *Chit* only.

Q: But creation, preservation and dissolution are functions requiring the use of limbs and material? *A:* It is so with workers of limited powers and objectives. This holds good for gross bodies; but in dreams the gross bodies do not act and there are no means nor objectives, yet worlds are created, transactions go on, battles are fought, and empires won and lost; it is *Chit* that causes it all. If there had been material before creation with which to create the *jagat,* such material should be eternal and exempt from being created. Then Iswara must be accepted to be the creator of a part of the *jagat;* this contradicts His being the all-creator. Also being only the effective cause and not the material cause of the *jagat,* He can no more be Iswara (than a magnified artisan). Kshemarâjâcharya says: "Those who admit Iswara to be the effective cause only place Him on a par with a profligate enmeshed in the lures of a wanton woman other than his wife." Those who imagine a starting-point for the creation (the *ârambha vadis*) assert that Iswara is only the effective cause and the effect *(jagat)* cannot come into being afresh. Before creation, *paramânus* (fundamental, indivisible, subtle particles) were present. By Iswara's will they united with each other and creation took place.

But this cannot be. It is seen that only a sentient being responds to the wishes of another, but not an inert object. The *paramânus* being insentient cannot react to Iswara's will. *Objection:* Such is the wonderful power of Iswara as to make even the inert *paramânus* obedient to His will. *A:* True, that Iswara's powers are immeasurable and infinite. It is because of His extraordinary powers that He creates the *jagat* even in total absence of material for it. If in spite of this, *paramânus* be said to be the material cause it is thanks to duality-minded obstinacy! Hereby is refuted the theistic (Sânkhya) school, *i.e.,* Patanjala or Yoga School.

There is not the least incongruity in our system based solely on the agamas declaring the all-powerful Supreme Being fully capable of conducting the totality of actions, transactions, etc. *Objection:* In order to explain the different grades of beings, etc.,

and also obviate the charges of partiality and cruelty to Iswara,
every school of thought admits *karma* to be the cause of differences. This admission by *you* vitiates *your* position, for, there is
karma needed for creation in addition to Iswara. So He is not all-
powerful. *A:* True, that this contention remains insuperable to
the dualists. As for the non-dualists the *jagat* is contained in *Chit*
like images in a mirror; so also *karma;* it is not external to the
infinite Supreme Intelligence (Parameswara) and there is not
the slightest discrepancy in our contention. *Objection:* Even then,
it is seen that a pot is made by a potter; he is the maker of the
pot; and therefore Iswara is not the all-creator. *A:* The potter is
not external to Iswara. Again just as the king remains the sole
administrator, even though his servants act on the spot, so also
Iswara acts through His agents. *Conclusion:* The Supreme Being
is only One Solid Intelligence, nameless, formless, bodiless, infinite, non-dual, and Blissful. This being incomprehensible to
impure minds is apprehended in various forms according to the
capacities of individuals. Nevertheless devotion to any form or
name of God purifies the mind so that the individual is ultimately resolved into the Supreme Being.

to Chapter IX
Nature of Pure Knowledge

Even after much effort the Self remains unrealized because
the *sâdhak* is not acquainted with it and so does not recognise it
even in Its presence. Now listen, the mind when checked
remains inert for some time. At the end of it darkness is perceived. Before darkness supervenes there is an interval of pure
knowledge which is quite unaware of the body or environment;
only this pure Knowledge shines along with objects when the
mind is active; when the mind is checked it shines of Itself. This
state of pure Knowledge is called the residual state *(sesha bhâva)*.
This can by no means be eliminated because being self-resplendent, it shines of Itself, as is experienced by one just risen from

sleep who says "For long I remained unaware of anything." This residual state is the one of pure Knowledge void of objects. Always contemplate 'I am.' That is the state of Bliss beyond the ken of great pandits, yogis or even sâdhakas of a sort.

Though the *jagat* is variegated the whole of it can be classified under the two heads, Knowledge and the knowable. Of these the knowable is established by direct perception, inference, etc. and it is always the non-self. Being non-self, it is not worthwhile investigating; therefore knowledge alone will be examined here. Being self-evident, it requires no external evidence. In its absence nothing else can exist. Being the background of all, like a mirror of the images reflected in it, nothing can shine without it; so it cannot in any way be obviated. *Objection:* Unreasonable to say that nothing else can exist without it, because the proven is proved by proofs. *A:* If the proof be valid the proven is established by it. The validity of the proof is known by the proven. To say so is absurd, being interdependent. But without the knower the proof does not gain authority, *i.e.,* the knowable cannot be said to be. A proof only proves a fact but is not the fact. If you object saying that the knower[1] also can be known only by a proof, I reply there must be equally a knower to deny the knower as to know him. Therefore, we say that the knower is self-proven and does not require extraneous proof to establish its Being. Being conscious, being always self-shining it requires no proof like the self-shining sun requiring no candle light to illumine it. Were one to deny pure Knowledge itself—the knowable is dependent on knowledge and it cannot be in the absence of knowledge; therefore he cannot raise the question nor expect an answer, *i.e.,* to say, he is out of consideration.

Pure knowledge means the state of awareness free from objective knowledge; it is knowledge remaining unmoded. This state forms the interval between deep sleep and waking state; it must be distinguished from the other two. Deep sleep means the dormant state of mind; waking consists of a series of broken knowledge; in it objects are perceived by the senses external to

1. Knower is the same as Knowledge.

the mind whereas in dream the mind is at one with the senses and its latencies are objectified and perceived within itself like particles of dust in water. In deep sleep supervening after dream the mind together with the senses merges into its source— *prakriti*; then the tamasic or dull aspect of *prakrti* remains predominant on overwhelming the *satvic* and *râjasic* aspects. In this state the Self shines only very indistinct like the sun behind very heavy clouds. In the interval between deep sleep and waking the mind continues to be inward turned and cannot reflect objects external to it; at the same time the *tamas* of *prakrti* has lost its solidity and does not hide the Self. In this manner the Self that is *Chit* shines unobjectified, *i.e.*, as unbroken knowledge.

In the same manner with the intervals of broken knowledge: the background namely pure knowledge remains unbroken in the interval of Knowledge of a pot, does not itself continue to subsist as that of a piece of cloth; the difference between the two is obvious. In the interval between the two kinds of knowledge, pure Knowledge persists devoid of the two forms: this cannot be denied. This is *samvit* (Knowledge) shining in its own merit.

Samvit is the seer or the ego. Just as the water in a tank passes through an outlet into a channel to irrigate a field and mixes with the water already in the field, so also at the instant of perception, the *samvit* of the seer passes through the senses to unite with the *samvit* of the object. In this case *Chit* remains as the body, mind, etc., of the seer; in the sky it remains as the sun; in the intervening space covered by it *samvit* is formless and this is its real state. All this indicates these intervals to be the seats of realization of the Self. The Self is no more than this. Pure *Chit* devoid of objective knowledge is the true Self. If this is realized as the Self the universe will appear to be just an image reflected in the mirror of *Chit* and so results the state of fearlessness, for to see a tiger reflected in a mirror does not cause fright.

to Chapter XI

Some say that the *jagat* is the product of invisible fundamental particles. Though remaining different from its source, it
vanishes altogether in the end. That the unitary, primary particles give rise to the binary particles is interred from the part-
ibility of the latter. According to them the process of creation is
as follows: The mature *adrshta* (results of previous *karma* per-
sisting in a subtle form) of the individuals together with the will
of Iswara causes the inert primary particles to be active; then
binary, tertiary, etc., particles are successively formed resulting
in the objects of the universe. The products are totally different
from the original cause. At the time of dissolution the universe
vanishes like the horns of a hare *(i.e.,* ceases to be).

Its refutation: It is not proper to say that a pot is non-existent
before creation; it is existent sometime; later it becomes non-
existent at dissolution because of the contrary existence and
non-existence of the same thing. *The Opponent:* Not so. Though
there is a contradiction in terms of being and non-being of the
same thing, there is no contradiction in terms of relationship
(samyoga) (e.g., a monkey is on the tree or a monkey is not on the
tree). *A:* No. "Being" pervades the object in entirety whereas in
relationship there is no such pervasiveness. This is certainly
opposed to non-being. The same object cannot be yellow and
not yellow at the same time. *Opponent:* The nature of an object
must be determined only from experience. Pervasiveness is
found applicable to the inseparable union of the material cause
of the object in space but it is not applicable to the existence or
the non-existence of the object in time; *e.g.,* a pot is or is not. *A:*
The same object cannot be both shining and non-shining at the
same time. On the other hand, (if you are thinking) of the contrary experiences at the same time such as a blue tamas is
moving, it is so because the same object by its *satvic* nature
reflects light and by its *tamasic* nature remains dark, thus making
it appear that light and darkness co-exist. This is not on all fours
with my statement that the same object cannot both be yellow

and not yellow at the same time. Therefore it is obvious that being and non-being certainly contradict each other both in time and space. *Opponent:* How can this rule apply to ascertain darkness to be, by seeing it with the light of the eye? It cannot. *A:* You are not right. To explain the facts of experience, different methods are adopted because the same rule may not apply in all cases.

In the doctrine of aggregation of particles before creation, other anomalies are also pointed out besides the above one. They are concerned with the imagined aggregation, *e.g.*, existence and non-existence of the same thing. Again the primary particles cannot be impartite or indivisible; also their separateness from one another cannot be proved because they mix together to form binary, etc., particles. *Opponent:* Defects in our doctrine are shared by us along with all others in their own doctrines. *A:* Quite so. It is common to all kinds of dualism but to advaita they become ornaments like the arrows aimed by Bhâgadattâ at Vasudeva which clung to Him like ornaments.

to Chapter XIV
Process of Creation

Creation being an empty fancy and *Chit* always unchanging, how can creation be said to originate from *Chit*?

A: The answer to this question is based on srutis. *Avidya (i.e.,* ignorance) being the root-cause of creation, its origin is first elucidated and it will be followed up by the thirty-six fundamentals. *Chit* is certainly changeless. A mirror is seen to reflect the sky in it; similarly *Chit* presents within itself something which (to us) signifies 'exterior.' But the external sky being merely an effective cause, its reflection is seen in the mirror, whereas the "exterior" in *Chit* is solely due to its inherent power. The difference lies in the intelligent nature of *Chit* and the inert nature of the mirror. Since the whole creation develops from this "exterior" it is said to be the first creation. This phenomenon is called *avidya* or *tamas* (ignorance or darkness). *Q: Chit* being impartite, how can this phenomenon arise as a part thereof? *A:* Quite so. Hence it is called a phenomenon. *And it is not a part but it looks like it.* When the unbroken WHOLE appears to be divided into parts, it is called a phenomenon (and not a fact). Parameswara is Pure Solid Intelligence altogether free from its counter-part; hence He is "independent." An inert thing is dependent on external aid to make known itself or another object; whereas the Supreme Intelligence is independent of external aid to make ITSELF known or other things. This factor "independence" is also called its *sakti, kriya* (action), *vimarsa* (deliberation) etc., which manifesting as *jagat* at the time of creation and after, yet remains as pure Being only, because awareness of pure Being continues unbroken till the time of dissolution. Therefor such "independence" is the ever-inseparable characteristic of Siva. At the end of dissolution the same uniting with the *adrshta* now mature, presents the Self *(svarupa)* as fragmented, *i.e.,* limited; this is otherwise said to be the manifestation of the "exterior." The manifestation of limitation is obviously the manifestation of space *(akâsa)* distinct from the Self. When one's arm is broken in two, the broken piece is no longer identified as 'I'; similarly the 'exterior' is no longer identified as ' I '; it is distinct from 'I'; it is no longer meant by 'I.' Such unfolding of the non-self is said to be that of space, of the seed, *i.e., jagat* in dormancy, or *jadasakti* (inert power). In this manner the perfect *Chit* by its own power presenting within Itself the phenomenon of *avidyâ* as distinct from Itself is called the first 'step' to creation. The Vedantists call this the root *avidyâ —mula-avidyâ.* What is here designated as "independence" is nothing but the power of *Chit* (freewill). This assumes three states. In dissolution, it remains purely as power (that is latent) because it is *nirvikalpa (i.e.,* the state of no modification or manifestation); just before creation, *i.e.,* before the objects take shape this power is said to be *mâyâ;* when shapes are manifest the same power is called *jadasakti.* All these names signify the same *sakti.* Sri Krishna has said, "Earth, air, fire, water, ether, mind, intellect and ego constitute my lower *prakrti;* distinct from it is my *para prakrti* which is of the form of *jivas* and preserves the *jagat.*" The former eight-fold *prakrti* constitutes the *jada* aspect as *kârya* whereas the latter *para prakrti* is *Chit Sakti* forming the background for the *jagat* like a mirror to the images reflected in it. Hence the statement: "By whom the eight-fold *prakrti* is supported." Nevertheless we have to admit that even before the appearance of the inert power the eight-fold *prakrti*, the *Chit Sakti* ("free will") already co-exists with the *adrshta* of the individuals and the time matures the *adrshta*. Otherwise the charge of partiality and cruelty and other stigma will attach (to Iswara). But the admission of *adrshta* lands us in duality and time is yet another (thorn). Is time the nature of Iswara or is it distinct? In any case, since in dissolution there is no *upadhi* to distinguish one from another and the same principle remains uniform from the beginning of dissolution to the end of it, the *adrshta* of the individuals remaining merged in *avidya* may perhaps mature the very next instant of dissolution and creation start untimely. In answer to this the *sadkarya vâdis* say: Before creation all *kâryas* remain merged in *mâyâ* in a subtle form; now that time and *adrshta* are together in a subtle form in *mâyâ*, the subtle *adrshta* matures in subtle time; *mâyâ* being the sakti of the Self, *i.e., Chit,* it is not distinct and therefore the advaita doctrine becomes tenable. Others declare that creation resembles dream or day-dreaming or magic requiring no explanation like the mirage-water unfit for discussion. For the same reason the accounts of creation are bound to differ from one another in different srutis. They are meant to impress on the mind that the Self alone is and creation is not distinct from it. Hence the declaration in the Parameswara Agama: "No creation; no cycle of births; no preservation; or any *krama* (regulation). Only solid Intelligence-Bliss is. This is the Self."

to Chapter XVI
The Ego

The Self is luminous owing to its self-shining nature. At the instant of perception of objects, such as a pot, the ego-sense of identity with the body vanishes. There is no experience of the

complexion of the body (for instance) simultaneous with perception of objects. Otherwise one would be thinking, "I am fair
or brown," even while perceiving a pot. In other words, when an
object is perceived it is as non-self, like the body known as
'mine' (my body).

It should not be said that the Self does not shine as 'I' simultaneously with the perception of objects. If so, the objects
cannot be perceived. For when there are no lights to illumine
objects they are not perceived. It should not also be said—yet
there is no ' I' sparkling *(spurthi)*. For it implies some distinctive
form of shining and not the sheen of pure light; this will also
imply inertness. Therefore the Self shines as pure 'I.' On
account of this, those who hold that knowledge is self-evident,
admit the experience "I know the pot" (but not 'I have the
knowledge of the pot'). *(Ghatam aham jânami* but not *Ghata jnâ-
navan aham).*

If the Self be not admitted to shine of itself even during our
objective perceptions, it will not be proper to reject the doubt
whether 'I am or not.' Nor should it be said that simultaneously
with objective perception the ego shines *(i.e.,* manifests) identical with body, etc. If in the perception of an object the form of
the object does not manifest, the body cannot manifest itself at
the time of sensing the body, etc. It does not follow that in the
knowledge 'He is Chaitra,' the *intelligence* namely the Self of
Chaitra is signified by the word 'he' and manifests transcending
his body-ego; for, to him Chaitra's ego remains unimpaired *(i.e.,*
he feels his ego-sense all the same).

In deep sleep and *samâdhi* the 'I' cannot be denied existence. All admit its continued existence in those states also
because of the recollection of the experience (in those two
states). True, the Self remains continuous in those states but it
cannot be denoted by 'I' for the former is unmodified
Consciousness and the latter is a mode of consciousness. The
answer to such an objection is according to the sages well-versed
in agamâs, as follows: 'I' is of two kinds, moded and unmoded
intelligence. Mode means differentiation; therefore moded
intelligence is differentiated intelligence. The other one is
undifferentiated and is therefore unmoded. When objectified

as bodies, etc., the ego is moded and differentiated. But in deep sleep and *samâdhi.* Consciousness remains unobjectified and undifferentiated; therefore it is unmoded. It does not follow from this that the admission of 'I' in *samâdhi* will amount to admission of the triads (*e.g.,* cogniser, cognition and the cognised). Since 'I' remains as the residue devoid of "non-I" there are no triads there. It is said in Pratyabhijna, "Although I shine as Pure Light yet it is word in a subtle form *(parayak)."* This ego is not a mode. Such is the doctrine of advaita.

This (unmoded Intelligence) is just the knowledge of "I-I." The agamas speak of it as Perfect EGO or Perfect Knowledge. Because this state later finds expression to describe it, it is said to be 'word' (vâk); but it does not mean audible word. It is 'word' in a subtle form, remaining unspoken.

Perfect Ego cannot be denied in the unmoded Consciousness for it will amount to inertness, Bhagavan Harina has said, "Should 'word' mean differentiation in the ever-Present Light, it would amount to saying the Sight does not shine (of itself)." On the other hand, 'word' signifies "profound contemplation." Pratyabhijna says "Deliberation makes clear the Self-shining Light. Were it not so, *i.e.,* if light should shine only in contact with an object, it would be inert like a crystal." Bhagavan Sri Sankara also says that the Self, namely *Chit,* is always shining as 'I.' In *Viveka Chudamani* it is found, "That which constantly shines forth as 'I' throughout infancy, etc., waking state, etc., which are super-imposed on it. . . ."

Dullness of Deep Sleep

Though the Self that is *Chit* is Pure Solid Intelligence, it is not like a solid rock for that would amount to inertness. It is pure, scintillating awareness. Its shining nature is distinct from that of bright objects such as a flame. This awareness is also called intelligence, deliberation, light of consciousness, activity, vibration, the supreme Ego, etc. Because of this nature the

Supreme Being is capable of creation and this also finds mention in *Soundarya Lahari* Sloka 1.

It is not correct to say that Paramasiva remains united with the power of *mâyâ* which is indescribable *(anirvâchaneeya)* and illusory. Should the *jagat* be false (non-existent) like a hare's horn, its creation must also be declared to be so. It is not proper to say that the Lord's nature is wasteful because it will end in a blank, *i.e., sunya.* If the *jagat* is said to be non-existent like a hare's horn, sruti declarations such as "Form whom all these elements, all these creatures have come forth, etc." would amount to a mad man's ravings. Nor is it proper to contend that acceptance of Supreme Intelligent Being followed by the denial of the reality of the *jagat* is *sunya vâda,* because false *jagat* inclusive of the Supreme Reality is self-contradictory. (The correct position is: the Supreme Being appears as or seems to be the *jagat.*) If you argue that this results in duality whereas the srutis declare, "There are not many here but only the Self," I say you do not understand the advaita sastra; nowhere do the sastras declare the *jagat* to be unreal. But yet they proclaim advaita to be certain. Srutis such as "He became all," "Only the non-dual Supreme Being shines as the universe," declare the *jagat* to be real and thereby non-duality is not impaired. Though the town reflected in a mirror seems distinct yet it cannot exist without the mirror and so is no other than the mirror; in the same manner the *jagat* though seeming distinct is no other than the Supreme Self. So non-duality is unimpaired.

As in the sruti cited by you, "there are not many here," the denial relates to duality only and nothing else. Therefore it is a sign of ignorance to declare the *jagat* to be unreal. The sages know that true knowledge consists in realizing that "all is Siva." Suta Samhita says, "to say pot, etc., are unreal, is ignorance. Correctly to say pot, etc., is real, is true knowledge."

Thus the supreme Intelligent Being by its own supreme power of *mâyâ* manifests Itself as this wonderful universe. In the universe thus manifested to see the *jiva* distinct from the Supreme is duality and constitutes the bondage of the individual. Knowledge of non-duality constitutes liberation. His "independence" *(svatantra,* free will), reflection of the universe, reflection of the individual selves, reflection of the bondage, reflection of liberation are all presented within Himself by His own independent power. Like a day-dream, all these depend upon His power of manifestation which however is not distinct from the Supreme Intelligence. So our system is free from any stigma. Power of deliberation always remains constant with the Supreme Being. However in deep sleep the reflection of inertness *(jada sakti)* veils it and renders it weak; though the Supreme Being or *Chit* is then shining in full, the sages have proclaimed the state to be one of inertness or dullness.

to Chapter XVII
The Nature of Vijnana

The knowledge gained by hearing is only indirect. Then reasoning in conformity with the sruti texts, it must be ascertained whether indirect knowledge concerns one's own self or not. By reflection all doubts will vanish. After thus ascertaining by reflection that the Self remains non-dual, contemplate the Self, that is to say, keep the mind one-pointedly on the Self. If the mind becomes restless, train it even forcibly. Be not effortless in this direction. Yoga Vasishta says: "Even with hands clenched and teeth ground, pressing the limbs and forcibly withdrawing the senses, the mind must first be brought under control." So the utmost effort must be made. Also the breath must forcibly be controlled, if necessary by means of prânâyâma (regulation of breath). One-pointedness must be gained at all costs. How long is effort necessary? Until direct experience is gained. Thus by contemplation the inmost Self is realized. Then contemplate 'I am Brahman.' This is known as Recognition of the Self as Brahman *(Pratyabhijna Jnâna)*. Although this amounts to unmoded *samâdhi (nirvikalpa)* because it is unbroken uniform knowledge, yet owing to the difference in the methods and results, it must be recognised that these two states are distinct. Such knowledge of the non-dual Self annihilates ignorance.

The same is further explained. First ascertain the Self to be real by means of *sravana* and *manana* (hearing and reflection); then contemplate; realization results and it is *nirvikalpa samâdhi.* This is the idea: Dhyâna is only one; it goes by the name of *savikalpa samâdhi* and of *nirvikalpa samâdhi* according to its stages of development. On resolving to keep the mind still for a particular duration of time and continuing on the trail of the resolve without forgetting it, the period during which the contemplated object remains uninterrupted, is said to be the duration of dhyana. If by long practice the contemplated object remains steady for the intended period it is *savikalpa samâdhi* (moded *samâdhi*). If again by repeated practice of the same the mind remains in unbroken contemplation even without the initial resolve and its continued memory, it is said to be *nirvikalpa* or unmoded *samâdhi.* The following explanation is found in a book *Paramânanda:* "Contemplation with series of breaks is dhyana; the same without break is *savikalpa samâdhi*; stillness of mind without contemplation and break is *nirvikalpa samâdhi.* Dhyana maturing and ending in *nirvikalpa samâdhi,* the inmost Self is realized. On breaking away from it, to remember the experience of the inmost Self, to recall to mind the description of the Supreme Being in the holy texts and to identify the one with the other, forms recognition *(Prathyabhijna Jnâna)."*

Q: For such recognition, recollection is a necessary ingredient; recollection is of the mental impression already formed; impression can be produced only in moded knowledge and not in the unmoded state of *nirvikalpa samâdhi* of one uniform unmoded Light of Consciousness. *A:* You are right. Unmoded light simply illumines objects like a pot, etc.; it cannot produce any impression on the mind to be reproduced later on. Otherwise a wayfarer will be able to remember all that he saw on the way; but it is not so. Only the moded knowledge such as "this is a pot, this is a piece of cloth" is later recollected. Hence, whatever subtle modes appeared in the unmoded state (*e.g.,* here is a man; here is Devadatta) are alone later recollected. By way of explanation some say that the end of the *nirvikalpa* state is followed by a moment of *savikalpa* and this helps formation of impressions to be recollected later.

Others: Since the pure inmost Self cannot form the object of experience even in *savikalpa samâdhi,* they say that recollection is of the experience of the *samâdhi* itself. (Because the *savikalpa samâdhi* of the nature of a resolve and cannot have the Pure Self for its object) it cannot be maintained that in *savikalpa samâdhi* the Pure Self forms the object of experience. But how can the recollection arise directly from *nirvikalpa samâdhi?* There is no rule that *savikalpa* alone should give rise to later recollection. Vikalpa means appearance of differentiation. A wayfarer takes in very subtle impressions of things seen on the way and recollects some of them. This alone can explain the recollection of deep sleep after waking from it. To the objection that recollection cannot arise from *nirvikalpa samâdhi,* the reply is: In any knowledge whichever factor is clearly seen, the same will later be recollected along with that knowledge. In recollecting a panorama all objects in it are not clearly seen. But as it is said in *Pratyabhijna Sâstra,* "According to taste and according to desire" the recollection is limited to them. In this way all differentiation is solely a mental mode. Yet pandits think in different ways. Therefore some say that there cannot be a recollection of *nirvikalpa samâdhi.* For details refer to *Pratyabhijna Sâstra* and its commentaries.

to Chapter XIX
Characteristic of Samâdhi

After realizing the Self as unmoded Consciousness in *nirvikalpa samâdhi,* Self-Realized beings keep on recollecting it deliberately; this results in withdrawal by them in perfect repose; this by the wise is said to be their *samâdhi.* This is the secret of *vijnana:* The hatha yogis who have not realized the Self by *sravana,* etc., fall into two groups; one of them is accomplished in the eight-fold yoga of Patanjali; the other after gradually finishing the stage of prânâyâma (control of breath), practises it more and more so that the *kundalini* is aroused to go up and open out the *sushumna nâdi*. The former, before entering *samâdhi*, resolves to avoid all thought of the non-self, succeeds gradually in avoiding extraneous thoughts, then contemplates the absence of all thoughts and then, released from contemplation as well, he is left as a residual being. The other, with great effort makes the vital air enter the *sushumna;* owing to the effort there is fatigue; however having entered the *sushumna* the fatigue vanishes; he feels refreshed like a man relieved of a heavy burden. Then his mind remains as if stupefied.

Both these classes of sadhakas experience Bliss like that of deep sleep in their own time.

As for the jnâna yogis who have realized the unmoded knowledge—Self by *sravana*, etc.—even before attaining *samâdhi* the veil of ignorance is removed and unmoded Knowledge-Self is found always scintillating as the various objects like reflections in a mirror. Not only this but also before *samâdhi*, the modes of mind vanish leaving the residual mind as the witness of the disappearance of the objects and he remains as unmoded knowledge only. The hatha yogis' experience is not this. Only to the jnâna-yogis does *ajnâna* (ignorance) vanish altogether in *samâdhi* along with its veiling and projecting or confusing powers, whereas for the hatha yogi, although the projecting power vanishes, the other power continues to veil the Self. To the jnâna yogi the veiling aspect is done away with in the process of contemplation of itself, leaving nothing of it in the culminating state of *samâdhi*.

Q: What is then the difference between deep sleep and *samâdhi* of a hatha yogi? *A:* In his deep sleep the Self remains hidden by the massive ignorance of darkness like the sun behind very heavy dark clouds; in the *samâdhi* state, the Self, though revealed by the satvic mind, will not yet be clear but be like the sun behind thin white clouds.

In the case of the *Jnâni*, his mind becomes satvic in *toto*, and thus dispels the veiling of ignorance, so that the Self shines perfectly clear like the sun in a clear sky. The Self-Realized know this to be the right Realization of the Self. *Jnâna samâdhi* is thus the true *samâdhi* (it means that in spite of the sâtvic mind developed by the hatha yogis, their *âvarna* (*i.e.*, veiling) remains without being dispelled).

to Chapter XXII
The Prarabdha of the Jnanis

The pleasures and pains of the individual are inferred to be the results of an invisible cause, *i.e.*, the past karma. Since it is noticed that *jnânis* also live like others, it is said that the *prârabdha* is not undone by one's *jnana*. This holds good for the lowest order of *jnânis* only, for they are seen to react to environment; it does not apply to the higher orders. The feeling of happiness affecting the mind of the individual can be the effect of karma. The middle and the highest classes of *jnânis* are not subject to fluctuations of mind. You cannot dispute this point because such fluctuations are completely absent in *samâdhi*. On arising from *samâdhi* all the non-self (*i.e.*, the *jagat*) shines only as Pure Knowledge (*i.e.*, the Self) just as the images are not distinct from the mirror reflecting them; happiness, etc., thus becoming one with the Self cannot then be felt as 'my happiness,' etc.; it follows that the Self itself cannot be said to be 'effects' and no corresponding karma can be postulated.

Q: Though his personal pleasures and pains are not there, yet he sees others enjoy pleasures and suffer pains; his reaction must be due to *prârabdha*. *A:* No. Others' pleasures and pains are not identified as 'mine.' But they are perceived as one perceives a pot; they cannot be the effects of *prârabdha*. Since there is no pleasure or pain to be called 'effects' for him, the *jnâni* cannot be said to have residual karma.

As for the lowest order of *jnânis,* when he engages himself in the daily routine of life, he is likely to forget that all is Self and takes himself to be the enjoyer; since pleasure and pain seem to be 'effects' to him, he is certainly having the fruits of his past karma. Some say that such knowledge as cannot stand the stress of daily life cannot have a lasting value. Others say otherwise.

Simultaneously with the rise of Supreme Knowledge, the veiling power of ignorance is at an end. Only the projecting power is operative for some time, owing to *prârabdha*. It will quickly exhaust itself and no more karma will be left to cling to new bodies (by rebirth); ignorance being at an end there, no fresh karma will accumulate; for the same reason there will not be any mode of mind, for it vanishes like fire which has burnt up its fuel; hence no fresh bodies will attach to him. Therefore the Pure Being is left over and thus liberation is inevitable. It is only too true that lapses from Knowledge do not constitute Knowledge in perfection. Hence the *Sâstras* distinguish the *jnâni* from a *jivanmukta, i.e.,* one liberated while alive.

Q: According to the dictum that a man will be reborn according to his last thought, that the *jnani* of the lowest order will also be reborn because his *prârabdha* is not completely ended, recollection of the non-self (by *viparita smarana*) must lead to rebirth. *A:* No. Recollection of the non-self is unavoidable to the higher order of *jivanmukta* also. The dictum you cited does not apply to *jnani* of any sort. Simultaneous with the rise of Knowledge there is complete loss of ignorance; therefore pleasures and pains no longer constitute 'effects' of karma; they are only transitory phenomena; *prârabdha* is conjectured simply to explain this phenomenon; but *prârabdha* no longer remains for a *jnâni* of any order and no recollection of non-self will arise in the last moment of his life.

Therefore the difference between a mere *jnani* and a *jivanmukta* lies in their reaction to the pains and pleasures of life. It is said that since liberation is simultaneous with the rise of Knowledge, it is immaterial when and how the *jnani* dies, either near holy places or in strange homes or other places, or taken unaware by death. If he knows perfectly even once the supreme state of Siva by means of reflection or by sastras or by Guru's grace, he is a Self-Realized man. And nothing more remains for him to do.

Bliss of Self

Cease thinking of the non-self; then blank prevails; the knower or the witness of this is pure knowledge without any modes; such is the Supreme Knowledge *(Para Samvit)*. This is full of Bliss and therefore the highest goal *(purushârtha)*. This state is one of solid Bliss. The reason is: Misery is the result of upâdhi which is totally absent in the Self. This *samvit* is the condensation of the sum total of bliss, consequent on all the forms of enjoyment by all living beings put together. For *samvit* is desired by one and all living beings.

Q: Is it not pleasure from objects that is thus desired? How can it take the form of the enjoyer? *A:* Since it is desired by all, the Self must be of the nature of Bliss. Otherwise it will not be desired by all equally.

Q: If it be the Self alone that is desired by all, how can the desires be various, *e.g.,* for the body, wealth, woman, etc.? *A:* The desire is not really for objects since it is for one's own sake. Hence those desirous of heaven, etc., undergo fasts, etc., and willingly leave their bodies, etc. So the Self is never that which is not desired. Therefore it must be Bliss itself.

Q: Pleasure is obvious in the enjoyment of objects, whereas the other bliss cannot be proved to be; therefore the Self cannot be admitted to be Bliss. *A:* The *agamâs* (holy texts) declare that all sensual pleasures are but fractions of the Bliss of the Self. This means: Just as ether though not itself visible is yet known to yield room for a pot, etc., and thus seems divisible by other adjuncts such as actions, etc., so also *Chit* though not visible yet appears divided by objects seeming to be the source of sensual pleasure (which in reality are only fractions of the Bliss of the Self).

Q: Your statements prove only the desire for pleasure by the self, and not itself being bliss. *A:* Only the natural bliss of the Self prevails at the instant of relief of one's burden and in deep sleep. This means: As soon as one is relieved of one's heavy load, one surely feels refreshed; this cannot be denied; but here are no objects to give pleasure and how could it be felt unless it is from within, *i.e.,* from the Self?

Q: It is due to the strain of load being removed. *A:* Removal is negative; how can a negation yield a positive result such as pleasure? It must therefore be admitted to be of the Self.

Q: Relief from strain amounts to relief from pain. And this *seems* to be pleasure to him. *A:* But in deep sleep there is no strain to be removed and yet there is the bliss of sleep. This cannot be denied because there is the recollection of the bliss of sleep after waking from it. This bliss cannot but of the Self.

Q: There is no such bliss of deep sleep. *A:* Why then do all beings desire to sleep and also prepare for it?

Q: If the Self be bliss, why is it not always apparent? *A:* Although there is noise constantly produced within the body, it is not usually heard; but if you plug your ears to prevent the intrusion of external noises; the noise is distinctly heard from within. Similarly with the bliss of Self. It is at present obstructed by the pains generated by the fire of desires and other latencies. These latencies lie dormant in their sources at the time of deep sleep and then the bliss of the Self becomes apparent like the internal sound on plugging the ears. While bearing the load the pain caused by it over-powers the common misery of current vasanas and thus predominates for the time being. As soon as the load is thrown down, the pain relating to it disappears and in the short interval before the rise of the current vasanas, the bliss of Self is felt. Similarly with the other sensual pleasures. Innumerable vasanas always remain in the heart pricking like thorns all the while. With the rise of a desire for an object the force of it overpowers the other vasanas which await their turn. When the desired object is attained, the immediate pain of its desire is at an end; in the short interval before the other vasanas manifest, the bliss of Self prevails. Hence it is said what always all desire is only the Bliss of the Self.

Q: How then do all not understand that the sought-for pleasures are really only the Self? *A:* Owing to their ignorance of the fact that only the bliss of the Self manifests as the pleasure of sensual enjoyments, their attention being on the objects which are transitory; they believe that as the enjoyments are transitory, their bliss also is co-eval with them.

Refutation of the Doctrine of Void

The followers of this school of thought declare that illusion can and does arise even in the absence of any background *(niradhishtâna)*. In the case of a piece of shell appearing as silver, they say that the knowledge of silver is groundless *(i.e.,* void); similarly with the knowledge of the Self. Their position is briefly put as follows: On the firm conviction that the *jagat* is non-existent, by a prolonged contemplation on the void, the thought of *jagat* completely vanishing, void prevails and this is liberation.

Now to refute it—denial of the *jagat* is imperfect knowledge. Just as a pot is not altogether false but is real as clay, so also is *jagat* not altogether false but is real as intelligence. Therefore to deny the *jagat* as being non-existent is only illusory knowledge. Its non-existence cannot be established by any proofs. Because the *jagat* shines as knowledge from which the individual who proves the *jagat* to be real or unreal, is not distinct; also the *jagat* though denied yet persists. Though a pot may be denied, its material clay cannot be so denied. Similarly though the *jagat* may be denied, its existence as knowledge cannot be denied. The same relationship holds between the *jagat* and consciousness as between a pot and clay. However the adherents of the school of void stick to void and deny all the perceptible as being void. But *he* is also contained in the *jagat* which is denied by him. Then what is left of him beyond denial is knowledge; this cannot be denied. They mean to say that the moded consciousness constitutes samsara whereas unmoded consciousness void of all else including the *pramanas* to prove it, constitutes liberation. But our objection is that the one who denies the *jagat* cannot deny himself and the *jagat* does not cease to exist simply because one curses it. Our objection is valid because consciousness subsists unimpaired in the unmoded state after denying all else to exist.

Q: (Granting your view point) what is there to be eliminated and how is non-duality established? *A:* The Vedantists say that the Supreme *Sat-Chit* seems to be the *asat* (false) *jagat* like the false reflection in a mirror; this is *anirvâchaniya, i.e.,* inexpressible; non-duality consists in removing this confusion and so this *jagat* is eliminated. But we say—the *jagat* appears like the images in a mirror. Just as these images are no other than the mirror, the *jagat* is no other than the *Sat-Chit.*

Q: If so, what remains to be eliminated? *A:* The sense of duality. *Q:* Is this duality included in *jagat?* Or is it exclusive of it? If the former, it is real as *jagat* and cannot be negated; if the latter, it leads to *anirvâchaniya. A:* It is included in *jagat.*

Q: How then is it eliminated? *A:* Listen! Duality is to believe that the illuminant and the illumined are different from each other. Since duality is nothing but illusion, denial of it puts an end to the illusion and thus to itself. Hence it was said, "As a matter of fact unity is not different from diversity. One reality alone shines forth as both."

Now let me turn round and question the Vedantists:

Q: Is negation indescribable or real? If the former, *jagat* cannot be negated; if the latter, duality results. Nor can you maintain that negation of the phenomenon resolves itself as the substratum so that the negation of *Jagat* results in its substratum, Brahman. Of course to admit the non-self-looking negation is simply included in the Self and the whole *jagat* is nothing but the Self, is not opposed to our view. But negation is negative in character and it cannot be said to resolve itself into its substratum—the Reality. The *jagat* can be established to exist according to the dictum—*the non-self is also the Self.* The point is only to gain *purushartha* by whatever means—negation or any other. *It is useless to engage in disputes. 'The mumukshu' and the 'sâd-hakas' are warned not to enter into controversies with other systems or religions.*

The *jagat* being of consciousness, like the images in a mirror not being different from a mirror, it is real. Simply because *jagat* is declared to be of the nature of consciousness, it should not be taken that *jagat* is consciousness itself. Such assumption will be equivalent to saying that *avidyâ* is, because it is said to be inexpressible. Just as you cannot raise the question if *avidyâ* is in order to be inexpressible, so also the question cannot arise if *jagat* is in order to be indistinct from Consciousness. In this manner to know that all is *sattamâtra* is perfect *Vinjana*.

Sri Ramanarpanâmastu

OM

Index

Nirvikalpa Samâdhi, 75, 112-113,
  115-118, 147, 151, 182, 205-
  206
Nivritta, 7
Niyati, 89
nondual Knowledge, 121, 125,
  166, 171, 183
Nondual realization, 150-152

Objective knowledge, 64, 113,
  120, 151, 169, 195-196
Obligation, 9-10
Obligatory action, 7-9
One Consciousness, 13, 88, 125,
  178
Origin of Universe, 43

Pandit, 56, 159
Parasara, 147
perceptions, 57, 101, 103, 108,
  180, 201
Perfect Ego, 172, 202
Perfect state, 62, 160
Perfection, 59, 61, 68, 87, 97,
  102, 112, 117-118, 121-122,
  124, 126, 128, 160, 168-169,
  172, 177, 209
Pleasure, 2, 4-6, 18, 20-21, 23-25,
  28, 32, 34, 37-38, 46, 48, 51,
  54, 58, 60, 63, 76, 90, 103,
  110-111, 116, 140, 143, 154,
  157-158, 160, 164, 168, 170,
  175-176, 180, 189, 208, 210-
  211
Pracheta, 147
Practice of Yoga, 76, 85
Prakriti, 89-90, 196
Prânâyâma, 145, 204, 206
prârabdha, 208-209
Pratyabhijna jnana, 151

Predispositions, 133-135, 137-
  138, 142, 152-153, 156, 161,
  169, 176
Primal Being, 46, 90
Primal Cause, 43
Primal condition, 116, 152
Prince, 16-18, 20, 22-25, 28-29,
  33, 37-38, 54, 57, 61, 75, 98,
  162-167, 171
Puranas, 139
Pure being, 58, 91, 109, 149,
  199, 209

Rajas, 67, 90, 190
Rama, 7, 11-15, 26, 71, 73, 94,
  99, 123, 126, 128, 130, 134,
  136, 142, 158
Ramanaka, 86
Ranjit Singh, 71
raptures, 110
raptures of happiness, 110
Ratnangada, 161
Ravana, 11-12
Realization, 3, 9, 50, 52-54, 56,
  62, 73, 82, 103-105, 111, 114-
  116, 118, 121, 127, 129, 133,
  135, 138, 141-142, 144, 149-
  152, 154-156, 159-160, 163,
  168, 170-171, 177, 196, 205,
  207
Reality, 57, 70, 73, 91, 98, 107-
  108, 122-124, 126, 130-133,
  135, 153, 169, 175, 183-184,
  186, 203, 210, 213
Reflections, 56-57, 69-70, 103,
  121, 167, 190, 207
Rope, 49, 71, 124, 130-132, 167,
  187
Rukmangada, 161, 164

sacrifice, 7, 74, 76, 95-96, 141
Sadasiva Tattva, 173

Other Titles on Hinduism
by World Wisdom

A Christian Pilgrim in India:
The Spiritual Journey of Swami Abhishiktananda (Henri Le Saux),
by Harry Oldmeadow, 2008

The Essential Sri Anandamayi Ma:
Life and Teachings of a 20th Century Indian Saint,
by Alexander Lipski and Sri Anandamayi Ma, 2007

The Essential Swami Ramdas: Commemorative Edition,
compiled by Susunaga Weeraperuma, 2005

The Essential Vedanta:
A New Source Book of Advaita Vedanta,
edited by Eliot Deutsch and Rohit Dalvi, 2004

A Guide to Hindu Spirituality,
by Arvind Sharma, 2006

Introduction to Hindu Dharma,
by the 68th Jagadguru of Kanchi,
HH Sri Chandrasekharendra Saraswati Swamigal,
edited by Michael Oren Fitzgerald, 2008

Lamp of Non-Dual Knowledge & Cream of Liberation:
Two Jewels of Indian Wisdom,
translated by Swami Sri Ramanananda Saraswathi, 2003

The Original Gospel of Ramakrishna:
Based on M's English Text, Abridged
edited by Swami Abhedananda and Joseph A. Fitzgerald, 2012

Paths to Transcendence:
According to Shankara, Ibn Arabi & Meister Eckhart,
by Reza Shah-Kazemi, 2006

The Power of the Sacred Name:
Indian Spirituality Inspired by Mantras
by Venkataraman Raghavan, edited by William J. Jackson, 2011

Timeless in Time: Sri Ramana Maharshi,
by A.R. Natarajan, 2006

Unveiling the Garden of Love:
Mystical Symbolism in Layla Majnun & Gitagovinda,
by Lalita Sinha, 2009

The Wisdom of Ananda Coomaraswamy:
Selected Reflections on Indian Art, Life, and Religion
by Ananda K. Coomaraswamy,
edited by S. Durai Raja Singam and Joseph A. Fitzgerald, 2011

Other Titles in the Spiritual Classics Series by World Wisdom

The Buddha Eye:
An Anthology of the Kyoto School and Its Contemporaries,
edited by Frederick Franck, 2004

A Christian Woman's Secret:
A Modern-Day Journey to God,
by Lilian Staveley, 2009

Gospel of the Redman,
compiled by Ernest Thompson Seton &
Julia M. Seton, 2005

Introduction to Sufi Doctrine,
by Titus Burckhardt, 2008

Lamp of Non-Dual Knowledge & Cream of Liberation:
Two Jewels of Indian Wisdom,
by Sri Swami Karapatra and Swami Tandavaraya,
translated by Swami Sri Ramanananda Saraswathi, 2003

Light on the Indian World:
The Essential Writings of Charles Eastman (Ohiyesa),
edited by Michael Oren Fitzgerald, 2002

Music of the Sky:
An Anthology of Spiritual Poetry,
edited by Patrick Laude and Barry McDonald, 2004

The Mystics of Islam,
by Reynold A. Nicholson, 2002

Naturalness: A Classic of Shin Buddhism,
by Kenryo Kanamatsu, 2002

The Path of Muhammad:
A Book on Islamic Morals and Ethics by Imam Birgivi,
interpreted by Shaykh Tosun Bayrak, 2005

Pray Without Ceasing:
The Way of the Invocation in World Religions,
edited by Patrick Laude, 2006

The Quiet Way:
A Christian Path to Inner Peace,
by Gerhard Tersteegen, translated by Emily Chisholm, 2008

The Way and the Mountain:
Tibet, Buddhism, and Tradition,
by Marco Pallis, 2008